Handsworth Revolution

THE ODYSSEY OF A SCHOOL

by

David Winkley

dlm

To Linda with love

First published in 2002
by Giles de la Mare Publishers Limited
53 Dartmouth Park Hill, London NW5 1JD

Typeset by Tom Knott
Printed in Great Britain
by Advance Book Printing

A CIP record of this book is available from the British Library

ISBN 1-900357-21-6 paperback

HANDSWORTH REVOLUTION

Sir David Winkley was head of Grove School, Handsworth, from 1974 to 1997, and was founder of the National Primary Trust in 1987, of which he is currently President. He has been a member of the present Government's educational Standards Task Force, and has served as advisor to several other Department for Education Advisory Committees. He has been a fellow of Nuffield College, Oxford, and since 1999 an honorary professor at the University of Birmingham. Originally a graduate of the University of Cambridge, he has a University of Oxford doctorate in philosophy and honorary doctorates from the Universities of Birmingham and Central England. His books include *Diplomats and Detectives: LEA Advisors at Work* (1985) and *Business Planning for Schools* (co-author with R. Puffitt and B. Stoten, 1992), and he has written over sixty articles on various learned subjects.

Contents

Acknowledgements

I would like to thank, especially, Cedric Cullingford, Ann Low-Beer, Virginia Makins and Simon Szreter for their generous help and advice – and their unfailing encouragement – throughout the writing of this book. Their persuasive observations have made for countless improvements. Virginia Makins has been an enormous help in editing the final drafts. Thanks also, for invaluable comments on the book, to Edward Daley, Nigel Fortune, Donal Knipe, Ann Lance, Martin Lawn, Ethan and Joanne Lipsig, Pamela Matty, Ranjit Sondhi and Dulcie Szreter. My wife, Linda, has been a continuous support, and without her enthusiasm it might never have been written.

A different kind of thanks must go, too, to the many dozens of teachers and hundreds of children of Grove School, who are the true heroes of this story.

Note

I have retained the true names of most of the adults who feature in this book; eight names have been changed, and the identities of the individuals concerned have been disguised. The names of most of the children have been changed.

Winter

The First Year

I

The Interview

It is a curious thing applying for a job you are not sure you want. I'm sitting in the corridor at the Council House outside Interview Room B on a small hard chair lined up in a row with the other candidates, and wondering whether to stay or to leave. It's an October Wednesday and it's raining heavily outside. We're all nervous, and it shows. Maybe I should walk down the windowless corridor, down the flights of stairs and out into the street, and forget the whole thing.

One of the other two candidates is considerably older than me and looks tired, or slightly depressed. His stiff collar is too tight and he tries to loosen it from time to time to escape from strangulation. His hair is spiky, his face round; he is a small man with small hands and an attractive smile. He glances across at me and says suddenly, 'I think it's yours.'

I am not sure if he's addressing me or the third of the candidates, who sits peculiarly still and upright, staring in front of me, preparing to go over the top at the first hint of the whistle, to rush at the door and get the business over with as soon as possible. At one point he stands up and goes to the toilet which is marked Members Only.

Mr Jay, the older man, smiles at me. I see his hair is going grey. He's one of those honest-to-God teachers who were emergency-trained during the teacher-shortage crisis soon after the war. He tells me he was once a secondary PE teacher who decided that his career prospects might be brighter in a primary school. Mr Bettingham, the third candidate, returns, sits down and sighs. He is – as all three of us are – in his Sunday best, in a sober-dark suit of almost funereal aspect. His shirt is white, his tie colourless; his shoes gleam bright black.

'Is this your first?' he asks.

'Yup,' I say, with a casual air, trying to give the impression I've been thrown into this, Musketeer-style, through the encouragement of others, and am not at all clear about what I am letting myself in for. 'You?'

'Fourth,' he says. 'Came near with the last one. Pipped at the post.'

'Fifteenth,' says Mr Jay. 'Can you believe it?'

I stare at him in disbelief.

'Spread over the year,' he adds smiling, unperturbed; 'I'm the make-up man.'

'Really?'

'When they're short on the ground they need someone to make up the numbers. 'Three,' he says. 'Less than three and it doesn't look good.'

'Are they short on the ground?'

'Why should anybody want that hell hole?' he says.

'Oh come on.'

'Have you seen it?'

'Oh yes.'

He leans forward and surveys me with interest.

'So you know what it's like?'

I'd made a short visit to the school late one afternoon earlier in the week. I'd walked round with the deputy head and noticed nothing untoward. The children were all in class and seemed to be working. Perhaps I was being fooled and they had been on their best behaviour.

'And you can face it?'

'Why not?'

Mr Jay blows a raspberry. 'I only hope you know what you're doing, that's all.'

'You know of course,' says Mr Bettingham, 'it's Councillor O'Connelly in the chair.'

'Don't know him.'

'Famous,' says Mr Bettingham.

Bettingham leans forward.

'Once he nodded off after an interview with one of the candidates. The next candidate was called. While she was gathering her thoughts waiting for the first question, Councillor O'Connelly woke up, smiled and said, "Thank you very much for coming, Miss So and So. We'll be in touch with you after Committee has deliberated. No need to wait."

'The lady looked puzzled but left without so much as a single question being asked. The clerk then rushed out of the room to fetch her back, but by this time she was so miffed that she said they could keep their job if this was the way she was going to be treated. Councillor O'Connelly replied that if that was how she felt then *tough* – he didn't much like the look of her anyway.'

Mr Bettingham chuckles.

'Another time,' he says, 'they invited a man called Smith from St Bernard's School to an interview for a headship – the wrong Smith. This Smith was very young and had only been a deputy for six months. He was very surprised to be on the short list, especially as he hadn't applied for the job. He was interviewed and appointed. Then they realized they'd sent for the wrong Smith.'

'What did they do?'

'They covered it up of course. People were astonished at the rise of young Smith, but there you are.' Bettingham leans back. 'Cock-ups all over the fucking place. You never know. That's what keeps you going.'

As it turns out, the chair isn't Councillor O'Connelly at all, but a sweet, elderly lady, who's sharp as mustard and seems to have a very clear view that the job on offer isn't at all easy. It's a large panel, ten or more people, many of them local councillors. Union representatives are here, and also the Senior Inspector for the area, a plump, smartly dressed lady, all in blue.

After I've been questioned for some time, the chair leans forward and says, 'Mr Winkley, we are concerned about this school. As you know, the present head has been there eighteen months and is moving for health reasons. I want to ask, if we offer you the job, that you will agree to stay for at least two years.'

Two years? I consider. Mostly they ask you to stay for a lifetime.

'Of course,' I say confidently with what I think is a winning smile. I suspect the interview has gone well, and increasingly as I talk I feel that, after all, maybe I want this job, and anyway what's two years? I could chalk it up as experience.

So it was that I found myself being appointed headteacher of this school, a job that nobody else wanted. It was only later that I found out that the staff, having briefly seen the candidates on a visit to the school, had had bets on who was going to get the job, and that I was the long-odds man on account of my visible youth. Mr Hurling, a young teacher, a shrewd punter, had apparently won a fair bit on me, the dark horse on the outside track.

2

Handsworth

If, on a fine day, you take a flight over Birmingham, travelling north-west to Handsworth, you can easily be mistaken in thinking that this is an upmarket residential suburb of unspoilt, spacious houses, in glittering redbrick. At its heart is a Victorian park: slightly run down, but still retaining some of its ancient glory. Its bandstand is still in place – its lake with its Canada geese surrounded by old willows. Its rolling parkland has clusters of elegant flowerbeds, and an old clock-towered house where the park-manager once lived. At one time there had been boating on the pond, round its bird-sanctuary island. Now the greatest activity is on the edge, where children play on swings and chutes at the play centre.

Grove School used to lie at the centre of a respectable

middle-class enclave, three hundred yards from a small town with its own town hall. At one time Handsworth was an Edwardian suburb of upright folk; and it is not hard to imagine businessmen, artisans and white-collar workers flooding out of their charming redbrick terraced houses to catch the yellow trams clanking into the middle of the city, and children in smocks heading for school.

This respectability survived the war, but the monster of the city of Birmingham was beginning to overwhelm the Handsworth suburb. The town hall was abandoned to become a cinema, and then in the 1980s it was glamorously rebuilt as a Sikh Gurdwara. The old trams metamorphosed for a short while into trolley buses, which themselves finally disappeared in the great car expansion of the 1960s, at the time of the city's appalling destruction of its nineteenth-century heritage. Massive American-style ring roads were laid out and trashily built high-rise flats sprang up around the inner city suburbs. Handsworth was left relatively unscathed like some forgotten old lady, its networks of Edwardian houses still in place even as the area went into social decline.

Then came the immigrants, each new arrival, it seemed, replacing a retreating middle-class white resident. Year by year the locals trickled out to the 'white highlands', first to Handsworth Wood, a smart area on the periphery of Handsworth, and eventually to the safe suburb of Sutton Coldfield. Some of the white residents who were left behind started to campaign, marching with banners down the main roads, past the shops – the unrestrained protest of the corralled provincials, later to be mirrored and mocked by out-and-out riots by the young and disadvantaged. This was the last gasp of the old white community and the local and national press made everything they could of it. 'Coloured children set increasing problems,' wailed the *Sunday Times* in February 1962. 'Immigrant children threaten classroom standards,' wrote the *Sunday Mercury* in the September of the same year.

Grove School at the centre of the area reflected the changing residential population, and raised the alarm in its own way. Its headteacher in 1965 was an elderly lady who wrote to the *Birmingham Evening Mail* that:

> In 1957 we only had one immigrant in the school, and he was Cypriot. Now all we do is lose white children and take in immigrant ones. It's a shame that Handsworth should have been allowed to get to its present condition.

And the *Guardian* reported in November 1965 that:

> Parents of children at Grove Primary, where 80% of the 418 pupils are coloured, decided last night to postpone their threatened boycott of the school.

With its nose for a scandal, the *News of the World* gave a two-page spread to the school and expressed outrage at its 'decline'.

All this coincided with the 1967 Plowden Report on Primary Education which seriously underestimated the problems, arguing that 'racism' or 'prejudice', as it was called, was not of too much concern:

> ... most primary schools do not think that colour prejudice causes much difficulty.

By 1974, when I was appointed to be headteacher at the school, Handsworth's population was around 65,000, of whom 58% were of Afro-Caribbean or Asian descent. Male unemployment was 4%, but it was soon to increase rapidly and within a decade was double Birmingham's average and three times the national rate. By the late 1970s, an average of thirty-five people were applying for every job advertised at the Handsworth Job Centre, and 91% of local youths had never worked. Taking into account the multiple indicators of disadvantage, unemployment, overcrowding, households lacking in the exclusive use of basic amenities, health standards and the number of single-parent households, the Soho ward where the school was located was, according to the Department of the Environment, the most deprived district in Birmingham and amongst the most deprived 10% in the European Community. The crime rate was high, especially burglary and street crime carried out by youths, and many people were genuinely frightened by the place.

The area of Handsworth around the school would have seemed to a casual visitor to be peaceful enough: a busy shopping centre, a bustling little market, shops that fell out colourfully across the pavement, with exotic spicy smells in the air. But it was not simple. It had three parishes but even these, different though they were, didn't capture its diversity. It had a political constituency, 'Handsworth', that cut off great chunks of the heart of the geographical Handsworth and had a past featuring interesting MPs, including the Rt Hon Sir Edward Boyle, one-time Tory Minister of Education. The real Handsworth consisted of villages that were more or less demarcated by its primary schools, with invisible and permeable boundaries between them known only to those who understood the area well. Each 'village' had its different make-up, some being slightly more Asian, and some more Afro-Caribbean, some Bengali, some more Sikh, and some more Muslim. There were differences in the character of its roads, some of them being privately owned, some with housing-trust property along them. The condition of its house frontages varied greatly. Some were without gardens; some gardens were trampled into the ground, and some were beautifully kept. The better off tended to move out of the rougher villages and into the better ones. The wealthiest moved out of Handsworth altogether. There were subtle differences even between people within the same religious traditions: between, for example, those who attended one Gurdwara and another. The divides between these villages were incomplete: no part of Handsworth was in any way monocultural. But there were real differences for all that, indicated in crime rates, sickness and mortality statistics, and school academic performance. The overall momentum of the area was, as estate agents would say, down rather than up – like an old crone, still elegant on the outside, but deteriorating within.

I didn't know Handsworth well and the weekend after being offered the job as head of Grove School, an innocent abroad, I visited this part of Handsworth, parking the car off the main road, and I walked about. On that cold day I wandered down Grove Lane and up Dawson Road, looking in at the school from the outside. Not a child was in sight and it seemed as if it had been locked up for the last eighty years: behind its high windows I imagined roomfuls of spiders, and dust, and old memories. I realized I was far from fully aware what I was taking on, and just now I didn't want to give it too much thought.

My immediate response to the area was not in fact that it was a place that was aged and ageing. Rather the opposite. I walked around the park and then on to the main shopping centre. Everywhere was teeming with young people, hanging over fences and sitting on steps, out at the play centre, congregating in little groups in the streets, tiny children with older children, girls accompanying their little sisters, a blaze of bright dresses and saris, everyone rattling on in a variety of languages. Were these pupils, or potential pupils? Some were very handsome, bubbling. There was youthful energy here, even in the cool and the rain: it was all something of an adventure.

3
The School

The Junior School is in a late Edwardian building; it had once been an elementary school that dated back to the turn of the twentieth century. From a distance it resembles a church, its bell-tower and elegantly gabled roofs commanding a view from high above the community. At its side is an Infant School, which had been a secondary school for girls in the 1920s and 1930s. There are playgrounds to the front and back of the building, surrounded by spiked green railings at the front and at the back by high wire fences, full of holes, that cut the school off from the abandoned St Peter's Church next door. The local vicar, an extreme high-churchman, had simply shut it up and let it die as a gesture, he argued, to the new, non-Christian immigrant community.

The 'yards' are bleak and far too small, surely, for the number of children at the school. Years ago they would have lined up in their pinafores and knee-length trousers, and marched in orderly fashion through the boys' and girls' doorways which are still marked out severely in carved stone. At other times they would have practised military PE exercises in full sight of passers-by, jumping up and down in neatly drilled lines. But how do children in the 1970s find room to play, especially as a terrapin classroom has been stuck in the middle of the front playground, next to the kitchens, and takes up a chunk of space in the already very small yard?

Right now it all seems very abandoned in the freezing January weather. The caretaker has for the moment salted a track across the uneven tarmac to prevent people skidding over.

I go inside, into a high main hall with magnificent iron girders sweeping across the domed roof, and with skylights either side. There's an old stage at one end, added at a later date, on which the headteacher is presumably expected to stand during assemblies. I imagine myself climbing the steps to address the sea of faces below, hanging, I would hope, upon my every word. The floor of polished wood blocks smells strongly of fresh scented wood-oil and the corridors glisten, slippery and overbuffed. All the classrooms are set off the main hall, so that the children would need to pass through the hall to go wherever they wanted to go. Here is a communal gathering place, noisy, busy, constantly in use: the focal point of the school.

At the north end, up some rickety stairs, is a staff-room overlooking the roof with an ancient little kitchen smelling strongly of gas. At the south end there is another staircase leading to a roof room used by Bob, the deputy, for storing the stock. The boys' toilets are at the back of the school near the cloakroom at the bottom of the staff stairs, and the girls' toilets open out onto the front playground, which will ensure even more complicated movements to and fro through the hall, and up and down the corridors. At the north end, too, at the end of the corridor are the secretary's office and the headteacher's study, with its windows overlooking the busy traffic of Grove Lane. From here I can see the terraced houses opposite, the bus stop, the grocery store on the corner.

It is just a few days before term starts. I have the vaguest feeling of being like a squire coming to a new estate, my staff – or at least some of them – faintly apprehensive about their new boss. We're getting ready for the Easter term and Christmas is still in evidence, with a few jaded decorations hanging about, and the odd homemade Christmas card stuck to the wall alongside a wilting Christmassy painting.

It all looks under control. Some of the teachers are there to greet me. Bob is a gentleman of the old-fashioned kind, not so far off sixty, impeccably dressed, white-haired and good humoured: he has the wry smile of someone who can't understand why a person like me, with so young and innocent an air, should want to be the head. I guess I look even younger than my thirty years. Teachers are pottering in and out of their classrooms, and occasionally amble over and chat about holidays and stock and the business of the first day to come. I stand gossiping, uneasily aware of the thousand and one things I'm supposed to be doing.

I don't ask the questions I want to ask. What is it really like here? Why does the school have such an alarming reputation?

Beneath the school there's a great cellar which the caretaker insists on showing me. It stretches the entire length of the building and is piled high with ancient desks and tables that are covered in thick layers of dust and old books, reading primers, ancient textbooks, old registers and school records. Down here, he claims, we have one of the oldest central-heating systems in the city, resembling the engine of an old iron ship, with a massive hand-operated thermostat hanging on a rope – with its lever to increase and decrease the temperature. When lit, the oil-fired burner bursts into life, fire visibly spurting out. It is a huge rocket-shaped affair that emits great roaring noises and looks as though it might at any moment start moving across the stone floor, shaking itself away from its huge, elegantly-forged bolts and fixtures. The heating works, but it tends to be either too hot or too cold, and will provide interesting future challenges.

We emerge from the darkness covered in dust and I resume my wanderings. People are very pleasant and courteous, attempting to help. They know I'm trying to get a feel of things, and they're understandably hoping to get a handle on me – what they should expect, what I'm going to change, what impact I'm going to have.

My little office is already piled high with a mountain of correspondence bound up in elastic bands, gathered over the Christmas holidays and put on my desk for my attention.

My secretary Eva, a sweet-natured elderly lady, is somewhat highly strung and Bob tells me, confidentially, that she has difficulty coping with anything new. I make a passing reference to the possibility of a dictaphone, and she looks distinctly alarmed. Indeed, she seems stressed just at seeing me, and I wonder how long she will stay. I notice that the whole north-west section of the school, her room and mine, is slowly collapsing and that large cracks are beginning to appear in the yellow walls.

I make one immediate and significant decision: to move my desk from its current position in the middle of the room, where the head normally sits like a superannuated managing director, to the side against the wall, thus opening up the room and removing a barrier. I've never been a lover of headteachers' desks, or, come to that, of anything else that stands as the apparatus of power. On the other hand, I *am* now a headteacher, and the headteacher in this small world is a genuinely powerful person: you feel it in the air if you didn't know it already. Am I getting edgy about it all?

I'm aware now of a rising adrenalin flow, the excitement of my very new entry into this very new territory and I begin to feel ever more confident, like a Sheriff riding alone into town.

4

The Assembly

A few days later, on a cold January Thursday, the children came back to school, streaming through the side gates in their hundreds, with a sprinkling of parents standing out in the yard. The older children hung around waiting for the morning bell. Directly opposite Grove School is an old church foundation Grammar School for boys with an intake of overwhelmingly white pupils, who travel in from their middle-class homes, many of them brought by car. There was an enormous daily conflux of traffic, cars crawling in from all directions down the icy roads and jamming up the junctions as they emptied their loads. With its sudden congregation of fifteen hundred youngsters, all arriving at the same point at the same time, the neighbourhood became a circus, an explosion of youth of all ages heading in different directions.

I stood in the playground. My responsibilities suddenly seemed awesome. The shock of it made me feel I should do something. Speak to someone. Make a decision.

I stared into the breeze, recognized by no one. Here I was, the person responsible for this flow of young humanity, with roots from all over the world, the migrants, the children of people who extraordinarily and courageously uprooted themselves to come to a country with a miserable cold climate on a kiss and a hope – a stratagem of high risk. These people, and immigrants everywhere, were perhaps the bravest of their generation.

I might have given half a thought to my own species of risk. Deep down for all my posturing I was cautious, guarded, wondering how long I would survive.

But now I had arrived, there was no turning back, nowhere to hide.

'Are you the head?' says a little girl. She has two plaits into which a kaleidoscope of coloured beads are sewn, and a bright orange cagoule; she looks in her brilliant colours like some tropical bird, out of place in the cold. She eyes me with interest, and I think that a girl with the nerve to check out her new headteacher without fear or favour has a future in life.

'Well, yes, I am.'

'Hallo then. I'm Mavis.'

'Hallo Mavis.'

'It's him – that one – I told you it was him,' Mavis shouts to her friend.

Other children eye me with renewed interest. 'You coulda

fooled me,' says one, in a voice that I was not supposed to hear.

'What's your name?' asks another child.

'Winkley,' I say, 'Mr Winkley.'

'Oh,' says the child, caught, it would seem, between indifference and disappointment.

At 9.15, a girl rings the bell and class by class the children slowly crocodile out of their classrooms into the hall, lining up facing the front with their teachers at the end of each class line, the youngest in front, the oldest at the back.

There's some restlessness; some classes are noisier and more pushy than others. The deputy stands at the back of the room sporting his grey waistcoat and he is ushering classes to their places and admonishing the occasional child in a loud voice. 'Take that gum out of your mouth, Wesley. No chewing, you hear, boy?'

Staring at the hundreds of unfamiliar black and brown faces and spotlighted in turn by the scrutinizing eyes, I am a great deal less than sure how to pitch this. I stare at the waiting children as they fall quiet. The majority are probably Christian, let's say at a guess 60% – young blacks who go to the local Pentecostal, Seventh Day Adventist, Baptist Churches. The rest are a mix of Sikhs and Hindus, with a sprinkling of Muslims and (I had been told) one black Jew. Assemblies in England were traditionally of a vaguely Christian flavour, more moral than theological. Schools had hardly caught up with the challenges of the newly emergent immigrant society; but then few children opted out of assembly as was their right to do if they so wished. None did at this school. Most children went to church on Sundays. The Gurdwaras and Mosques were establishing themselves in the area, and there was a tiny Buddhist Temple in one of the terraced houses in Arthur Road. The white children were predominantly Catholics.

It's a moment of anticipation, when all the participants are edgy. The children look clean, well presented, some in smart, fresh school uniforms. It registers in my mind that school uniform itself may be an issue. Did parents approve – or, like *Guardian* readers, largely disapprove? I wonder how the children are feeling as they settle and stare forwards. I stand in the front, slightly unnerved by the silence, a *weighing up* silence in which the youngsters are no doubt assessing the form of their new headmaster.

Determined to break this tension, I walk briskly over to the piano and begin playing a blues tune, spreading my fingers across the keyboard in long slow rhythmic chords – knowing instinctively that such quirky and unexpected demonstrations are always attractive to children, who are easily bored, sometimes with good reason. I grab their attention – I sense it – and I play for a few moments and then stop, stand up again, and greet them with a firm, 'Good morning children.'

'Good morning Mr ... Wilky, Winky, Winkerly, Wimply, Wibbly, Winkley.' The voices ring out in a chorus.

'Winkley. Mr Winkley. Shall we try again?'

I smile. 'Good morning children.'

'Good morning Mr Winkley. Good morning everyone.'

The first song they all sing, me playing the piano, is 'Love is Something if You Give it Away'. The children sing well, making quite a noise, especially after I stop and say, 'My goodness, that's good singing. But I think you can do even better.' The next verse raises the roof. They laugh along with this excessively young, slender and longhaired young man who would have looked in place on the 1968 Paris barricades. They have a sense, no doubt, of change in the air. A few think I'm a pushover. Perhaps I am.

I give the children my first story which I've made up myself, all about a poor child from an unknown village who turns up at the back of the Great Town Church on a particularly important occasion.

> 'Out you go, you scruffy little wretch,' they said, but somehow or other he managed to creep in and hide himself at the back.

> Anyhow, then the service – the church service, you know – began – and after a bit something amazing happened. Everything went dark and everyone felt dreadfully scared, so scared they went all shivery down their spines: you know how it feels when you're suddenly really scared of something? The whole place was Black as Night. Can you imagine? And then they noticed a light at the far end of the church in front of them, this light which got brighter and brighter until eventually everyone was staring at it, you know? – unable to look away. Then out of the light they saw this Mysterious Figure walking towards them. 'He's coming for me,' exclaimed the mayor excitedly, but the Mysterious Figure moved slowly past the mayor. 'Hey,' cried the mayor, 'I'm the mayor. Aren't you going to speak to me? I'm the most important person here. Don't you know that?' But the Figure moved slowly down the church and all the VIPs thought he was coming for them. Ever so slowly, he walked down the aisle, past all these posh people in their best clothes, all thinking how wonderful they were. Everyone was looking behind them in astonishment, overcome as the Mysterious Figure picked up the little boy gently in his arms and carried him down the aisle, back towards the light, which was too dazzling for the eyes of the people. Like the sun, you couldn't look at it. The Figure walked straight into the light and completely disappeared.

It's the end of the story and I pause for a moment for it to sink in. The children are totally still, a silent capitulation to the story, a shade of acknowledgement. Then they sing another song and the assembly is over. The atmosphere feels more relaxed.

Now I say I hope everyone had a terrific holiday and how I am looking forward to meeting them in due course and how I will be coming round all the classes. I smile. I feel that they are enjoying the assembly, and I feel genuinely too that they are smart-looking children, with a lot to say for themselves. 'I like people who come up to talk to me,' I say, wondering if the staff weren't thinking that I was beginning to sound too much like a soft touch. No, I convince myself, I've worked with tough kids before, in northern district housing estates, in difficult schools. I know what children are capable of; I know the children here have a reputation running before them. But there's nothing like being positive when making a start.

The assembly is over and the teachers begin to lead their classes away.

One little girl says to me, 'You goina play some more stuff?'

'How do you mean?'

It's a stupid question.

'On the piano.'

'If you like,' I say, and sit back down and start playing a jolly variation on one of the hymns.

'That's great, man,' says another girl.

'Not "man", Myrtle,' says her teacher, 'Mr Winkley.'

'Ain't he a man?', says the girl cheekily and I stop playing.

'Myrtle,' I say. 'Questions yes. Rudeness no. I bet you're not really a rude girl.'

'You don't know her,' says a boy, and the girl stares furiously at him.

'Now then, now then,' says the teacher and the class disappears into its classroom.

One teacher, the remedial specialist, an elderly unassuming man of small height who arrives each morning in a neat trilby hat, which he dutifully puts on a peg outside the staffroom at precisely eight-thirty, comes up to me after the assembly and says, 'That was excellent. Just the job.'

It was a kind, memorably thoughtful remark at a difficult moment.

5
Walking About

The children are back in their rooms by now, and there's a chance for me to walk around the school to get a feel for the place. In every school there are as many differences between the feel of classrooms as there are differences between teachers. You pick up this anecdotally, surreptitiously.

Most of the classes are off the main hall, as I have said, but Mr Coker's class is in the temporary hut in the yard – thirty-five children in a room that is much too small. It had been temporary for years: temporariness with the look of permanence. There was nowhere else for the children to go.

'Hi sir,' says a boy, running across the yard, almost bumping into me. 'How's it going?'

'OK,' I say, 'so far.'

'Don' worry, man,' says the boy with a grin; 'it'll change.'

Five minutes into the day, Mr Coker is having his problems. He is a small man with a fierce red face that fails to help him with his discipline. You can see through the window that the children play him up dreadfully, and his voice is rising. I wonder what passers-by can see and hear from the road. He edges himself into the classroom, where the children are still milling around, hanging their coats up and messing about, twenty minutes after assembly, and he fusses over the register.

I sidle into the classroom, with not much reaction from the children, creep to the back of the room and position myself on a vacant chair. The desks are in groups rather than rows, and I closet myself with a table of six children. I don't believe Mr Coker has noticed I'm there. He is, right now, calling the register, but everyone's still talking, and no one's taking much notice.

'I think you should be listening to Mr Coker,' I suggest mildly, leaning over the desk and speaking to the children within arm's length, who are heatedly discussing what they've been up to in the holidays.

'Oh, Coker,' a boy says, 'he can't teach.'

'He can't run, that's for sure,' says another boy.

'How d'you mean?'

'He chases us round the classroom, but he can't catch us.'

'Jamie once climbed right out of the window.'

'Good heavens, what did Mr Coker do?'

'He never saw.'

'What happened to Jamie?'

'Dunno – he went.'

'How d'you mean? He didn't come back?'

'Nope. He just went.'

'Didn't anyone say anything?'

'Nope.'

'I see.'

'You goina teach us sir?'

'You want me to?'

They stare at me. What kind of question is that? What are headteachers doing asking such questions? You can see it in his eye: heads are there to tell you what to do and punish you if you don't do it. Like the recusant Jamie, I stalk out of the room. Unlike Jamie I have every intention of coming back.

In the main building again, I continue my patrol. Some rooms are noisy and children wander aimlessly about the room, pursuing tasks of varying quality. Other classes are sitting in rows and beavering away in silence. The teachers here, like teachers everywhere, by and large go their own way – at least in relation to how they manage the class.

Over the next few weeks I spend some time assessing every class, getting to know the children and the teachers, listening at doors, peeping through windows, entering rooms and noticing the frisson in the response: children instantly go quieter, glancing in my direction. The presence of another adult, especially the head, totally changes the atmosphere.

I continue to sit at the backs of classes, trying to get a feel for what it is like to be here as a child. Bit by bit, I start to piece together what I think is a reasonably good picture of how things were going. Or not going.

The curriculum at the school seems to operate according to unwritten conventions. Every teacher teaches a considerable amount of maths and language, using similar books and materials. The children work out of books or on worksheets, and are engaged in lots of repetitive work, doing their pages of sums and comprehension exercises. Smart commercial materials are in vogue, often tarted up versions of old-fashioned word-filling exercises, in glossy format. Many of these are American and packaged in glossy boxes. They are a great fall-back for teachers at 'in-between moments', and help keep the children occupied all day long.

As with the conventions of eighteenth-century classical music, there's a clear understanding of what the rules are: reading, writing and maths are very much the priority. There are a few syllabuses about, which are made up of broad generalizations as to what teachers ought, in principle at least, to pursue. In my past experience syllabuses were usually left to rot in teachers' desks. Apart from maths and English, what's left to teach is largely driven by the teachers' enthusiasms and interests. Environmental studies, what there is of it – snippets of geography, history, science – is unpredictable. Art is variable. Music, the little that takes place, is sometimes interesting. A Welsh teacher runs a choir which performs with gusto and the children love singing in the hall.

Every teacher has his or her own way of going about things and everything that is taught is filtered, refined or minced through the teacher's mind. Minds – involving the ability to think, as well as the skill to make things interesting and to occupy and discipline a class – vary enormously.

There is a kind of teacher who is both competent and half-committed. One colleague, for example, fulfilled all his duties, and in the event of an inspection, which at that time was a rare event, would have shifted his lessons up a few grades, rather like the sudden swift movements he was capable of during his Sunday league games on the rugby field; and he would have emerged safely in the highly competent bracket. But some teachers lack internal energy. Worse, they lack passion, a curiously important component in teaching. It is possible, I suspect, to succeed in many jobs without passion, but not in teaching. Passion demands a long-term commitment to the pupils. It requires an intensity of interest both in the children themselves and in the subjects that you are teaching. It acts as an inner fire, burning away. This may not show in the teacher's eyes, or manner. A passionate teacher may be quiet and fastidious just as she may be tough and vigorous; but the pupils know about teachers who are committed to them, and forgive them a lot. Teachers may punish, berate, drive, enforce, and even once in a while be unreasonable; but the fire, the bothering, gives children a feel of security and animation: they sense that the experience is worth having. The caring is not a vague abstraction; it is a particular, animate thing: you must care about me, not just about the class as a whole. You must care about what I do, how I behave, how I work. Such caring is signalled in a large number of small matters. It matters how you speak to me, how you mark my work, how you look at me. There is a distinctive warmth and interest in those who care – nothing phoney about it. The child makes a ruthless distinction between caring and indifference. Caring motivates. It not only makes you feel better; it makes you work better. It oils the relationships in the classroom. It enhances the way you value yourself.

Caring is not the same as kindness. It is possible to be kind but not caring. As a matter of fact most of the teachers in the school now seem kind. There is currently in the air, for example, the makings of a great debate about racism. Much criticism in the press explicitly blames teachers for creating and enhancing racism. This is not evident at Grove

School. Having worked in other schools, mostly with all-white children, I can't see any striking difference in the way the teachers treat these mostly black children. There are no visible signs of racism, not even in the staff room where it might become most apparent. On the contrary, there is a pervasive atmosphere of kindness. Most teachers come into the job because they like children and want to help them. Their own lives, self-esteem, sense of achievement are profoundly linked to the successes of the children. Even those teachers who are pretty incompetent in the classroom will spend time playing cricket with them after school, or running football teams on Saturdays. It is certainly true that there are children teachers dislike, children they will be angry – even dismissive – about; but these are the ones who disrupt their classes or behave in appalling ways to each other. They are 'unpleasant' children.

There are teachers who tend to judge all children as though they are emotionally the same: there is an expectation of conformity which may result in a pragmatic approach to managing them, based, reasonably enough, on intuited and sometimes imagined principles of good parenting. Not that all these teachers would make good parents. Some harangue far too much. Some are rigid and too severe. Some fail to listen to perfectly reasonable points that children make. Some let them get away with murder. They flail about in the classroom like desperate windmills, the children running rings round them.

There is one elderly teacher who in her quiet way is both kind and committed. She cares profoundly about the children's welfare and in an old-fashioned way prepares and delivers her work meticulously. She suffers from personal ill health but is never away. Nalini, from South India, is reliable and gentle. She has a way with children that is insistent but polite. If she feels a child should be chastized she will say so with regret, and without fear or favour. But there is a maturity there, a calmness and commonsense, that impresses the children and strengthens the staff. She is competent, unpretentious, a person who keeps the wheels moving, turning up day after day, year after year, until finally she gives up through ill health and exhaustion. Settled in her ways, safe in her performance, she delivers a repetitive programme of carefully prepared work. And the children learn in so far as they are settled and feel safe. They internalize her personal strengths, and because she is at heart both democratically inclined, and liberal in approach, children with imagination can ease themselves forward out of the circle of routines, and learn quite effectively.

She is very small in height and gives an appearance of frailty. Her voice is quiet and low, and she maintains a deep respect for the children, accentuated by a formality of rhythm and routine in the way she works. She begins each day by expecting each child – many children towering over her – to stand upright next to their desk and to reply in chorus to her 'good morning children' before being officially allowed to sit down. The work has been prepared on the board and the children sit in rows, her authority being one of respect; and it would be all too easy to underrate the contribution she makes to these children's lives.

I am impatient, though. There are others on the staff who are less distinguished.

There were some wholly unacceptable things that I was going to have to deal with. The children in Mr Coker's class were regularly climbing out of the window, and from time to time, in a fit of despair, he chased some of them around the classroom with a stick in his hand. There were classes on the edge of being out of control, and others where there was high tension in the air, children being slapped or shouted into submission.

I take note. Maybe it will be possible in due course to replace some of the staff with more able practitioners. But I try to think positive. As a matter of fact I've seen much worse. For a year or so I was a supply teacher going the rounds from school to school. At one school I went to, there was a class teacher, short in height, who always taught in a little peaked Andy Capp hat, and who set children writing tasks at the beginning of the day which freed him up to pursue his interest in woodwork at the front of the class, while his large baglady of a wife sat at the back, leaping up from time to time to smack recalcitrant pupils with a ruler. At another school, a Falstaffian character of a man, a retired merchant seaman, used to set up a periscope in a high window, leaving the children working in silence while he went off for a smoke. The children would eye this periscope with trepidation, and woe betide anyone who spoke while he was out. In another school, a lady who was particularly fond of black clothing, regularly found it hard to track down her own classroom. Other teachers, seeing her dismally circling the playground after morning break, would shout out of their rooms: 'This way Mrs Mac.' It became a school mantra. 'This way Mrs Mac,' the children chanted.

Many schools have a handful of such problems that have been inherited over the years. They are often of the generation of those emergency teachers who were crash-coursed into teaching in the chronic post-war teacher shortage. While this process picked up many women of unusual talent, some of the men, usually ex-servicemen, were almost comically disastrous, though often greatly loved. I am aware that it is extremely difficult to get rid of unsatisfactory staff. The Local Authority has a forked tongue in such matters, failing to back you up when it comes to the crunch, and scared of the unions. The best they can offer is to encourage a 'transfer', which means sharing your disasters out round other schools. Another plan is to move them, 'the one-legged brigade', as one politically incorrect Inspector calls them, into supply teaching, or into one of the peripatetic outfits where these oddballs can do least harm. The successful head, I know, needs to take all this into account and to pursue his line of attack with considerable cunning.

The most successful teachers operate a kind of *realpolitik*, based on establishing firm control and a strongly directive approach to teaching. I am already on the look out for points of light, exemplars, opportunities.

Avril is an inventive teacher who explores new educational territory with her children by means of a curious mix of ruthless discipline and unusual and stimulating work activity. She has a particular way with the big girls, an ability to demand standards of behaviour but at the same time attract them as friends – mothering them. They know there are no holds barred if they mess her about: they'll be in big trouble. But they love her, carry her bag, visit her sometimes at home, and come back year after year to see her after they've left the school. She takes them camping and keeps telling them how good they are. She is, as the children describe her, a tough cookie. Lady Plowden would have been shocked by her tactics. But they work like beavers in her class, and in interesting ways. Her children are polite and clearly like coming to school. The parents think she is wonderful. The artwork she produces is monumental and stunning, of a quality that I have rarely seen. She is, above all, memorable.

On one occasion an elderly lady, the senior editor of a major publishing house, comes to visit me, and we pass through a hall in which Avril is engaged in a PE lesson with her thirty-five large adolescent-looking children. Avril, not saying a word, holds up her hand, snaps her fingers and the children freeze in their places. There's absolute silence as the visitor and I sweep through the room. Even I am slightly taken aback by this slightly fearful example of managerial efficiency.

'You run a tight ship, Mr Winkley,' says the lady, not, I feel, altogether approvingly.

6
The Children

What then of the children? The ability range is evidently very wide and as I go round on my daily tour of duty, I am alarmingly aware that some children can do very little. Many, perhaps as many as a third, are way behind their age group. And yet there are some very able children, too, who can read like adults and write exceptionally well. The gaps are wide by the age of seven, and cavernous at the age of eleven. In this respect the school is no different from many inner city schools.

I have insufficient firm data on the children (I am soon to gather it), but the evidence strongly suggests – as in every inner city school I have ever taught in – that the literacy skills of a minority, maybe a substantial minority, of the children are poor. There's also the substantial issue of children learning English as a second language, of which we have a great number.

Whatever my misgivings may be about there being too narrow an emphasis on 'standards', a shifty nineteenth-century educational concept, with a host of disputable meanings, the fact is that some children's achievements are so far behind those of others that their life chances must surely be affected. One boy has a problem remembering his own name. Each day he is asked by everyone what his name is, and he pauses for some time to reflect. He has good days and bad days, and on bad days he is Peter or Tom or someone else; on good days he gets his own name, Michael. Some children can scarcely keep up with the normal curriculum, and resort to staring out of the window, messing about, or crayoning – an activity which seems to me a form of mindlessness. Why do teachers make children crayon things in? It may keep them quiet but it takes them nowhere. I devise a word for it – *cruising*. There seems to me to be a point at which such children will dissociate themselves from school and all it offers, and a coincidental point at which the teachers will decide that they can spend no more time and energy coping with children who are so manifestly disenfranchised from the main class activities.

I have no illusions that solving these children's problems is going to be easy. At one time I ran a remedial department for slow learners, and I am well aware of just what an Everest for them it can be making progress after the age of seven, and what a complex of factors holds these youngsters back. Lurking in the back of my mind, however, as my insecure thoughts evolve, there is an intuition that something different must surely be called for, some breaking of the mould, some way of improving things for them.

The children come, of course, from a huge variety of cultures. I try to project myself into their minds. These are youngsters who have for the most part been born in England; born, moreover, in a seething, changing Western city with its own dying traditions. The great industrial train bolstered by two wars of armament manufacture and the huge, antiquated car industry are disappearing as fast as the old communities. The children are from countries still bound up in post-colonialism. Their parents came over here carrying pictures of the Queen. They were tempted by advertisements in the 1950s and 1960s for nurses and other workers.

It strikes me, once again, how painful it must be to uproot yourself from one culture to enter another. Especially one that proves to be a mixed blessing: these invited guests are in no time at all seen as invaders.

Through this act of immigration the newcomers, a multicultural and polymathically diverse group, were forging the world of the new Western cities. Birmingham has every claim to be ahead of the field and to have become the most amicably receptive of communities, extending its long tradition of absorbing immigrants from Ireland, Wales, or wherever it may be, since the industrial explosion at the turn of the twentieth century. This is not to say that those who came to Birmingham found it easy. But maybe, in some small ways, this place has proved to be more accommodating than most.

Their children are in a sense in a cultural no-man's-land, *between* cultures. Viewed differently, they have an excess of culture. They have their own home culture, their religion, their style of upbringing. But they also live and breathe the air of a Western city.

It's hard to say quite what 'Western culture' is. The term expresses unstated values, behaviour, presumptions, attitudes that have been transmitted through the texture of daily life, particularly perhaps through television. I once asked in assembly how many children had stayed up the night before to watch TV. Most had been watching after the 9 p.m. watershed. Strict home discipline in some families may give way to periods of neglectful tolerance, especially when it comes to bedtime. Adult films are grist to the mill of these youngsters. But one young Muslim girl was marched to school by her irate mother who had found her playing hooky from school one afternoon to watch an episode she had secretly videoed the night before of *Coronation Street*.

Culture is not a quiet, passive thing, something to be preserved in aspic. It shifts and changes, and is a sounding board against which we discover and test out who we are. 'Tradition,' said Stravinsky, 'is not a relic of a past that is irretrievably gone; it is a living force that animates and reinforces the present.'[1]

I understand how, in their quest for a strong sense of identity, these children find themselves at the cutting edge of different traditions. At too young an age they have to mould and adapt them for themselves. Things do not necessarily make sense for them.

You hear the occasional bursts of abuse in the playground.

'You Paki, Cooby.'

But in what sense is Yacoub a Paki? And would he be

called 'Cooby' in Islamabad? It's possible he's been to Pakistan, but it would only have been for a holiday. Some children go to school out East, but they are mostly horrified at the appallingly strict teaching methods there and can't wait to come back to England. Yacoub was born in Dudley Road Hospital Maternity Unit. At home his parents speak Urdu, and every night he spends an hour or two at the mosque. But to his friends he speaks street-English. English is the language at school and his teachers mostly exude Englishness. Inside his head he is internalizing a flow of television, all Anglo-American. His daily life is a routine of endless translations from one sphere to another, occupying some strange middle ground where multiple streams meet and collide.

One day I come into a class and see a group of black girls. Many people would call them 'Jamaican', but to me they are not in any clear sense Jamaican. Most of them were born in England, Jamaica being little more than a distant prospect. The girls, sitting in a line on a bench at the front of the class, are watching a science programme which is referring to the idea of 'evolution' – showing pictures of turtles on the Galapagos. And the row of girls have their fingers in their ears and their eyes tightly closed, to avoid, presumably, hearing the word of the Devil. The Seventh Day Adventist church – their church – does not approve of such ideas. It is transparently clear to them that God, as he manifestly says in *Genesis*, put Adam and Eve on the earth, and that was that. The girls are adopting a highly defensive and righteous posture. I suspect that behind their noble act of defiance there is a healthy touch of ironic naughtiness. It could be a cunning use of religion as a tease. But the girls are equally aware that there are other overriding considerations – for instance that their parents would be horrified at such behaviour in the face of the teacher, who is there to be respected. At home there is the slipper and the strap to deal with such outrages should I unwisely summon mum or dad. Realizing the complexities of the situation, I say nothing.

There are in fact plenty of happy-go-lucky youngsters here, with big smiles and confident, good-humoured rivers of words. But there are also some children who are deeply uneasy with themselves. Some of them are living with aunts and uncles, often temporarily, and sometimes unloved or half loved, or even, I sometimes suspect, neglected and abused.

I visit one family at about six o'clock one evening and the child, a large, attractive eleven-year-old black girl, is already in bed having committed some offence. She has been punished and I'm not allowed to see her. I'm shocked by the sudden flow of abuse about the girl from a well-dressed, good-looking woman, the girl's 'aunty'. She had been sent to England from Jamaica two years before to live with 'aunty' and aunty couldn't think of one good thing to say about her. The girl was a ne'er-do-well, a lazy, useless creature who would be better 'back home' where she'd get the punishments she deserved. This family isn't like some families I know, who are knock-about but warm, caring and good-hearted. The attack on the child is emotionally venomous, uncompromising in its dislike. I speak gently to her the next day, with two friends by her side, and I can read her deep unhappiness – she is scared even now of me, as I have been to her home. All she has are her friends, and I try to think of ways to comfort her. She is a Cinderella, detached from the friendly, cheerful world back home: how important the school must be for giving such a child a sense of pride in herself and of belonging to people who do care about her.

Other children may suffer from their parents' separation or insecurity. Fathers are out of work. There have been bad experiences with accommodation; or alienating rudeness and inexplicable racism from employers, landlords, strangers in the street; or difficulties in finding jobs; or unanticipated experiences of hostility and unhelpfulness. All of these can lead to guardedness, suspicion – or worse still to paranoia or complete emotional breakdown.

There is the added danger here that some teachers, wholly

unfamiliar with the worlds of these youngsters, and commuting as most of them do from middle-class suburbia, are all too quick to generalize. The children are all this or that. 'Can't swim.' 'Good at running.' 'Not very bright.' Such generalizations are often expressed out of impatience, or sheer exhaustion, at the impossible behaviour of some child. All 'these children' are 'like this'. Some are inherently 'stupid' or 'bright' as the case may be. Some come from 'bad homes' and 'are neglected'. Teachers care all right, but they also make distinctions, as though these children 'from elsewhere' are not quite part of their world. From all of us not living in this community, not wanting to live in this community, there is inevitably an element of condescension towards the youngsters we teach, of being patronizing.

Children pick these things up. Their feelings are too easily ignored. For instance, some of them hate to be touched, even on the shoulder. It's as though they believe they're physically vulnerable, liable to fall apart. Which is why, perhaps, some of them are so aggressive physically, so hypersensitive to what they perceive to be an unfriendly look, a push, a hostile act, and so easily explode with fury, fists flying, pouring out streams of abuse. These are not easy children to deal with.

But, at the same time, it is possible to forget their strengths. Many of their families have come from rural communities in the Punjab, Jamaica, Barbados, St Kitts, communities with high levels of mutual community support. Such families, including extended families, will have offered an underlying security, with financial and other help when times got tough. It won't be long before the more enterprising folk round here build up businesses, and produce top-rate musicians; or buy up property and set up clothes outfitters and restaurants by the dozen. Some have real ambitions, a determination to succeed, and striking energy. The different religions provide powerful forms of bonding, helping forge new communities – emerging from an age of insecurity. Above all, many of these families are ambitious for their children. They send them to school to learn, and they expect them to be properly taught. They have faith that the school will provide.

Once stripped of cultural and class distinctions, each child has his or her own character, his or her own integrity. Acknowledgement must be made of their individuality: the teacher's responsibilities must go beyond culture, race and class towards something like comradeship and friendship. You admire people for what they are; you teach them for what they can be. Their virtues are the equal of yours; their potential is at least as great. The only difference between us is that my own responsibility is the more onerous one.

7
The Appraisal

In a well-publicized speech in Birmingham in the autumn of 1974, Sir Keith Joseph spoke trenchantly about the appalling standards of schools.[2] In a Jeremiad spirit of gloom, he argued that handouts to the poor merely increased their degeneracy, undermining their ability to help themselves. As for primary schools, these were sloppy, liberal places where children misbehaved and failed to learn to read. Joseph was not without unexpected supporters. A leading liberal at the time, Clement Freud, fired off his own volley at the Liberal Conference at Brighton that year. 30% of the children of Birmingham, he declared, can't read at all. 'Like old cars,' he said, 'head teachers should be tested regularly to see if they are fit for service.'

Delegates were appalled at such illiberality and Freud was much berated. Then the Conservative Manifesto came out with some unlikely proposals, intended to increase parental choice, to promote the centralization of the service and to launch a major drive on standards and a Parent's Charter. None of them would see light of day, we all thought. Not a chance.

There was gloom in the air. Sir Alec Clegg, one-time Chief Education Officer to the West Riding of Yorkshire, argued that the quality of many primary schools in the UK was internationally renowned. They were creative and civilizing places for people to learn. But his prognostications were not encouraging. He divined that they were, like the rest of the educational system, profoundly vulnerable. The cult of managerialism, a US import like much else, was gathering momentum.

> I suspect that at this moment in the development of the service it is with teachers that the main hope lies. What they do will determine whether they emerge as a fully-fledged profession in control of their own destinies or remain at the technician level where they will be told by lay members, administrators, advisers, examiners, professors and others how to do their jobs.[3]

At the far left of the spectrum was the Free School movement. Paulo Freire and his supporters took the view that all schools were anti-educational prisons producing uncritical factory (or cannon) fodder for a greedy society.

This was a time when the Plowden Report of 1967, *Children and their Primary Schools*, was still in the air. The report was known about, if not read, by many teachers and it was endlessly discussed and used as a template by a generation of Local Education Authority inspectors and advisers. It advocated child-centred education and the understanding of how much children bring to their own learning. There were, however, vociferous critics of Lady Plowden and all her works. The 'Black Papers', short radical essays published in the late 1960s and early 1970s, and seen by many in education as the eccentricities of right-wing fanatics, were produced by disillusioned academics and grammar-school teachers.[4] In truth, the Plowden Report had not been wholly in touch with the real world. The commonsense of the matter was that you had to find your own way to survive.

Only one in six teachers on the national scene could be described as 'Plowdenesque'. Research showed that there was a lot of whole-class teaching going on across the land (the national statistic produced by one researcher was approximately 20%), and a lot of individual work, with children beavering away in silence at desks on their own (national statistic, 40% of the time).[5] The cleverest teachers changed their approach according to need and engaged the children in conversation, in group activities, even in some choice of task. Even for them, control was always at the forefront of their minds. 50% of teachers nationally admitted to smacking children occasionally. Over 90% approved, as did most parents.

My assessment of real life at Grove – somehow none of these pronouncements, whether from right or left, seemed to be about real life – was that the teachers here were fairly representative of teachers everywhere. Overall, there wasn't much to set the world on fire. Teachers across the nation were, in general, conservative in the way they worked. It amused me to think that there were pundits who claimed that some schools were hotbeds of revolution, awash with hordes of long-haired Marxist-Leninist teachers promulgating insane, libertarian views to marauding kids who were crawling up the walls.

In reality, children talking too much, not listening, getting distracted and distracting others was by far the biggest problem teachers faced. It requires considerable skill to manage thirty-five or more children all day long in a small room. As for the children's behaviour at Grove, I detected obvious tensions, and even from time to time a note of fear, as though things might at any minute explode in unsuspected ways. They were sometimes harangued by the teachers, or spoken to furiously. It made for sudden bursts of noise, and rising blood-pressure. The children in turn were all too often aggressive with each other, some of them losing their temper at the drop of a hat. Then came raging confrontations and sulking.

There was frequently a fierce tension between child and child, child and adult, too much incomprehension and intolerance: too many moments when trivial matters took on the status of war. There were constant dangers that people would grievously hurt each other. There was constant pressure to exclude, reject, punish children. A few teachers saw me as over-protecting the children and encouraging, in some maverick way, the spirit of revolution.

I reminded myself that I had not been fazed by such things in the past. In a previous job as deputy head of a school on a rough council estate I'd had plenty of first-hand experience of managing very difficult kids (and some difficult staff). I was not going to throw in the towel easily.

8

Miss Minchin

'Well,' says Miss Minchin, glancing at her fingernails, 'and how are we getting on?'

Miss Minchin, the school inspector, is a buxom lady in her mid forties, smartly dressed in pigeon blue, wearing a small neat hat and swinging a handbag. She had, as a matter of fact, been the blue lady in on the appointment interview. But as she marches across the newly oiled wood-blocks, glancing from time to time through the glass tops of the classroom doors, I don't recognize her.

I look at her, faintly bemused, as she seems to know me. 'David, my dear boy,' she says and heads into my tiny office with its yellow walls and jagged crack in the wall, the whole place sinking an inch or two, year by year.

She glances around with the knowing eye of someone

whose business is assessing offices. For their sense of order, no doubt. For signs of timetables and pictures on the walls; of command – could she sense that this was the room of someone in charge, despite being insecure and excessively young? I rapidly work out that she is someone *from the office*, and after sitting herself in my chair (I'm in the armchair in a corner of the room), she wheels round and eyes me, hovering like a great blue bird above me, the desk chair being a few inches higher than the armchair.

'So how are things?' she asks.

'I'm settling in,' I murmur, 'it's early days yet.'

She humphs. 'I have an apology to make,' she says; 'I've made a few mistakes in the appointments here – as you've probably realized ... one has to admit it, when one makes a mistake – I'm quite open about it. I'm afraid it will fall to you to persuade people – one or two – to leave: one or two are surely not so very far off retirement, are they? That's always encouraging. We can probably offer a fairly generous package. My suggestion is ...' She pauses and makes the first of her useful suggestions, 'You *bypass* them.'

'How d'you mean?'

'I mean you find someone else, someone young and bright, something of a go-getter ...' she looks at me brightly, 'like yourself ...' She smiles.

'And you effectively treat that person as – well – having leadership potential ... someone with a B allowance. Give them their head.'

She smiles again.

'I'm not sure that I can see anyone on the current staff who quite fits the bill. Certainly, there's no getting away from the fact that you need help. One cannot do these things all on one's own.'

'No,' I agree.

'I understand exactly. Getting good staff – that's the problem ...'

Then Miss Minchin leans forward.

'I have one useful suggestion,' she says pleasantly. 'This

job is extremely stressful. I do realize. So my little suggestion is that on one day each week – let's say a Thursday morning – you take assembly, make sure everything's settled down, and then take the bus to town: isn't it the number 76 goes from here? Or of course a taxi if you feel up to it ... and go off to Rackham's and have a nice cup of coffee – there's a very nice coffee bar on the third floor – head through the ladies' dress section to the back, and there you'll find it ... Just a short break ... once a week; you take my advice.'

She smiles again. 'We don't want to lose you now we've got you, do we?'

I never took this advice and I sometimes regretted it. It wasn't as crazy as it sounded. Running a school is a job where reflection and personal balance are at a premium because there is so little space to think, and because the ferocity of school activity chips away at you each day. The job induces a kind of blindness, to yourself, to the world outside. This evolves into a sense of indispensability – this place can't do without me – which is made worse by the undeniable need of young children to feel secure, to have a father-figure present. The subconscious life of children is full of defences against the dreadful fear of desertion. My realization that the children need me and so I must be there for them turns, at worst, into a form of guilt that demands my continuous presence. My knowledge that both staff and children need to feel that I am holding them in mind is easily puffed up into a conviction that they require my continuous, resolute, sacrificial attendance and that without me things will fall apart.

Miss Minchin stands up and for a moment admires the view from the window.

'Well,' she says; 'must be going. I expect you've got lots to do.'

I want to talk more about what I've seen: the staff, the children, my first appraisal of how things are.

'There are plenty of problems,' I say.

'*Challenges*,' she says. 'See them as challenges. It's a nicer word, don't you think?'

With that she picks up her handbag and, after a very long delay in the poky Ladies toilet upstairs, sets off down the corridor saying hello to the Deputy on her way out, devious in her pastiche of cheeriness, telling him how splendidly he's doing, how wonderfully well everything seems to be going, adding, 'You will give Mr Winkley lots of support, won't you?' It's as though part of her believes that, should there be the slightest shift in the breeze, this all-too-young head, so frail, so inexperienced, so likely to be interested in better things, might fall by the wayside like his predecessor: not for health reasons but just by getting pissed off and not being able to cope. One more candidate doomed to a short stay. Yet another of her little mistakes.

9

The Riot

A small girl sings as she hops through the hall, holding her head on one side like a little bird, and eyeing me with a cheeky smile on her face, 'Getting to know you, getting to know all about you ...'

'You know Mr James, sir?' says her little friend.

'No, sorry – who's Mr James?'

'He's the head at my friend's school.'

Her friend's school was a mile or so away.

'He marches round the school with a big cane,' she says. 'My dad says the kids there are dead well behaved.'

There's a pause.

'But I'd hate it. It's shit there, man. Can Jazzie come here?'

'Who's Jazzie?'

'My friend, *silly*.'

She puts her hand to her mouth, appalled, suddenly, at what she's said. Her friend, Sadia, giggles.

'Sooorry,' she says, looking at me to judge my reaction.

Such things don't bother me and I smile. There's a sense of anticipation everywhere, amongst the children, amongst the staff. I guess I look too young to be a head, too untraditional.

John, the head here before me, had been a good man who liked the children, but had been exhausted and, I suspect, made ill by the strain of it all. I'd met him only once, and he'd said in a broad Welsh accent, 'Don't you stay here too long, my boy. You hear?'

It isn't long now before I have to start dealing with things. A boy comes rushing into my room.

'Sir, sir.'

'Yes?'

'There's a riot, sir.'

'How d'you mean? A *riot* ...?'

It was a nice word; it showed articulacy. I'm poised to approve. He smiles.

'I mean in the class,' says the boy, trying to give the impression it's urgent.

'Calm down, and explain properly.'

He stares at me, clearly astonished at the lack of managerial action.

'The kids are fighting,' he says with admirable clarity, 'getting out of hand, like ...' He pauses. 'You need to come and see.'

'OK, OK, OK,' I say, 'lead the way.'

We march together down the corridor, the sound of screaming voices flowing from the classroom into the hall, where it seems to resonate and amplify. The class is certainly a riot. The teacher, Nalini, is at the back calling for order in a high voice; two boys are fighting at the front; and the timid children are hiding under their desks. Others are gathered around, standing on desks and yelling support for one warrior or another. Two big girls are involved on the side, trying to help, cuffing one or other of the participants as they rebound off the desks or the walls, struggling with each other. One of the boys, in a wild temper, picks up the heavy duty pencil-sharpener, rips it from the desk where it's been screwed down, and throws this large piece of metal, say a pound weight of it, at the head of his opponent. It misses by a mile and sinks into the blackboard, making a great hole just underneath a row of sums which Nalini has written up for the children to work through. The boy, a tall gangly lad, then leaps on his victim and they both fall to the ground grappling on the floor – driven on by the audience. The shouting now turns into a name chant, as the hyped-up supporters get more and more into the excitement. And there I stand, at the door.

It would take more than me appearing at the door to quell the riot. Nalini looks overwhelmed with relief at seeing me come in, but the children react not at all. No sudden calming, no return to normality at the mere sight of their headteacher. Indeed, it's as though I'm not there.

There are times when I can myself react quickly. They don't yet know me. I don't look like a bruiser; on the contrary. But I can control wild children and make it look as though I mean business. Not for the first time I discover just how strong even small children can be in a state of mindless fury. It's as if they have access to a secret engine of furious strength that their brains can switch on once they've lost any sense of rational self-control.

It is now my turn to show an element of fury. It isn't like me to be particularly nasty, but a touch of drama is clearly useful here. I raise my voice, and wave my arms, and the children are clearly impressed. The spotlight turns on me, and I look all heated and faintly like a creature from a zoo, just released from behind bars – *dangerous*. It's a game, a performance; but I'm rather good at this. I have my own inner fire, determined that I'm going to get my way in such matters. Christ, this is my school, isn't it? I'm damned if I'm not going to be in control. That boy could have been killed. In my first week as head.

I turn on the class.

'Sit down,' I thunder.

Quietened now, they slink back to their desks.

'Out,' I order the boys, and the two girls.

I turn to Adam, the lad who's raised the alarm. My voice lowers, calmer.

'Well done.' I say, 'Have you heard the expression, "saving the day"? Well, you've saved the day. As for the rest of you. This was pitiful. *Pitiful.* What do you think your teacher feels? Can you imagine? All the work she's put in to help you, and look how you treat her? You think that's good? You think so? You think that's the way to behave? Is that right? What if your parents could see this? Suppose they'd been here? What on earth would they be thinking. You think they'd let you behave like this at home? I can't believe it. I tell you I can't believe it. I'm amazed; that's what I am, amazed. Is this what you're really like ...?'

There's a long pause. I draw a deep, deliberate breath.

'It's not what you're really like, is it?'

The children now sit silent, staring forward. They are large for their age, although it's possible that children grow in size, a curious emotionally-driven optical illusion, when things such as this happen. They seem more like twelve or thirteen years old. Nalini has returned to the front of the class. I am ready to hand things back over to her.

In my room are the four instigators.

'Well, what shall I do with you?'

'Smack us, sir.'

There was a pause.

'Please.'

'What do you mean, *please*?'

They look at me, quietly submissive, in surprise.

'You not goina tell our parents?'

'Of course I'm going to tell your parents.'

One of the girls begins to cry.

'Please don't.'

They stare at me, with dark ashen faces.

'Don't you think they ought to know?'

A long silence.

They don't understand. For the most part, what happens at school is what happens at school: that is to say, it does not happen at home. It should, therefore, in their ethical rule-based interpretation of the world, be dealt with at school. It is a surprise to me since I have never thought before that this might be an issue for a child – though, reflecting on my own childhood, I remember that the last thing I would ever want to happen was that my parents should find out about my misdemeanours at school.

As I stare at the miscreants standing there, I feel, not for the first time, like a judge. I might almost have worn a wig. Keep calm. Be sensible. Don't overreact. Don't underrate the hurting power of words. Don't overrate the ameliorating power of punishment. Never attack the child, focus on the behaviour. Don't lose perspective. If possible don't impose, negotiate. But don't forget, either, that in Nalini's silent class, the children are waiting to see what will happen. These are early days. They're all discovering a relationship. These children suddenly find themselves with a new father-figure – someone with authority. For some children (as they see it) *more* authority, in effect, than their own father. Can this prototype father cope?

The children stare back at me in my room, nervous, and wait and wonder. So they want to be smacked. I was to hear this more than once over the years, to the point where I realized that spanking for many children of that generation – maybe most of them – when confronted with the potential consequences of seriously out-of-order behaviour, was no big deal, and even in some circumstances preferred. For many of them, used to tightly observed rules of justice and delivery, it was seen as instant punishment making no waves and not rippling into emotional confrontations at home. It was the commonsensical way of the world, and pointless, except as a marker of moral disapproval, an effective signing-off of an incident of bad behaviour.

The children standing before me are not outrageously difficult. They are immature and bad-tempered. But when you get yourself into sticky positions like this you have to accept the consequences. I told them they would have to help pay for the damaged blackboard: they would be fined out of their pocket money and it would be spread over the next couple of weeks. They were now on probation: the incident would temporarily go on their record. One repetition and it wouldn't just be a smack; the whole ghastly episode would be relayed to all their parents.

'All for one and one for all. You know what that means?'

'No.'

'It's the Three Musketeers. You're like the Three Musketeers – well, in your case the Four Musketeers.'

They stare.

'It means, like the Three Musketeers, you're responsible for each other. You got each other into this mess; you've got to help each other get out of it. You make sure that you watch each other: you understand? If one person starts losing his temper, you deal with it. How do you deal with it?'

'Calm them down.'

'Right. Bang on.'

'And in addition, for you there'll be no breaks for a week. And a beautifully neat letter of apology to your teacher.'

The relief is tangible.

'If you go back to the class and look amused, I'll have you back. If I have you back, it'll be a big deal.'

They nod thoughtfully.

'You know what I mean by a big deal?'

'Tell our parents.'

'You got it in one.'

It was odd. I was closer to them; it was almost as though I was one of them. I felt, curiously, that I was getting under their skin, into the way they thought, the way I used to think at that age. I was beginning to communicate with these youngsters, to gain a feel for their language. I had tried to communicate my own response, directly, as though through the air, almost beyond words.

'The Three Musketeers used to fight for the French king, you know?' I say.

'I saw them on a film,' says Angela.

'Right. They looked after each other. They fought on the side of good. You ever see a Musketeer lose his temper?'

They shake their heads.

'Back to the class. Show me the letters before you give them to your teacher. Write them at lunchtime.'

'You're not telling our parents?'

'No. It's confidential. That's the end of the matter.'

They look back.

'Thanks, sir,' they say.

It's not until afterwards when I assess my performance in dealing with this first crisis that I realize I have made new friends. The class is visibly more relaxed. The chastened children look straight at me as they walk past, and smile and speak, and as a matter of record they did not re-offend. The incident has brought us closer together in some mysterious, clumsy way.

All that I now had to do was to counsel poor Nalini.

'I'm sorry,' she says confidentially to me late in the day. 'It blew up in my face.'

'You handled it brilliantly,' I say, not sure what else to say, and not seeing the point of saying anything else.

'You think so?'

'Getting Adam out was a brilliant move, exactly right.'

She smiles, a beautiful smile.

'Adam took himself out,' she says.

'Ah well,' I laugh; 'it turned out OK in the end.'

'I'm afraid things like this happen sometimes.'

'I'll get used to it. My last school wasn't a pushover you know.'

'I thought you were wonderful,' she says.

This was so typical of her: she was reassuring and encouraging me; and I saw then just how much the incident, for all my apparent calmness, had knocked me off my perch. It raised a multitude of questions. What could I do to prevent such things happening? Why were these children so edgy, so explosive? Was it a sign of insecurity, unhappiness, poor management, lack of discipline, the wrong teaching methods? Was it me making them insecure? Had I made a right shambles of the whole thing? Or was the incident like a tropical storm, not to be taken too seriously?

10

The Logbook

The Logbook was a large, thick volume in cracked dark-brown leather, worn down by the years, with heavy-duty pages that were more suited to the quill than the biro, and all locked up by its own tiny brass lock and key. You would have expected to read something sensational inside it but my predecessors' contributions turned out to be a disappointingly dry record of daily events, the names of teachers, dates of appointments punctiliously recorded, along with brief comments on trips, parties, accidents, serious misdemeanours and punishments and the names of school visitors. Every effort was made to put the school in a good light:

> Mr Green, after having lunch with the headteacher was taken on a guided tour of the school, and said how impressed he was by the wonderful behaviour of the children.

Such comments, of which there were a great many, could be taken with a pinch of salt. The book had none of the interest of a truly personal diary, nor the informative detail of a historical document. It gave no sense of real progress, no glimpse of a vision or purpose, no coverage of the unexpected hazards. It was supposed to be a record of events, and I was expected to fill it in regularly; but it was hardly ever looked at and, once full up, it was filed away in the local reference library.

The only person who ever asked to see the Logbook was an elderly ex-pupil visitor, Mr Smith from London's Carlton Club, who arrived one day in a chauffeur-driven Rolls Royce, which he parked in the front yard. This very elderly gentleman, immaculately dressed in navy-blue blazer, grey flannels and club tie, stood in the hall with its soaring iron beams, closed his eyes and was at once transported back to the 1920s, his head filled with recollections of old staff and friends. From that moment on, he was locked into a time-warp, and as I took him round the classes, he produced a flow of memories about his teacher, Miss Hay, with her whippy little cane, the huge map at the side of the room with its impressive mass of British Empire red, the head-teacher, a Boer War veteran, and his friend Herbert, who was killed in the Second World War.

Afterwards he sat in my room flicking through the Log-book as though it might remind him of something he had missed. It couldn't possibly have done so as it didn't go back more than three or four years.

'In the Central Reference Library,' I said, 'there are lots more of these.' He nodded. He was very wealthy, and had retired many years before from his business.

'It is,' he said over lunch in the New Inns on the Soho Road, 'very nice round here.'

I asked if he had noticed any changes. He looked surprised. Should he have? Then it struck me that he'd been round the school and into his old classrooms and hadn't noticed that, for example, most of the children were black. Changes? Maybe in the shadow of the lounge room he even saw me momentarily transformed into his old Boer War veteran headteacher.

'He was,' he said, 'a tall, thin, rather handsome man.'

He peered and leaned forward as he spoke.

'With a trim moustache.'

Just for a moment he looked at me, puzzled.

II

Mornings

At Mr Smith's suggestion, I now start to keep a diary of my first year: little more really than disorganized notes which one day I might be able to shape up into something more like a narrative.

February, 8.00 a.m. I've just arrived. The post has accumulated to the point where it can easily make you grind to a halt. I devise a system of reading through this correspondence by ignoring anything not urgent, and I reply to just one letter. The rest goes into the pending tray. *Pending* piles up, and I await enquiries, at which point I shall reply. Once a month, *Pending* is put into the bin. Nothing is ever heard again of 95% of the correspondence, a relief to my still stressed secretary who will soon be leaving.

I realize how important secretaries are: I must learn to look after them. The secretary is the first person you meet as you come into the school, the ambassador, and often the confidante for the parents, all of whose work has to be fitted in round the numerous phone-calls and register work and money collection.

February, 8.30 a.m. Phone-calls flow in, usually teachers registering in sick. Immediate action needs to be taken to replace missing staff, with supply teachers or by redeployment of the staff in the school. We tread a thin red line between survival and collapse at this point. One particularly dreadful, snowy day, when staff get snarled up in the traffic, I have to take eighty or more children in the hall for much of the day.

The supply service is managed by the Local Authority, but the school can't employ anybody until after the third day of a teacher's absence, so that when there's some crisis like, say, a flu epidemic, there are simply not enough teachers available. Even ships can manage with the odd sick seaman. Schools must cover their classes. Now, in the mid 1970s, many heads, especially of smaller schools, spend much of their time teaching in response to crises.

Once there is a teacher in each class, it's time for assembly. I have regular weekly hymn practices with the children, who sing lustily at high volume, especially tunes with good jazz rhythms. I also say prayers. My line is that these are, after all, children whose lives are saturated in religion. I am inclined to think, like some of them, that religion matters.

At the end of assembly I try not to pontificate about behaviour or school rules: I had enough of that in my own childhood. I think assemblies should be crisp and short. Children get bored sitting doing nothing crunched up in uncomfortable postures. It's a good idea to make jokes, which for children are like fireworks, crackling and sparkling, unexpected. It's easy to get them to laugh and applaud, and a joke or two or a funny story puts everyone in a good mood.

March, 9.15 a.m. After assembly, there's maths. The teaching of maths is ever more controversial these days: should children plough through acres of sums, master their tables by rote, be sharpened up by regular testing? Or does this turn them – especially the girls – off maths altogether? How do we deal with the problem that variations in ability in any class are so wide? How can a teacher ring the changes in a lesson to suit such a range of abilities in a class of thirty or more?

There's a great debate fermenting in the wider world of educational politics, somewhere in the ether above our heads. There are pressures from advisers to make maths more interesting, more practical and activity-based. Putting children into ability groups is frowned upon as 'streaming', but still quite common in a number of junior schools. Group work is seen as good news; teaching with chalk in hand to the whole class of very limited use. Inspectors are pressing for changes in maths teaching more than any other subject. There's nothing they would rather see than children bustling about with their metre rulers, counting bricks and checking weighing machines, or standing outside doing traffic surveys.

The maths teaching programme here is held together by Fletcher books, an up-to-date maths scheme. Fletcher books are everywhere, in piles of different stages with different colours, books with covers adrift from continuous use: every class has its supply and hundreds of spares are kept in cupboards and the corridors. Assessment is all about knowing which Fletcher book the child is on, so that an element of differentiation by ability is possible.

I'm having a bit of a battle with the staff over what's seen by some as my archaic preference for having maths taught across the school at the same time of day. Some think it's more a prejudice than a preference and there are complaints that there isn't enough apparatus to go round, which is fair enough. Some teachers argue that it undermines the principles of teacher choice, and modern theories of how young children learn, which demand flexible boundaries, shorter or longer lessons depending on circumstances, and recommend improvisation. My argument is that there's something in having a routine, in regular practice, in systematic consolidation from one day to the next. The only way to learn the piano for instance is to practise every day, even if it is sometimes boring. In any case, I'm sticking to my guns.

This is the quietest time of the day. The children are mostly settled, not too tired, and by and large engaged in their work. Any trouble usually comes in the last ten minutes of the lesson when they become restless. There are a few who are in a mental haze when it comes to maths, and for them the whole business is a pain, and the bell for break is a blessed release.

12

Break

April, 10.30 a.m. The playground facilities are miserable. Cars have to be parked in the front part of it which takes up much of the children's already limited play space. Play easily degenerates into children hurtling about like rockets and knocking each other over. There's a 1970s fashion for *kung fu*, and any attempt to play football seems to end up with girls getting hit by the ball: they either burst into tears, or engage in ferocious retribution. The teachers' cars are parked at the back of the yard, and from time to time get their side-mirrors knocked off, which involves me in a lot of hassle. But the worst thing, the thing that really worries me, is that every so often children become bored and throw stones.

It's break time and two boys have invented a game called Let's Bomb Grove Lane. This involves hurling bricks over the school fence from the back playground. They get away with it for a while without anyone noticing, and then one brick lands on a passing VW Beetle, smashing its windscreen. The driver loses control, and the car veers off the road and crashes into a lamp-post. Shaken, he climbs out, lucky to have survived.

He abandons his wrecked car and retrieves the brick as evidence (or maybe as a weapon). Then he heads into the school, oblivious to the hundreds of children who have by now stopped playing to come and peer over the fence. They are amazed to see him resurrected after such an almighty crash. Half the school is anxious to march the offenders – the two little boys – inside. I am appalled, and I apologize profusely to the young man and promise that I will *most certainly* deal severely with the offenders and *definitely* inform their parents. It is almost as if I had hurled the brick myself.

The young man turns out to be a youth-worker. He's pale and distressed, his hands shaking slightly. The perpetrators of the disaster stare miserably at their victim from a yard or two away. They make out that they're sorry, very sorry – and this causes him to feel guilty.

'Can I get you a cup of tea?' I suggest.

'No thank you,' he says meekly.

'Are you sure? You're looking a bit pale ...'

'No, I'm quite all right, really.'

He's looking at the boys, as they stand there, tears welling in their eyes.

'I would rather,' whispers the young man, 'that they were *not* punished, as a matter of fact ...'

He looks at me as though I'm Genghis Khan – *no wonder the poor kids do such things*. 'If you don't mind. Do you *have* to tell their parents?'

'The school is insured,' I say, trying to be matter-of-fact. 'You're not to worry.'

'It doesn't matter,' says the young man. 'Really it doesn't.'

'You must give me your full details, your address and so on, and I shall deal with it ... I'm so sorry. We are all sorry aren't we boys? How many times have you been told that throwing stones is forbidden? What if this gentleman had been killed? He could easily have been killed. Do you realize that?'

The boys survey me in silence and nod.

'It doesn't matter,' the young man repeats as though in a daze; and for a moment I wonder if he isn't a bit concussed. 'I'll give you my address, but I don't want you to make a thing of it.'

Then I see one of the boys grin to the other behind his back. So much for repentance.

After the young man has left I summon the whole school and bang on about the dire penalties that may – nay will – ensue.

> How many times have I told you how dangerous it is to throw stones? Don't you see that people can get killed? It's just lucky that the driver of that car wasn't killed, as a matter of fact; and what do you think he now feels about this school, about all of you, your behaviour?

The children sit listening patiently and probably wonder what this has got to do with them as only two of them had actually *thrown* any stones and both of them are still standing outside my room. But perhaps they suspect I'm right: it was serious; it might have been disastrous. And in an odd way we were all a little bit responsible. The bricks *were* a problem that had to be solved.

As I offload on the children, I'm all too aware that the playground is frequently littered with stones and that even if they are cleared up one day, there will be a whole lot more of them the next. Playtimes present almost irresistible temptations to the children. It will have to be a long-term project for me to try to get to grips with the environment: putting in plants, say, and play equipment, and maybe as an option allowing children to stay inside.

At the moment all I can do is threaten dire penalties for any stone-throwers to scare them off. I also need to have another go at the caretaker to have the playgrounds more effectively cleared.

May, 10.45 a.m. Break, in bright spring sunlight, ends after fifteen minutes. I arrive in the hall to find hundreds of children, who have just come in from the playground, milling about unsupervised and noisy, moving casually into their classes. The deputy is standing, as he always stands, at the back of the hall, facing the throng but quite unable to impose any kind of order.

'Bob,' I say, 'where are the teachers?'

'I've rung the bell,' he complains, 'but they've not appeared.'

He summons a little girl.

'Claudia,' he says, patiently, 'would you ring the bell *again* please?'

Unmanned classrooms are a risk. Teachers have a responsibility to be there, ready to receive the children.

'No,' I interrupt urgently, 'why don't you go up to the staff-room and tell them the children are already in?'

He heads up the narrow wooden stairway that leads to the staff-room, high up in the roof of the school. I march slightly manically round the hall, exhorting children to go into their classrooms, to sit down and get some work out.

'Where are the teachers?' asks one bright soul.

'On their way,' I say. 'Don't worry. They'll be here soon.'

'They're late,' says one child smartly.

'Don't be silly,' I say getting hot under the collar.

'But they are.'

'Be patient.'

'Mr Winkley's getting cross,' says a girl to her friend. 'His face is going red.'

The staff were not on their way. Bob returns and lowers his voice with the bad news.

'Where the hell *are* they?' I hiss. 'They're still not here. Am I supposed to manage the entire school *all on my own*?'

Bad temper was always lost on Bob, though a bubble of sweat has appeared on his forehead.

'They're locked in,' he says.

'How d'you mean, locked in?'

'In the staff-room. Someone's locked them in.'

'Well, let them out for Christ's sake.'

'I can't,' he says. 'Someone's taken my keys.' He pauses. 'Do you know where *your* keys are?'

It takes the rest of the morning to find Bob's keys which have been hidden under the coats in the cloakroom. As for the identity of the young Zorro, I suspect a boy called Wesley.

'Know anything about keys, Wes?'

'Nope,' says Wesley with a smile.

'Just asking.'

13

Literacy and Lunchtime

June, 11.00 a.m. Much of the rest of the morning is spent on reading and writing. Some teachers 'integrate' this into humanities subjects such as history and geography. There is a current tradition in teacher-training of encouraging the teacher to let the child simply 'get on with things'. This seems to me to be likely to lead to what I call 'too much tolerance'. The teacher will be in danger of disengaging with what the child is doing, and the child will then simply go round in circles.

I'm fascinated by teachers like Jenny, an extraordinary new addition to the school, who manages to talk constructively to children about their writing, and has mastered the trick of focusing clearly on the needs of children of different abilities. She's got to be our model, who will lead us out of the wood in this difficult business of developing literacy. She's also an exceptional teacher of reading: the children not only seem to read a good deal in her class, but they read constructively, with Jenny frequently intervening and asking questions.

There are some teachers who impose death by the worksheet. These are just as ineffective as those who allow tracts of unconsidered free-range writing to spread randomly across acres of paper, much of which gets lost. We've still a long way to go in this area, and we're miles from dealing adequately with the problems of the slower pupils.

October, 12.30 p.m. The bell goes for the lunch break. For me it is the worst time of the day. The children line up in long crocodiles and play in the two small concrete playgrounds. Balls are constantly flying out into the road or into the broken-down autumnal churchyard at the back of the school. I keep thinking of forbidding ball games; but what else is there for the children to do? I've got no money to buy any equipment for the playgrounds.

The children crush into the dining-hall, collecting their meals on trays from the counter: they are stolid affairs, with regular offerings of cabbage and pickled beetroot. But everything is freshly cooked. Bernie, the Irish chief cook, is sometimes a bit overexcitable but is good-hearted, kind to the children, wholly reliable. Her staff are a mixed bag and often give her a lot of angst. Sometimes I catch her sitting miserably on a stool amid the vats of cooking-oil shaking her head.

A dinner lady comes to see me.

'Mr Winkley, can I have a word in confidence?'

'Sure. What is it?'

'I wonder if you've noticed the white children are getting more food than the black children?'

'What?'

'You watch the servers.'

'Good God.'

I place myself at a strategic point in the dining-hall. It is true. One tiny boy called Mark is served such a mountain of food that it is far too much to eat, and he weeps when the dinner-lady goes on at him about finishing it up. I discover that under Bernie's nose, trays of pies are being cunningly removed from the counter, and the servers – all of whom are white – shake their heads and claim that things have 'run out'. The last twenty or so children often seem to get nothing much except a handful of shredded cheese in a sandwich.

I check this out urgently. Rumour has it that the National Front has infiltrated the staff and that there's been a plot to give the white children bigger helpings than the rest. What had blown this into the open was the fact that they had tried to recruit the new white dinner-lady not realizing that she was married to a black guy. And now she's the person who has come to me and blown the gaff.

The accused deny that anything untoward has happened. The white child in question is under-size and, they argue, he needs the extra food. The pies would have otherwise been wasted. There was certainly no malice aforethought. How could anyone think that? On the contrary, they had been acting out of genuine compassion. But one particular cook's political views were well known and it was she who seemed to have instigated the whole business, although she denied everything. No one is inclined to believe her, not even Bernie who, now she's found out what's been going on, is duly appalled.

'Oh, Mr Winkley, what shall we do?' she laments, shaking her head furiously, and sitting down on her stool.

I go to see a Senior Education Officer about the matter. What can you do with such insubstantial evidence? But the cook's employer was the Local Education Authority's School Meals Department. Could she not, therefore, be moved to a school which urgently needed help? Especially if she could be offered promotion – say, in an all-white school?

'A long way away,' I suggest.

The good news is that the cook has left. She hated the journey on three different buses to the school, which was on the other side of the city, and has finally resigned her post with the Authority. Everything in the kitchens is back to normal. Two black cooks are being appointed in her place.

The teachers have a rota to supervise the children during

the dinner hour, and they receive a free meal as compensation. The deputy and I are almost permanently on duty. Without the help of some teachers, who give up their own time, it would be virtually impossible to manage. There are regular fights and arguments, children climbing on the roof, and misbehaving in all manner of ways. They're lined up for me to deal with once the bell has gone. Wet days are even more of a nightmare because the children are shut up inside with nothing much to do. The staff do in fact set up wet-day boxes of toys and games which helps, but they have to stay in their classrooms, which puts an end to their lunch break; and I find myself on permanent patrol dealing with children running round the hall – boys creeping into the girls toilets, or disappearing to the sweet shop round the corner.

One boy climbs onto the church roof and like a cat can't get down. The fire brigade has to be brought in. A Vietnamese boy chops his finger in half on the school gate. Three girls who were supposed to stay for school dinner creep off pinching make-up and money for food. They paint their faces in modish ways, dress up and organize a party with chips and coca cola, dancing round their house and leaving the place in a terrible mess.

Understandably concerned, the parents come to the school and shout at me: why did I let the children out?

'This isn't a zoo,' I protest; 'I can't lock them up.'

'They're your responsibility,' says the irate father. And he was right, of course. 'You better make sure you punish them,' he says.

'She is your child ...'

He shakes his head.

'Your responsibility,' he says. 'During lunch hour. My responsibility when she's home. OK?'

By one-thirty, when the bell goes, I've had enough. I often go without lunch or end up grabbing a last-minute sandwich myself.

14
Afternoons

December, 1.30 p.m. The afternoon has a variety of activities going on, often chosen at random – depending on the teachers' own interests. A teacher may be interested in pottery or Indian culture, folk songs or the history of newts – there's little rhyme or reason to it. Often this seems to be the time the children enjoy most. Maybe it's because there's more freedom for them to move around the classroom, to get involved in hands-on activities. A couple of hours, then, to focus on music or art, or the catch-all umbrella called 'environmental studies'.

I realize now that some of our results are coming on, are even occasionally impressive. Everything depends on the ability of a teacher, absorbed in the subject, to carry a vivid, inventive idea to the bitter end, and allow time enough to get things properly finished. The weakest teachers let the children ramble on, unfocused. The most impressive set a ball in motion and continually intervene as the pupils work, not so much – or not just – telling them what to do as prompting, then tinkering, asking questions, suggesting, arguing, persuading.

Some of the children are getting bored and naughty, and are causing trouble. Some are sent out for me to deal with. The truth is that by this time of the day I am fed up with naughty children and I'm not always sure how best to deal with them. Naughtiness seems to me to be too often a function of undirected freedom, a lack of focus in lessons. Why should I chastize a child? Sometimes I'm simply not clear in my mind. The fact is that sometimes you can move a difficult child from one teacher to another and his (usually his) problems largely go away. They don't always, of course. There are a few children I'm getting to know well who are like kettles steaming away, always on the brink of boiling over. These are a challenge to everyone: genuine and disturbing disrupters, who are able to test the patience of a saint.

December, 3.30 p.m. The bell rings for home-time. The parents are gathering, some with prams and babies, and there are also grandmothers, aunts and big sisters, unemployed dads, and people who've rushed out from work and parked their cars on the double yellow lines. Some of them wander into the classes and disrupt them by plunging in to grab their child. Out-of-control toddlers swing dangerously on the PE wall bars, and I wander around trying to get them down, or else I try to calm parents or search for missing coats for weeping children. The children themselves rush off, bags in hand, pushing and shoving out of the classrooms; filling the hall with noise; unwrapping crisps and sweets and pulling their coats on; spinning away in all directions back to their homes, or to the park and the play-centre.

This is not the end of the day for the teachers. There's a brief respite for them to gather breath in the staff-room. Then they're preparing work for the next day, tidying up, marking. Some are running clubs, practising football or netball in the yard, or badminton in the hall, all of them voluntary activities of one sort or another. A few teachers go home early. Most do additional work at home to complete and prepare work for the next day. In due course I aim to set up a facility for the children, where they can be looked after until their mums have finished work, with tea and games and proper supervision. Occasionally we have to take forgotten children home ourselves, late into the evening.

It's an intensely wearing schedule. Teachers are unusually susceptible to illness, some as the result of stress, some from sheer exhaustion. Some I realize, without regret, are on the way out.

I'm almost at the end of my first year. My first Christmas

comes soon, with all the school's traditional celebrations: Christmas decorations, parties and Father Christmas, who I discover to my alarm is expected to be me.

'Aaaaah, it's Mr Winkley,' the children guffaw, pulling my beard as I hand out their presents from my big red sack, flushed and sweating beneath my furry gown.

Looking back, I think I've made some progress. Things are, despite everything, settling down a little. I feel more on top of the job. There is a long way to go, but I have survived. I do believe, after all, that I am going to be able to cope.

15
Utopia

Keep going, our elderly visitor from the Carlton Club had said. But it was so hard to focus on any one task, to complete anything, to come to feel that you had achieved something specific and worthwhile at the end of the day.

I would often go home drained, my head buzzing with various incidents which, disconcertingly, seemed to grow noisier and become more pressing the further I was away from them. And in the back of my mind I knew perfectly well that just keeping going, keeping things as they were, was not good enough.

The aim had to be *improvement*. Was that possible? Was this job just a matter of survival, as my predecessor had suggested? How many misjudgements had I made during the day? What would the mother of the child who yesterday climbed on the school railings and stuck a spike through her arm, say to me tomorrow? What was I to do about the class which was manifestly going under, not learning anything? How many staff was I going to have if the weaker and more exhausted ones moved on, given the problem of recruiting teachers to work in Handsworth? Should I have told the end of the cliff-hanger assembly story to the child who tried to bribe me with crisps for a private account of it? What should I do with the boy who stole the dinner money?

I woke up in the night, the school working away inside my head.

Over the next decade, school improvement was to be prodigiously examined and institutionalized, with a mushrooming of conferences and networks of school-improvement departments. Michael Rutter and his colleagues were already at work on their comparative survey of secondary schools, which was published in 1979 as *15,000 Hours*.[6] Their argument was that schools can make a real difference to pupil performance, and that it is possible to identify key indicators that characterize effective schools.

But 'improvement' requires an underpinning vision, some deeper sense of purpose. It is as much about values as tactics. If the *routine* is the daily management of the ship, the *vision* is the sense of direction, the maps, the compass bearings: the vision needed to come from the headteacher. There should be a sensitive awareness of the expectations of the local community, who will benefit from or suffer the consequences.

So how far to Utopia? Where does it lie? How do we get there?

The *staff* are certainly important. If you have 100% high-quality teachers you will be perhaps 90% of the way there ... *Teacher morale* ... and *excellent leadership*: this surely goes without saying. I must aim at the kind of leadership that offers practical ideas, but unites the crew with a sense of being part of a great enterprise ... We must not neglect issues of class size, the availability of good equipment, the importance of a spacious, stimulating environment in which to work. All these are dependent on *resources* ... For these, we have to fight.

> We should aim for an across-the-board achievement in *basic skills*, and to attain this we must engineer a high-quality *teaching programme* to which the teachers are fully committed … All must be carried out in a spirit of *imagination and inventiveness*, so that the school is exhilarating for everyone … We must demand an out-of-the ordinary *sense of caring* for the pupils' feelings … We must set out to evolve a truly *democratic culture* … This will require building up *trust* and involving parents …

All these abstractions, these hopes, these possibilities. Each objective raises a host of technical problems and strategic considerations. There are four principles underpinning everything. First, the children must feel safe, and peacefulness must reign. Second, they must enjoy coming to school. Third, they must learn something. Fourth, they must feel that what they learn is worthwhile.

Poor judgement on even a minor matter could bring the house tumbling down. There were always the seeds of dissent in the community that could grow at any sign of potential trouble. The Socialist Workers Party, small and chaotic though it was, was highly organized round here and well practised in fanning trouble that might benefit its cause. Like other minority organizations in the area it was made up of people of high intelligence, some of whom were youngsters feeling their way into the public arena, who had significant careers in front of them. Some, who were quite dangerous, were bright but mad. The most threatening of them all were the single-issue fanatics. In one nearby school, a relatively minor episode had led to a parent accusing the head, and the school, of provocative racism. This school found itself petitioned day and night by groups camping outside the school gates, who brought in the press and TV, and magnifying the problems of one small boy into a great and noble cause. In such situations, the pressure on the school becomes extreme and seriously damaging.

The problem was how to get from A to B: how best to

steer the ship to the promised land. I was fond of outlining plans on bits of paper: writing and drawings would sweep across the page, hurriedly expressed. I started shaping up a list of plans for staff and parents, with headings for curriculum planning, ability setting, parent meetings, information flow, staff structure, new appointments. We needed to look at curriculum programmes, the unevenness of the way different teachers taught different subjects, the behaviour problems of the children, and cultural insecurities and insensitivities.

There was a note on the bottom of the page:

> There is no point in doing anything unless it makes a difference to the children.

I sit back in my room at the end of the day. The school out there is absolutely silent: everyone seems to have gone home. The dark evenings are with us. I need to do some sharp thinking, to turn vague aspirations into practical plans. I'm going to require patience (which I lack) and, very likely, nerves of steel (and I'm not really sure how courageous I am). The changes of the kind we will have to deliver will not please everyone.

I switch the corridor lights on. A figure at the other end steams down towards me, glowing bright orange as the ceiling light shines off her coat: it is the lollipop lady who's left her job helping children cross the road to come and find me. It looks frighteningly urgent as she pounds along, large lady that she is, waving her stick around and shouting volubly that if it carries on like this she'll be handing in her cards.

'Oh dear,' I say.

'Some of your boys …' she pauses. '… Well, you won't believe this.'

'Oh dear. Come on then Mrs Swift, spit it out.'

'Some of your boys …' She pauses again, confronting me fiercely. 'They've invented this game.'

'What …?'

'*Let's see how long we can lie across Grove Lane before a car comes.*'

'What?'

'What they do is lie end to end across the road – can you believe it – trying to join up hands ... can you believe it ... before the next car comes. There was a bus ... I tell you it was a bloody good thing it saw them ... The driver was effing and blinding ... but of course by now they're up and away, aren't they ... And there's me standing there like a patsy to cross them over ... '

'Who were they ...?' I sound alarmed. I *am* alarmed.

'Well, I know one of them, that Norman Briggs. My God what I'd do to them if I lay my hands on them ...'

'Calm down, Mrs Swift ... you leave them to me ...'

She looks at me with little sign of confidence.

'Ha,' she says, 'I know what some of these kids need ... I won't say it ...'

She lifts her lollipop off the floor and starts to walk away as if ready to clop the first person she meets on the head with it.

'I tell you one thing's for sure: you need to be crazy to work here.'

It's now well past five'o'clock and dark, and most of the children have gone. I'll see the game players in the morning. What on earth were they up to: did they have the faintest idea of the risk they were taking? Whatever you thought about them, it was a kind of mad courage to be lying across Grove Lane with all the traffic trundling down the road. Maybe Mrs Swift's right: crazy is what you need to be to work here.

16

The Film

How could I find time in the hectic flow of the school day to discuss my vision, and set out a blueprint for future action? Evening meetings were all very well, but teachers were tired then and there was never enough time to get your teeth into things. The level of primary-school funding meant that teachers had a 95% class-teaching load. When you took into account the seasonal hazards of illness, and crisis, and the need for teachers to go out on courses (when their classes had to be covered), this worked out in practice as 100% non-stop teaching for most of the week. Creating the opportunities for us to engage in serious seminar-style discussion in which real issues were debated in depth, required a good deal of lateral thinking.

The weather was drizzly and bitterly cold, which kept the children inside for much of the day. We had thermometers in every classroom since the central heating system, roaring away beneath us, had problems piping its heat into the ancient radiators. There were days when both children and teachers wore coats and scarves all day long. There was an official temperature below which we were not supposed to work, but the thermometers would move up and down unpredictably; they would vary from class to class for no apparent reason, and tantalizingly hover over the red-light temperature. People stayed in school working, mostly without complaint, out of an admirable sense of solidarity. Meanwhile, I reassured them, I was fighting for improved heating: more radiators in the hall, and in some classrooms as well.

The children often got agitated in such weather as though they were mysteriously in touch with the movement of the seasons. They were emotionally affected by snow, which alerted them and brightened the spirit, and rain, which depressed them, and wind, which brought a strange restlessness.

The staff came up with the bright idea of having an occasional staff meeting on a Friday afternoon. Maybe someone had twigged that the staff-room was the warmest place to be. The double whammy was that a distinct role could then be found for Bob. In another life he would have made an excellent administrator or accountant. He was a woodworker of modest aspirations. He was, moreover, a good man, good-humoured, kind and modest; he offered in subtle ways a touch of gentlemanliness, even gentleness, to the school. He was totally reliable, loyal and never absent. He was certainly willing to help on the idea for an afternoon staff meeting by taking the whole school for a session all on his own.

One of Bob's passions was the 16-millimetre film-projector which was set up on rare wet days and the last days of term as a special treat. It was almost unused, and it was kept in a storeroom containing thousands of books, many of which dated back decades. The storeroom was Bob's gold mine. He took pride in bringing out various objects and machines which he would fondly dust and polish.

The projector was relatively new. It required considerable expertise to get it ready, with reels of film threaded round a maze of tiny notches and wheels. It had a habit of sticking and burning the film out and of literally setting the film on fire. But, once it got going, it could project sound movies very effectively onto the large sheet-screen which hung over the stage. There were ancient blackout curtains over all the windows, operated by immensely long and temperamental curtain pulls which more or less darkened the hall.

Bob was never happier than when he was putting his projector and his screen together, and slowly and meticulously moving round the room to pull down the blackout screens. His enthusiasm for the plan for a Friday staff meeting was infectious. Preparation would take a good slow-moving hour, the whole lunchtime. But Bob was always generous with his time and his goodwill.

A Friday afternoon is fixed when Bob can get the projector in place, black out the hall, and show the children some films. Bob has sent off for film catalogues from such places as the British Film Institute, and spent a lot of time preparing for the show.

'Laurel and Hardy,' I suggest, 'or Buster Keaton ... That kind of thing ... or maybe a cowboy film ...?'

'I'm not sure that they watch Hoppalong Cassidy round here,' says Bob.

'They should,' I argue; 'it'll widen their experience. There's some good stuff in the catalogues which they'll never see on the TV ... especially the comedies ... How about hiring *The General*: you know, it's a Buster Keaton movie ...?'

'Good idea,' says Bob; 'I'll look into it.'

By 1.30 that Friday afternoon he has assembled the gleaming projector with all its complicated little cogs and wheels, and its two huge reel-holders. The screen itself is a large affair, encased in a black wooden frame. The caretaker has been high up in the roof risking his life to release stuck blackouts. The bell is rung and the children pile in, all excited.

The staff meeting takes place up in the staff-room, a long way away from the children, and I start with what I estimate to be provocative thoughts about key themes that we need to discuss in depth.

'We need to put our cards on the table,' I begin. 'Don't be afraid to say what you really think. Everything's up for grabs.'

So the discussion gets under way, thoughts flying backwards and forwards. Was it debate or dispute? Some people say very little, but that always happens in meetings. Others are vociferous. Some are more interested in extremely practical matters. 'So what shall I do if someone throws a chair across the room?' 'How do I deal with that wretched Mrs

Brown – you know, Cheryl's mum – who comes into the class every day at about twenty-past-three and grabs the girl to take her home? "Can't wait no longer; you keep them in too long," she says ...'

'We are, quite simply, not doing enough needlework,' says one of the classroom assistants ...

There are those who think that we might start establishing some systems, new ways of working in the classrooms. 'Trying out' is the thing: it is a particularly useful approach, as everyone understands what it means and it is, put this way, not too threatening.

'Nothing,' I say, 'is for ever.'

One teacher has an interesting idea for setting up individual tutorials with the children, as happens with university students. I think it has some mileage. There's agreement that teachers need to work on planning so that there is continuity between one year and the next, and between one class and another. 'Without losing our independence,' says someone else. 'Of course not,' comes the reply. I start to feel pleased with the rising level of the debate. Key themes steadily emerge, and they are pretty predictable: improving behaviour management, working more closely with parents, and breaking down emotional barriers, which seem to invisibly separate the school from the community. People are talking about the curriculum, and how they might improve their planning of class activities and develop some commonality of approach in a professional world which is highly individualistic. The staff are arguing constructively, and with good humour. It's in this kind of relaxed, playful atmosphere that the best ideas begin to flow ...

At this point, it occurs to me that it might be a good idea to check how Bob's getting on managing the whole school. So I leave the meeting and trundle back downstairs, edging my way cautiously into the hall.

There's a rising sound of chattering voices and I can see some of the older children sprawling across the floor, one or two of them shouting at each other, and one group playing cards: is it *poker*? Surely not. When I get into the hall itself the problem is starkly apparent. *Where is the film?* Bob has dropped off to sleep on his chair next to the projector and at some point his elbow has knocked it so that the film has jogged off the big screen and is whirring away incoherently up the wall, making the room flicker like a disco. The children have given up, and all things considered, they're holding themselves together remarkably well. They clap when they notice my tentative entrance and I gently wake Bob up and move the film back onto the screen. He watches it for a moment or two, listening to its loud, scratchy soundtrack.

'Bob, what *is* this?'

'*The History of the German Oil Industry*.'

'It's not Buster Keaton.'

'No.'

'But I thought ... we agreed ...'

'Ah,' says Bob, pointing out that he also carries responsibility for the School Fund, which is in a pretty grievous state. 'But it came *for free*.'

'I see,' I say, and say no more. I have realized by now that this is definitely going to put an end to any contribution I might make to the staff meeting. The film stops, the lights go on; I stay in the hall with the children and improvise a Richmal Crompton story about the subversive adventures of young William Brown to finish off the afternoon, while Bob happily packs away his beloved projector.

'Worked like a dream,' he says, patting it tenderly.

17

Building the Team

A successful head has to be constantly on the search for the best teachers in the business. The profession was, right now, a mixed bag and I wondered whether it might in the 1970s have been better described as an emergent or quasi-profession. Some teachers were rather thinly trained and had come into the job late, having a background in other employment. There was also a growing number of young teachers who had taken a four-year BEd course, a route into teaching which was coming under scrutiny because it was thought they were disseminating 'overly liberal' values, and giving theory precedence over practice.

An alternative route into teaching was via a first degree and a one-year postgraduate certificate in education, which in primary schools had produced another group of relatively superficially trained teachers, whose first year in front of a class tended to be highly experimental. But despite these hazards, individual talents were capable of overcoming inexperience: a good teacher can come from any direction, and excellence seemed to be as much to do with sheer intelligence, emotional balance and natural communication and management skills as anything else.

It was also true of course that a poor – or what is perhaps best described as an *unsuitable* – teacher can come from any background. Some people are simply not up to the job, and too many have been pushed through the training process into what is for them, and the children, a discouraging career.

Incompetence in teaching is generally difficult to hide. Everyone can see it, most of all the unfortunate pupils. But getting rid of such people was by no means easy. One was by promoting these hopeless folk to another school, and being less than economical with the truth. That was why you learnt to treat references with considerable caution.

It was certainly true that one of a headteacher's biggest headaches was dealing with staff 'problems', that is the kind of teacher who disrupts, behaves destructively, is bored, tired, unfit or simply incompetent; and I was bit by bit having to find my own way of encouraging unsuitable teachers to move out of the profession. (My first experience had been at my previous school where I was deputy, and was told to get rid of one particularly dire teacher 'at any cost'. 'Get him to be a *librarian* – or a *poet* – for God's sake,' said the despairing head. The victim was a young man with the fatal habit of only speaking to the front row of the class. He was my first 'success', and did indeed eventually become a librarian.)

There were many teachers who had talents of one sort or another but never made the most of them. Some were 'stuck-in-the-mud', in permanent third gear. Some simply didn't have the physical or mental stamina to survive: I had teachers who regularly took a day a week off, month in and month out, and always got flu at times of high pressure, thus increasing everyone else's stress. One teacher was invariably injured in his rugby match each weekend, which led to his absence on Monday. One talented young teacher suddenly took to dancing round the school with manic cheerfulness, coaxing children from other colleagues' classes into her own. She announced to the children that she was pregnant and started a campaign to get them to knit baby clothes for her fictional baby. She was clearly mentally ill, but her GP was pompously uncooperative, informing me, despite all the evidence, that there was nothing wrong with her.

I discussed the matter with the Inspector, Miss Minchin. She adjusted her hat and showed concern.

'It's not obvious what we should do,' she declared.

She had watched the lady teach. The children seemed to find their teacher hypnotic, like a snake-charmer, who mystified them into a kind of submission. No child or parent had complained yet. However, concerned reports from other members of staff were accumulating.

'But we must do something,' I said, desperately.

She looked round the room.

'You could take a risk on it and suspend her.' There was a pause, 'But of course then you're on your own.'

The gods were on my side. Three days before the end of

the term the teacher came to see me, planting herself on a chair by my side and putting her feet on the bookshelf. All she needed was a long cigarette to complete a scene from *The Long Goodbye*.

'I'm so sorry,' she said, smiling, 'I'm letting you down.'

I eyed her quizzically.

'We're leaving. We're going abroad.'

'Abroad?'

'Is there any problem: I mean about giving notice and so on?'

'Good heavens, no ... Of course you must go. But where ...?'

'I feel terrible about this,' she said, standing up, looking round the room, picking a book up off my desk, and smiling radiantly. 'I can't imagine what people will think of me ...'

I envisaged her in some happy place like Bali or Tahiti.

'Ah. Don't you worry,' I said dreamily. 'They'll understand.'

Three months later a headteacher from down south rang up. Our teacher had been admitted to hospital suffering from severe hypomania and was very ill.

The whole business of appointing and dealing with staff is awash with paradox. What do you make of the young teacher in the Infant School who seems to be appallingly disorganized – papers higgledy-piggledy on her desk, art paper spewing out of cupboards, books scattered around the room, things falling off the walls – whose ability to communicate with the minds of six-year-olds is impressive. Year after year, her class comes into the Juniors better taught, more mature, more enthused by learning than the classes of anyone else. Or the teacher who is always cheerful, works his socks off running the football team, and cricket and sports, but is all over the place in the classroom? Or the teacher who is outstanding at teaching, say, maths, but hasn't a clue about anything to do with the arts and has no ability to get the children to paint or develop musically?

Or the teacher who is far too strict with the children but produces good academic results?

Such unevenness won't do. Casualness in teaching is damaging. So is a lack of mental alertness, and an inability to constantly re-think what you're about and to tinker with your approach to things, to work on your weak points – to *know* your weak points.

How do we engage everyone with a systematic approach in such a way that it doesn't create an excess of dull conformity? How do we cross-fertilize the good ideas and the good practices? How do we pick up on the fact that Avril is a phenomenal teacher of art, and a class manager of the highest order, and use this knowledge to improve class management and art-teaching right across the school? We have Jenny, one of the finest teachers of English I have ever seen. How can she have an impact way beyond her own classroom?

We do have what are called 'responsibility posts' which put people in charge of particular curriculum areas, but there is still not enough time to arrange formal meetings to exchange ideas.

We won't be able to repeat the film experiment too often, so I work on devices such as elongating assemblies, extending playtimes, and grabbing quick lunchtime meetings. 'Responsibility posts' too often entail little more than writing a short 'policy statement', administering equipment and ordering books for the 'department'. The danger is, especially when there's considerable unevenness of talent, that people trundle along the way they've always trundled. And then there's also the hazard of impatience, especially from me, which leads to an excess of direction, a conviction that everything can be planned, that dumbheads and recalcitrants can be Told What to Do. It is, you learn, an illusion that a school culture of the kind that truly engages intellectual energy and exchange can be entirely planned and delivered from on high.

But traditions, 'ways of doing things', do in fact start to evolve. Heads have the enormous power of patronage. They can identify and spotlight talent rather as a theatre director casts a show.

An odd mixture of persuasion and arduous discussion can be linked to the matter of showing quite clearly what you think seems to be working, or not working. The focus must be not mainly on failure, on the pathetic and dull, but on the smart things, the pinpoints of light. High-quality practices are invariably more complex and intellectually challenging than low-quality ones, which are often lazy, with low outputs of energy and thinking. I am fairly tough on incompetence and I do gradually manage to encourage people who don't fit in to leave. I think I can communicate these things by implication, by a 'withdrawal of patronage'. But a tiny minority of people dig in even so and refuse to go; and most schools have one or two of these teachers clogging up the works. With such people you have to do what you can.

I talk a lot to the people who are really tremendous, and exactly the kind of teachers we want. Future management initiatives will be weakened if we fail to use the powers of these folk, to consult them, to use them to improve schools for everyone. There is a great danger in focusing obsessively on the negative features of the system. You bring down morale, tarring everyone with the same brush. My criterion is: would I want my own child taught here, in this way, by this person? (Eventually my own children *will* come here.) I wish I could be more expressively, more directly *admiring*. Why do I find it so difficult just to say it right out: 'You can't believe how important you are to me, to this school; how remarkable your performance is?' But despite my hopelessness at doing this, I think they know. They stay. They start to gel as a team.

I suffer from a restless sense of urgency. Once I see something good I want to go for it; I want it everywhere. And when we fail to get where I think we should, I overreact by becoming far too critical. I do the same with myself. In private I find myself a continual disappointment. *Could do better ...*

It's easy too to underrate the imponderable, the less conscious and more intuitive elements in building up a team. It's a management trick, especially a male-management trick, to think that empathy, mood, states of feeling, are of little consequence. But here I think I am stronger: I can pick up the feelings in a group, and connect with individual teachers and children.

It seems self-evident to me that a culture where people enjoy themselves and come to work feeling positive will be more effective in the long run. In this respect teaching is highly theatrical: we are here as professionals to be committed to playing a part. For there are times when all of us have to keep going despite difficulties. Teachers seem to me to be by and large admirable in this way; they are astonishingly patient, tolerant folk, even as they (often histrionically) mutter and complain.

One of our difficulties is appreciating what living all day with young children can do to us. There's a strange and interesting tension between being mature and immature. Often the best teachers are precariously but precisely balanced between the two: in touch with a childlike part of themselves but equally able to move into an adult role. Children seem to have an extraordinary intuitive sense of this. But most of all teaching calls for balance, inner strength and contentment, even toughness, in your character for you to be able to withstand the unpredictabilities of daily life in a school like this: a determination not to let things get to you too much, without at the same time – and there's the trick – losing a sense of openness, of vulnerability. It's a magical feat to pull off.

The final quality of the teachers I aim to seek out, is specialist skill: they must be not just good at maths, English, art, or what have you, but possess an ability to transform the way the whole school thinks about its practices. A great pottery teacher conveys an enthusiasm for pottery but also knows how to teach you the practical competences that enable you to make worthwhile articles. A great drama teacher creates a world, and gives you techniques that lead finally to high-quality performances. Enthusiasm transfers. It sets in motion traditions which bed in and create their own momentum. When the teachers move on from the school the quality of their work can then be replicated.

The more people leave this creative residue behind them, the finer the school will become. Which is why 'traditions' of practice, changing constantly, modifying as new people take over, require *continuity*; and why one of the roles of the head is to ensure that such good things evolve to the point where they fully establish themselves in the school as a whole.

18

New Blood

Appointing good teachers is a murky business, not at all the rational process you might think it ought to be. It's more like playing poker with a group of strangers in a smoke-filled room, pitting your wits against the rest of the world, and being hugely dependent on the run of the cards.

I begin to headhunt, and to search the system for star performers. This isn't so easy: we're lucky if there are more than a couple of applicants for any job we advertise. Who wants to come and teach in downtown Handsworth, with its dismal reputation? Will anyone come here just for the money? No, they will not.

I have contacts from other schools I have worked at, old comrades, and receive reliable recommendations down the grapevine. I am learning to become a mite devious. One of the best heads I ever knew taught me this: 'Kill to get the best staff you can in the business', he used to say.

One head rings me in a ferocious temper, 'I've heard you're trying to poach one of my staff ...'

'Oh dear, she gave me the impression she was looking for promotion ... I only suggested ... there might be a post coming up here ...'

'Don't you give me that, young man,' comes this hard-bitten lady's voice down the phone. 'I'm an old hand. Keep off my patch, you hear?'

I encouraged some people to leave because they really deserved promotion and a wider career experience: a good school ought to be a training ground for high-quality teachers. It was great if people did feel their time here was a springboard. But getting the right people in the first place is the secret of success. I'm in the business of recruiting by hook and by crook, by phone calls and visits, by persuasion and pleading, battering doors down to find people who can make things happen, and above all can work as a team.

I hit my first big problem with the Local Authority in fighting to get one teacher I especially wanted. Here was a highly intelligent young man, a mathematician, well balanced, talented, someone I had worked with before. He was crucial right now to building up the team. There was a system of scale points for staff, each point offering extra money and seniority; and you could 'spend' up to seven. This teacher, if I could get him, would take two points. The Local Education Authority was unhelpful.

'You're a point short,' says the staffing officer with brutal precision ... 'Anyway,' she continued, 'you can't appoint anyone you like just like that ... have you discussed the matter with your inspector ...? You'll need an interview ... It's out of the question anyway because you're a point short ...'

'I'm not giving up,' I say; 'this appointment is essential to this school ... You understand? I must have him ... He's available, he wants to come. All I need to do is confirm the post ...'

'Out of the question ...'

The lady is adamant.

It's my first real battle. I set about ringing various officers at Margaret Street.

Margaret Street, in Birmingham city centre, is the Local Education Authority base and from here everything is managed. It was the age of powerful Chief Officers, working to powerful local education committees. As Birmingham's Chief Officer, Ken Brooksbank, said, speaking for Chief Officers everywhere, 'I am ultimately responsible for the control of my schools.'[7]

An officer of middle rank, well down the line, was required to carry out stipulations, regulations and directions as formulated by the Local Authority. The inspectors monitored the headteachers and were expected to keep them in order. But this is a long way from me, happy to forget that I'm part of a wider controlling management system. I explain that if I don't have enough points now, I will by September, since the numbers of children are going up and so more points will be allocated.

'This is not September,' says the staffing officer. 'That's purely speculative.'

'But likely ...'

'All kind of things are possible ... It is now April ...'

'If I leave it until September, he will no longer be available ...'

'You must realize that we have to work – you have to work – within the rules ...'

'I don't think you quite realize ...' I say, 'I am appointing him.'

'You can't.'

'I can ...'

There's a deep breath.

Miss Minchin comes out on one of her visits, sits down in my room and, after the door has been securely closed, she smiles gently.

'I hear,' she says, 'you have been a rather naughty boy.'

'I've appointed him,' I say.

'You can't.'

'I can ... I *have*.'

'Oh dear,' she says. She smiles again. 'Never mind, let's not worry too much about it, shall we?' Miss Minchin is a lady who worries very little. But when it matters she's admirably cool. There would be much head shaking at Margaret Street. It would be noted that I needed watching. This is, of course, out of order, but then again there will probably be more points for the school in September. I ring my new appointment that evening. 'We're there, Edward,' I say. 'You can start.'

There are other appointments: we're on a roll. Fraser, an art-specialist from a secondary school, shows us how to produce remarkable work from children. His approach is to constrain in order to create: just sufficiently to focus the child's inventiveness. The outcome is individual pieces, never stereotypes. More astonishingly he can transmit his ideas to other teachers. A succession of artistically gifted teachers, Judith, Verna, Ingrid, Lynn, will follow in his wake over the coming years. An art exhibition will become part of the school year with an explosion of original art work appearing across the walls of the halls and classrooms. Later there's Donal, who shows what can be done by young children with clay. Wonderful masks, heads, models of all kinds begin to emerge, which make me ask the question: how many young children get such an opportunity to use clay?

There are others with different skills like Vivienne, Sue and Cheryl who have an ability to deal with difficult children with good humoured patience, and can offer a haven of good parenting experience in a turbulent world. I have particular admiration for such teachers, with the skills to manage, to control and to re-direct the energies of difficult, restless pupils.

One class I cover for the day impresses me with its

bravura confidence and command. Each child is responsible for someone else, and expected to check, chide and reassure. I have not been long in the class, and am taking the register, during which time the children already have a bevy of tasks to perform, when a child confides in me: 'You know sir, Lucy isn't doing what she's supposed to be doing.'

The depth of organization extends to illustrations being put up round the walls. Parts of the walls are allocated to pairs of children, rather in the way that you might parcel up a garden; and there are all manner of rules and recommendations for how the children may display their work. The result has to be interesting, provocative, and make others in the class ask questions. It has to be easy to read and good-looking, and from time to time it has to be developed and changed, though not in class time. Children are given the freedom to stay in the lunch break and after school to get a grip on this particular obligation. Rare indeed is the experience on another occasion of being told by a little girl that 'her partner', a large boy with a macho style and a notorious background with his leather-jacketed gangster brothers, 'is not behaving himself properly'. The little girl points the boy out openly, and adds, slightly primly, but without an ounce of doubt or fear, 'I think you should do something about it.' But before I say a word, the boy slopes off guiltily back to his work.

How many other teachers can manage so sophisticated an operation? How dependent is it on *genius*? I hold in my mind from now on the *possibility* of such an achievement, this shred of Utopia. I encourage others to think about display in this way – the active displaying of work so that it means something to the children.

I am confirmed in my belief that young children can manage much more than they are given credit for. They can even deal with some of the problems of badly behaved compatriots in the class. They need to see the point of what they are doing, to be able to connect the jigsaw of their day-today learning experiences into a larger picture. They need to think incisively and ask questions for themselves, to stand on their own feet and, when necessary, speak out fearlessly. All this can be accommodated within the desirable principles of whole-class teaching. When I tell Nicky's class to be quiet and listen, there is, within seconds, absolute attention: they're looking and watching, even when they are not seated at their desks. *Remarkable.* There are other classes, however, where, when you call them to order, it's as though they haven't heard a word you've said, or don't care a toss anyway.

There's nothing so reassuring as seeing something that you believe in happen in practice. You can stash the experience away in your mind like so much swag as a potential reference point for training future teachers, and thinking about the children. I doubt whether, these days, I can achieve such levels of practice myself. It's too easy to become de-skilled in teaching a class. I can teach, say, music, or writing, or drama. Or even at a push, maths. But a whole class all day long? In the way that the best teachers manage? I need to remind myself (and don't remind myself anything like often enough) just how difficult this is. Once someone stops practising, then their skills atrophy.

But paradoxically, I feel more confident now about what *might* be achieved – bearing in mind that teachers themselves will sometimes have despaired when considering how difficult it was to master what they believed could be mastered, *if only they could get it right.*

Good teachers set balls rolling. New ideas have begun to flow. We are exploring ways in which we can make the teaching more interesting, and how the children can get more involved, and maybe even make some decisions for themselves. We experiment with our one-to-one tutorial system involving what we call a 'work schedule', which is a record of work for each child, that is accumulated and assessed each week. Edward starts looking at new ways of teaching maths, getting away from the straitjacket of Fletcher textbooks and working on the perennial problem of teaching large classes with a huge range of ability. The idea is to build up a knowledge base, to discover what the children can and can't do, and then focus on skills that matter.

I am developing an obsession with *knowing*. I want to know how the children are getting on, what their parents think of the school. I want to know what might define success or failure.

We begin to gather data about the children's performance which maps out the proportions of children of high, average and low achievement in maths and language skills. There are interesting questions that follow – so long as we treat the data with considerable care. Data invariably raises questions rather than answering them. For example, it helps provide an evidence base for analysing your practice. Why is it, for instance, that Maggie seems to be such a good maths teacher? Maths is of all subjects the easiest in which to measure progress, and Edward has gathered data which shows that the children in Maggie's class improve their maths year on year more than they do with any other teacher. Why? What is the magic formula? We videoed her teaching with the good services of a slightly eccentric man from the film and media department of the local Polytechnic.

The film turns out to be a revelation unveiling a maestro of the teaching art. On the surface of things, she appears as old-fashioned and didactic as they come, but she still creates an exploration of her maths theme that is driven forward almost entirely by the intense engagement of the children. Each child makes a point or asks a question. As moment after moment goes by, the points pile up interconnected by her persuasive questions and explanations to form an ever-expanding narrative that captures the viewer's attention as well as the children's. It was great teaching; and Maggie, though not particularly strong on visual artistry, was to extend her considerable skills into other spheres, to drama, for instance. That same term she was responsible for one of the most memorable assembly performances, a production of *Toad of Toad Hall* concentrated into twenty minutes of clear diction, dramatic aplomb and absorbing effect. The children reached a staggering degree of professionalism. It made you realize what could be done.

19
William Tyndale

The William Tyndale School affair in 1976 had been a time-bomb waiting to explode. It resonated through the education system for years to come. It was seen as a horror story that showed the terrible state to which the 'permissive era' of the educational system had brought us. William Tyndale was a small junior school in Islington, at that time under the control of the Inner London Education Authority, and the school had a team of teachers committed to radical change. For us in Handsworth, caught up in changes of our own, here was an alarming example of how to get things wrong.

The London school broke down completely after the implementation of a highly permissive, child-centred discipline system (or lack of it) and a free-ranging curriculum that was built on the principle of trying to respond to what the children seemed to want regardless of what adults might have thought appropriate. It was, indeed, and in a way Plowden never intended, child-centred, and in the end all boundaries and barriers seemed to wither away, so that the place was left in a state of anarchy. It appeared to show how much freedom a school had to develop a wildly eccentric approach to education in any way that the teachers saw fit. Parents were up in arms, some children being taken away, and the Governors and staff had started to quarrel. An independent review was called for, and it was finally exposed to the public through the withering analysis of a lawyer, Robin Auld. In practice the public enquiry was probably unnecessary: if the affair had been left for the local community to deal with the outcome would have been no different. Sharper action from the Local Authority would have helped this along.

The William Tyndale school had begun with its own vision of utopia. It believed that the children should be set free from constraints – pure 'New Romanticism', as it was sometimes called[8] – and it put its beliefs into action on an unsuspecting, mainly working-class community with single-minded zeal.

Terry Ellis, the head, had a democratic view of how a school should be run, but he was nothing like clear enough about what it meant in practice, and about the role of leadership in the process of change. What effectively happened was that power was handed over to his deputy, Brian Haddow. As Auld remarked,

> Ellis's first action, sensibly enough, was to institute regular staff meetings. However, in the minds of some of the staff and possibly at times even in that of Mr Ellis, this was not just for the airing and eventually resolving of differences, but a first step in the withering away of the power of the head.[9]

Reading this, I tried to sum up where I was as leader, as director of the team, compared with Ellis – his principles, his ways of working. Democracy in any organization, and maybe especially in a school, seemed to me to need more than lip service. It was self-evident that people are infantilized in over-controlled environments. They grow emotionally and intellectually in proportion to the freedom they have to explore and fulfil their own potential. But this transformation requires carefully managing.

During my first year as head, I had become aware in subtle ways of my role changing. I was delegating more, especially to teachers with a bit of zip and drive, and was trying to encourage opportunism. But there is also a constant need not just for provoking and challenging but for *binding*, for ensuring that the team neither atrophies nor splinters. Ideas and initiatives need to flow into the mainstream of the school, and not remain the intellectual property of one or two people. In all this, there may be defensiveness, uncertainty, vulnerability, disagreement, reluctance. But a balanced team, working in a climate of freedom – trying new things out and then integrating or harmonizing them into existing practice – can in the end become strikingly productive. In practice Terry Ellis handed over power to other stronger members of staff and allowed his own judgement to be superseded. Revolutionary fervour collapsed into anarchy.

At Grove our principles were fundamentally different: we aimed to carry the parents with us; discipline was important; a structured curriculum was high on the agenda – despite the accompanying principle of democratizing the school. I began to realize that to change things in depth would take longer than I had thought.

Jim Rose, one of Her Majesty's national primary-school inspectors, paid us his first visit and observed that he thought that things were a bit less stressed, that there was less tension in the school and some good teaching going on. His report was, in a cautious way, encouraging. When you're not sure of yourself in the early days and know what a long way there is to go, this is just the kind of fillip you need. There was now a modest sense of momentum, of teachers feeling that they were reasonably settled in under the new regime.

But I knew perfectly well how much there was to do. I would sit and try to think out my principles clearly. I wanted to know what was best, what was right, to achieve a convergence of knowledge to the point where you could say: yes, this is it. *This* is the best way to go about teaching Inderjit how to read; to assess children's capabilities in maths; to help Mrs A become as good a teacher as Mrs B. It was typical headteacher behaviour, and basically about control, the need to have things tied up and neatly parcelled; and I was always in danger of becoming obsessive and pompous. On the other hand, acquiring the kind of knowledge that might *prove* something was invariably a problem.

The philosopher Thomas Weldon made a distinction between difficulties, problems and puzzles. A problem is a difficulty which we try to turn into a puzzle, sometimes by simply asking the right question – often without realizing it. A puzzle has definite rules and constraints which cannot be broken, and a potential solution. Our difficulty? We need to come closer to the parents, to be more responsive to their expectations. Our problem? How do we do this? We set ourselves objectives; we come up with ideas that might help, each one of which raises a host of queries and challenges. One problem turns into many. We wonder if we can crack any of them. But then we puzzle out specific tasks, timescales, action plans. For instance: we will meet parents more frequently. We will canvas their opinions and set up a PTA and a parents' room, and we will hope and learn, and perhaps we will change tack in the light of experience.

Teachers would sometimes complain of difficulties in the classroom: vague traumatic, overwhelming things that seemed unresolvable. They might be frustrated at not being able to communicate with the children, at a class edging out of control, at lack of equipment, at having nothing like enough time to get things done. I got into the habit of asking people to suggest answers. The secret seemed to lie in turning these overwhelming difficulties into theoretically manageable problems and then to conceive the problems as having practical limits, so that at least temporarily you could reduce them to puzzles.

The danger is that any external solution ('this is what you

do ...') helicopters people into forming conclusions that avoid the struggle of the further journey that is required to get there by themselves. You short-circuit. When anyone is told what to do, they're in danger of stopping wrestling with a problem for themselves. Conclusions are tidy, but the procedure of coming to conclusions, or resolving problems and puzzles – though often messy and unpredictable – is much more satisfying. At its heart lies a dilemma in the education system itself. Those in control, the managers of the system, increasingly want the security of tidiness, the evidence of conclusions, whilst those close to the ground, and most of all the learners themselves, want the fun of the chase.

There was another dilemma. Children unquestionably need certain skills. You can't play Bach on the violin without a lot of basic skills and hard work. And learning basic skills is painful, requiring repetition and boredom. For some of us discipline must be enforced: it must be banged into us. But the one thing that must not be allowed to happen is that the children should be put off the journey itself: they must have some glimpse of its purpose, of the excitement it creates, of things to come.

We wanted teaching that constantly engaged children's thinking on journeys full of problems and puzzles – teaching that offered new challenges at exactly the right moment. It was all about inventiveness and timing.

There were two sets of difficulties. One was imposed by circumstances – particularly by the size of classes and the need to differentiate between children of different abilities. The other lay in the capacity of each individual teacher to cope with the exceptional intellectual demands such teaching involves. It needed technical and specialist knowledge of subject areas; it needed a strong sense of appropriate language, of ways in which children's conceptual thinking could be widened and deepened. It needed emotional security and calmness. It required managerial skills of a high order; and a certain bloody-minded determination to make the children come with you on the journey.

The journey of learning moves from relative simplicity to relative complexity, with plateaux and moments of rest, when we prepare for a new climb. Sometimes we have to be accompanied by a teacher; sometimes we move on by ourselves. The best teachers encourage independent thinking. They press the learner to take risks, to have the courage to venture into unknown, or even threatening, intellectual or emotional territory. Different journeys require different mindsets. Some require convergence, and the elimination of irrelevant elements to penetrate to the core of what really matters; some require the opposite, divergence, the ability to step sideways, to expand, to invent.

Then there is the question of intensity. The best teachers engage our interest at a number of levels. I spent a day following a child around the school, sitting in on all his lessons. The experience of children in classrooms is extraordinarily patchy. At worst, the experience is like a bad movie, a dull narrative with derivative, unchallenging tasks – a yawn, as one child said.

But when things work well, the experience is riveting: the brain is provoked to work at full pelt, almost by *deception*. In that respect the great teacher is a species of magician. She may use planned strategies, immaculately prepared material, practised presentation, but the event itself may be hard, if not impossible, to copy. There is a kind of improvisation where one is aware of *tension*, as though at any minute we're going into the depths of the Amazon rainforest, or into a dark Venetian church where there may be wonderful discoveries, or back to the moment when Turing cracks one of his codes.

Learning of this kind is like Mozart's *Jupiter* symphony, inventive and yet oddly reassuring, plunging us into new musical territory, but from time to time pulling us back into familiar configurations of repetition and convention, before taking us ever further into new emotional and musical realms, with shocks, exultation and surprises.

We can't of course form more than the most general of

connections between the *Jupiter* symphony and the teacher facing thirty children on a Monday morning. But thinking about it highlights the fact that teaching is important, and difficult, and makes considerable intellectual and emotional demands. One of the best ways to start coping with them is to turn our day to day difficulties into something more like problems, and those problems into puzzles that can be solved.

Spring

1976–1979

20

Parents

One warm spring evening the whole staff sets out into the streets. The children are playing outside their houses, and are excited at seeing this unexpected procession. The area round the school is like a piazza, a meeting place, old folk mingling with rings of chasing children. People open their doors and invite us inside for sweet tea, chocolate biscuits, samosas, noodles; to meet grandparents, the baby, brothers and sisters, aunts and uncles. The children follow us, running or on roller skates or swinging round on bikes constantly calling out, or distributing our Spring Fair leaflets to baffled passers-by. The idea is to promote the Fair and persuade shops and homes to stick up posters. But as it turns out, more important is the walkabout itself. It is a sign to the community that the school matters, and that the community matters to us. It's a surprise to the locals that teachers are out here, wandering around. It is an unpompous way of breaking down barriers. Pretty well all the staff are there, chirpy, outward-going, and there's a raucous warmth about the evening.

The school has by now set up a community room for parents to meet, and we are having some twenty-four parents' evenings a year: some for the whole school, some for year-groups and at least one every term for each individual class. At these evenings the children speak about the work they are doing. There are demonstrations, slide-shows, dancing, little plays from the children, music, talks by the teachers; and I try to talk to as many parents as possible. Parents who don't come will get a visit at home.

The staff design a guide on *How to Talk to Parents on Parents' Evenings*. There's a certain amount of tension in the air: parents and teachers are equally nervous, which can easily lead to stand-offishness, or a tendency for us to be patronizing and the parents defensive. I'm aware that certain parents will take their children home and punish them after a 'bad report'. This has made some teachers cautious about saying anything critical at all about the children. The way forward here, we think, is to encourage teachers to ask parents questions such as 'How do you think your child is getting on? Are you happy with the way things are going? Is there anything more that we can do to help?'

It is important to ask whether children are doing any homework. The staff are already working on a homework policy, which is mandatory for every child. It's particularly important to enquire whether the child is reading at home. Reading, we want to say, is the key to learning. All the smartest, most successful learners have one thing in common: they read every book they can lay their hands on. Reading, you want to explain to the parents, makes you feel more powerful, more in control, more curious, more spacious: certainly as a thinker, probably as a person. The teachers tell the parents to read with the children, to encourage them, to be insistent, to switch the TV off from time to time.

Whole families are persuaded to come, as well as the children themselves. Often the child stares sweetly at you and smiles. *No, he wasn't reading much at home. Yes, he watched too much TV, and played about in the street too late at night. There was too much noise at home for him to do much homework.* Mothers smile and sigh, and pat their little ones on the head, and confess that they have, oh dear, little control over events. 'Bad enough,' some would say, 'to get them to bed.' Many mothers can't speak English, and we have the essential help of Punjabi- and Urdu-speaking classroom assistants, who live in the community, know the problems, know what it's like living round here. They are tough, straight-talking, matter-of-fact. Classroom assistants are an important resource, and need more recognition for what they do. In due course, they'll run clubs and develop specialist skills in teaching reading, counselling, special needs, and the management of information technology. The teachers begin to take note of any problems that look as though a home visit may be called for.

We are hoping the parents' evenings will become *events*. We are hoping they are interesting to come to, informative for teachers and parents, a step forward in building up links, common interests and feelings of mutual support.

A questionnaire assessing parent opinion about the school was distributed by an independent researcher from Birmingham University to a random sample of a hundred parents, and a hundred children. The results made intriguing reading. They showed a predictably strong support for homework, school uniform, firm discipline. One third of the parents felt discipline in the school was still not strict enough. There was a request from many of them for closer relationships between school and home, with the school playing a more active part in supporting the management of their children at home. The good news was that the vast majority of the children seemed to like school, with a high 'happiness' rating. Many of them too were expecting 'to do well', which was encouraging and gave us a lift.

In analysing the results more closely, you felt their answers reflected wider concerns. Was there proper acknowledgement of their own values and cultures? Would the children become corrupted through the low standards of behaviour they saw on the streets? The parents were particularly bothered about safety, control, appearance, behaviour. Their view of discipline clearly reflected personal experience of the much more authoritarian and physical discipline of schools in the West Indies, the Far East and India. Authority was important in their home cultures, and obedience necessary for the evolution of moral character. Poor behaviour expressed moral problems – more than mere naughtiness. It exposed the children to worldly dangers. The parents were prepared to support the teachers in an unexpected way so long as they were sure that the teacher was on the right side.

How was such trust to be established? Personal contact was invaluable, but I suspected that the main impact had to be made through the children. The little things count. They begin with civility and respect from the teachers; nothing phoney; respect that says: *You matter to me, I'm going to do the best I can for you. I may disagree, disapprove, punish, but I shall continue to consider you as special in your own right and special for positive reasons.* It's often a subliminal message, communicated in as little as a 'hallo' or a smile.

Some years later I wrote:

> We all have a fear of the anecdotal. It is too easy to bulldoze through to convenient generalizations. There is an intensity and physicality about working in a school like this one, that is hard to describe convincingly. There are dozens of inconsequential contacts and feelings that are much more like the daily life of a family, living in a lively little village. In the end the reputation of a school is built up from such moments, themselves the products of hundreds of children.[10]

Responding to the questionnaire, I began to make a few home visits myself. The school now had its first home-school liaison teacher, in his spare time an international rugby referee. For the first time, we had a teacher who could spend time visiting homes, picking up problems and responding to local needs. Over the next few years, a succession of these people came in and out of this post, all of them excellent, a huge asset to the school. To reinforce my determination to engage with the parents – and especially to respond to their request for 'more support in managing their children at home' – I gave my home phone number to one or two families, offering an 'on call' service in dealing with their naughty children.

One mother told me about the problems she'd been having with her four boys, all of them at the school. The father was as baffled as she was, though the truth was that he was often out of the house, running a newspaper shop; or else he was in the pub, and left his wife to manage or mismanage the four boys during the evening. Grandma also lived in the house and was by all accounts inclined to aggravate matters either by complaining or by taking the children's side. Mother, caught in the middle, was at her wits end. 'What shall I do?' she pleaded. 'What *can* I do?' tears flowing down her cheeks.

This was by no means an impoverished family. They had a good income, the children were well dressed, and they lived in a reasonably spacious four-bedroomed house with two sitting-rooms, one beautifully furnished, and two TVs, one in one of the boys' bedrooms. And at school the children were well behaved, bright as buttons, and popular in their classes: attractive, well-balanced boys who had every chance of a successful future.

But on arrival home they behaved appallingly. They ran in and out of the house as they pleased, either ate, or did not eat, their evening meal, raided the fridge when they were hungry at all times of the day and night, fought over the TV, drew cartoons on the wallpaper, charged round the house at all hours, refused to do any homework and kicked their mother when she tried to intervene. The poor woman had bruises all up her legs. They invented bizarre games, the most alarming of which was 'let's pull granny out of bed'.

I gathered together all the family, the boys, their father and mother and grandma for a serious discussion in the sitting-room. Two of the children apparently slept in grandma's room, and yet there was another bedroom that was completely vacant. This was easy to sort out. From now on no one was to be allowed to sleep with grandma. Two of the boys must move their bed into the spare-room. I laid down rules for the boys to keep. 'No kicking mother, no entering grandma's room; going to bed at a certain time, with no more TV after that, and completing homework. Is that understood?'

The boys stood in front of me, in a line, upright like little soldiers.

'What's more I shall be coming to visit in the evening to check out that everything's going OK. You understand?'

The boys, still in a line, all nodded.

'Furthermore ...' I watched their eyes, focusing intently, 'I'm giving mum a yellow card for each of you, and on this she will put a tick or a cross. A cross means that you've broken one of the rules. I want to see all your yellow cards when you arrive at school each morning, and I shall sign them to show you've been.'

The father translated all this into Punjabi.

'You've got it?'

The boys nodded.

'And your mum and dad have got my phone number. If they ring, I shall come round. I don't live that far away. It won't take me long ... and if they ring up ... wow ...'

I sucked in my breath and left it to their imagination.

It was my first use of a yellow card, which turned out to be very effective. The boys settled down almost at once. I visited once more and the mother was all over me with gratitude. After a couple of weeks, even the yellow card was abandoned. The problem simply seemed to go away.

There were other families that were too strict, and we tried to get parents to be more reasonable and not to beat their children for relatively trivial offences. Excessive and inconsistent discipline created a great many problems. In some cases I told parents that *under no condition* were they to smack their children: if they had a problem they should ring me up, and for the time being I'd deal with them myself, *in loco parentis*. There was sometimes a problem in reporting serious abuse to social services, and the 1970s saw the development of a procedure. I reported a number of cases, but I tried to be aware of the problems this could cause, one of which was that there would be a breakdown in my relationship with the family. Social services could be wildly inconsistent. One couple who whipped their eight-year-old son fifty times with a curtain rod ('they laid me across the bed and told me not to take my eyes off the wall') were told in future 'just to smack him'. Another whose (thoroughly spoilt) daughter was caught stealing and slapped, were taken away for videoed interviews and intensive investigations which stretched over two weeks, after she complained about her father to social services. The outcome was that the child was uncontrollable from then on, stole the family jewellery which she brought to school, and the father refused to go anywhere near her.

I learnt to be cautious. I needed to take into account local circumstances, cultures, likely outcomes, threats to family life, dangers for the children. One mother hit her child far too hard for a 'terrible thing she has done'. I went round at night and showed her the marks on the child. 'I've known you for years,' I said; 'she's a lovely girl. And I thought you were a sensible parent ...'

At first she blustered, then she wept. The child obviously felt terrible, no doubt blaming herself, and I sent her out of the room. The message was clear, and the mother understood. It wouldn't, and didn't, happen again.

It was all about balance, about commonsense, and understanding how difficult some children can be, what stress some families were under and most of all, maybe, what the children themselves felt.

21

Mr Afraz

'Ah,' says Mr Afraz, 'I am not happy.' Mr Afraz is elderly with white hair and baggy white trousers to match, wearing a little black hat.

'I'm not happy,' he says, 'about my daughter Safraz swimming with the boys, as they do on Wednesday. She is eight years old and for her, for my religion, this is a bad thing.'

He shakes his head, such things do not happen in Pakistan.

Mr Afraz vaguely threatens to take it higher if something is not done, by which he means getting the more senior Mullahs involved: maybe making a community issue of it as has happened at schools elsewhere in the area.

He seems to be in despair that the facts of the matter are not obvious. It strikes me that I won't get very far by telling him that swimming is a compulsory feature in the curriculum; that we don't have the staffing to take girls swimming separately; that it's a good thing for Safraz to learn to swim. His answer will be that school is there to educate his daughter, not to teach her to swim, and he has no intention of encouraging swimming. And he adds, 'There are too many girls at this school swim.' His English is not good, but his communication skills are considerable. He looks at me and wags his finger in front of his beard.

I invite Mr Afraz to sit down. He is a large man and his baggy pants billow like a tent around his legs. He wears thick-rimmed glasses and bends his back to lean forward.

'What I don't understand,' I say, 'is why you feel there's a problem with Safraz when your other daughter Alma passed through the school and went swimming like everyone else, and you said not a word.'

'Ah,' he says, 'but that was another time.'

Had Mr Afraz mysteriously changed his mind – or had someone in the family been getting at him? Most likely, Safraz had decided she didn't like swimming and was pressing her soft old dad to make a fuss so she could give it up.

'She's only eight, after all,' I argue. 'There are lots of other Muslim girls swimming. There are always two teachers there, separate changing-rooms, a lady teacher, the lot. Nothing to worry about.'

He pouts his lips. It was not right and it couldn't go on.

He has made up his mind on the matter. His daughter must be excused swimming.

'While others swim,' he suggests constructively, 'she likes to read.'

'It's in the curriculum,' I say now. 'It's out of my hands. They have to go swimming. It's the law.'

'You are the head,' he says, unconvinced. 'If you say, there is no swimming. I know that.'

I shake my head and he shakes his head and we smile at each other, getting nowhere.

I can see now that he's not comfortable in his chair. He is shuffling about and grunting.

'Are you all right?' I ask.

'It's my leg,' he says, 'It's paining me. For weeks.'

'Have you been to the doctor?'

He nods vigorously. 'Many times.'

'What treatment has he given you?'

He shakes his head again, mournfully.

'Only a little. A pill one time.'

'Who's your doctor?'

So I pick up the phone there and then and ring the GP. I tell him I'm worried about his patient Mr Afraz's leg and I want him referred as a matter of urgency to the orthopaedic department to have it properly checked. 'It's been bad for weeks,' I say. The GP was very responsive.

'I've got the doctor to fix an appointment. You need to have something done about that leg. I noticed you were limping. You must go straight to the doctor now, and he will tell you where to go.'

'It's true,' he says. 'It keeps me awake.'

He stands up and shakes me vigorously by the hand.

'Thank you,' he says.

'I'm pleased that something's being done. If you have any more trouble with the leg let me know. Don't hesitate.'

'Very kind,' he says, pausing at the door. 'Oh,' he says, 'the swimming.'

'Oh, yes.'

'Not important. I tell Safraz.'

'Oh, good,' I say, 'that's splendid. Don't you worry, she'll be fine.'

He smiles, shakes my hand again and limps away down the corridor.

22

Difficult Parents

Every school has some parents, a tiny minority, who from the teachers' point of view present problems. Some blow in like hurricanes, causing immense disruption. One demented mother took to hitting other parents as they brought their children to school, and she slapped another young mother in a classroom in front of the children. Another regularly marched through assembly, timing her entry like some Restoration comedy queen, a brood of children trailing behind her. Her shoes would clack like drumbeats across the wooden floor as she flounced past, and everything would have to stop until she was out of the way. The staring mass of children would view this performance for what it was, a crazy display that was best ignored. Occasionally a parent would show signs of paranoia. One took to writing letters at great length: she sent rambling missives not just from herself but from other members of the family as well, including a grandmother in Jamaica. The tiniest thing – the loss of a shoe, a child pushing another child in the playground, an altercation with a dinner-lady – could lead to a parental explosion and all hell could be let loose.

There was an incident at one Christmas Fayre when a local curate, who nobly volunteered for the Santa Claus role in the Christmassy dark room, made the fatal mistake of giving girls boy presents, and vice versa. This led to a punch up in the Father Christmas queue, which rapidly turned into a war between two families, everyone hitting everyone else. Children were chased by adults across the hall and around the room, attracting a large audience. The dispute reached the point where I rang the police and Laurie, the home school teacher, had to bring his large Alsatian dog to quieten things down.

On another occasion, Edward, now the deputy head, was out on duty at lunchtime when an irate Irish mother came into the Upper School playground with two enormous heavyweight female companions, each armed with a stiletto-heeled shoe. They surrounded him, waving their grotesque weapons in his face. The mum was a familiar figure, regularly mouthing off at teachers and using the playground as a walk-through: she would curse the children through the windows, 'Fuck off you little bastards ...'

I had her formally summoned to the Education Office, where we sat a long time waiting for her with a lady councillor, a member of the education committee, dolled up in a thick fur coat. A taxi had been sent to fetch her. But she failed to turn up.

'Two fingers to you,' she says to me, when I go round to her house one bright early spring day. She stands on her doorstep, arms folded, defending her territory.

'What's more,' she adds, 'my kids have to stand outside for dinners and them dinner ladies is racist.'

'Racist?' I say; 'I thought you were Irish.'

'Dat's my very point. Them – that lot – they hate the Irish. Fuckin' typical. Anyway I'm taking Celia away from this school. She's goin' to another school.'

'Ah,' I say, delighted at this news. 'What about the boys?'

She had two boys at the school.

'The boys is staying, that's for sure. They like it here.'

'Ah, well,' I say, thinking I'd get a point in here. 'I'll keep them only if you behave yourself. I'm not having you threatening the staff. If you want something you come straight to me. And if you threaten me I'll ...' I pause, wondering what

I would do. 'You know I've reported you to the Office. There's such a thing as a court order.'

At this she laughs loudly. It struck me that there was something I rather liked about her. Did she pick this feeling up? Did she smile at me? Were we suddenly on the same almost audible wavelength?

'You think I care about fucking court orders? They can put their court orders up their arses ...'

'Pity you couldn't tell them that.'

'How d'you mean?'

'I wanted them to meet you – I set up that meeting ...'

'Ha,' she says, 'I got better things to do.'

'You goina behave?' I say, slipping into the lingo. 'That's all I want to know.'

I watch her warily, realizing she could fell me with one blow of her enormous arms. I prepare myself for an *osoto-gari*, the hip-over-the-top throw which was my best defence in the days when I used to study judo at the old club in Erdington. I doubted if I could even shift her weight off the ground.

'Teach,' she says. 'De boys like you – you gotta keep them.'

'OK,' I say. 'Do I have a promise?'

'I don't make promises. You have a deal.'

'A deal will do,' I say. I turn to leave and look back with a smile. 'These kids see enough violence on television, don't you think? I mean, without us pushing it as well – I mean, giving bad examples.'

'Yeh,' she says, and for me right then 'Yeh' is enough, a kind of seal of agreement.

The head of the Infant School rang to say that she had reason to believe that a particular father who lived just around the corner was abusing his children, two boys and a girl, all in the Junior School. I had a duty to check this out, but there was not a hint of evidence I could find, not a bruise or a mark in sight, and the children complained about nothing. Nonetheless I considered calling the doctor in for a full examination.

It all filtered back to the parents under suspicion who came up in a rage. The father was a large man, with a reputation for violence. The men on the staff hung around in the corridor in case something untoward happened, and shouting could be heard a mile off. The father wanted me to stand up, get out of my chair, so that he could punch my head in. As he stood there screaming, I failed to react, and in the end he went away cursing and grumbling. Were we accusing him of violence? To his own children? Man, what fucking planet are we on?

But enquiries in the community confirmed the rumours that there was indeed something wrong. The father regularly beat up his wife and they both belted the children, who at school became increasingly disturbed and unmanageable. Here was a family in crisis: the social services got involved, and in a kind of paranoid revenge they created every possible disturbance. It was a whole-family madness. The mother took to invading the school at all times of the day, on one occasion arriving in slippers and her nightie at about 4.30 in the afternoon, catching me winding down on my own – playing jazz on the school piano. She let out a stream of abuse above my performance of Fat's Waller's *Ain't Misbehaving*, and I simply ignored her until I'd got to the end of the piece, by which time, with a bit of luck, she would have run out of breath. Eventually she stopped yelling and stood there suddenly silent, strangely frail and sad, wraithlike in her white nightie. Her hair was falling over her face, neglected, and her face was blotchy: she was an attractive woman who was losing all sense of pride in herself, all sense of proportion. She was falling apart, as the family fell apart.

Round the corner from the school there was a battered office called Harambee, run by some young marxist blacks, one of whose objectives was to monitor the behaviour of whites in the area, all whites being potential racists. The mother, after her moment of calm, headed straight off to complain to Harambee, not for the first time, and a smart young black guy turned up the following day to talk to me. His line was that the school was abusing her children. They had now turned the tables: I would now have to try defending myself.

'Really?' I said, 'Like how?'

'You made Joanna stand outside your room for half an hour during lunchtime.'

'Sure. Does that sound such a terrible thing?'

'Injustice is a terrible thing. Man, for something like that there has to be justification.'

'How about telling a dinner lady that she's a cunt, and if she says anything to her she'll get her dad to cut her up.'

'She abuse this kid, this woman? You checked that out? She called the kid trash or something? Kids don't just say things for no reason.'

'She's black this dinner lady. You want to talk to her? She's very religious – goes to the Baptist Church ... In the circumstances, I think she's been pretty reasonable.'

I added, 'You know this mother isn't exactly popular. You talk to the locals. I had one mum who came in recently saying she knew how to deal with that mad woman. She said she kept a knife in her stockings and she pulled her dress right up to show me.'

The young guy suddenly smiled. 'OK, man,' he said. 'I get the message. We'll keep an eye on things.'

And to my surprise they did, visiting the home, and quizzing the parents. There then appeared to have been an almighty row and one night the whole family disappeared from the house in a midnight flit to another part of the city. The odd thing was that, before leaving, they painted all the windows white, as though hiding something dangerous, sinister, inside, which no one was allowed to see.

The business of running a school is a strange mixture of routines and these sudden alarming squalls. One bright

April day just before school starts, I'm in my room laying out my correspondence in the pending tray when I hear a tremendous noise in the corridor. It isn't time for the bell, but the children are already streaming wildly into school, pounding breathlessly down the corridor, rushing to find me.

'Sir, sir, sir, sir, there's a mad woman in the playground.'

More children come rushing in. Others have run out of the playground back into the road. A woman of about forty, large and buxom, wearing a green sari has come into the Old School yard as the children are trickling in, ready for school, and she's pulled out a long knife from under her clothes and is starting to swing it around in all directions.

Everyone's screaming and running away. She ignores them and takes one or two steps forward and back continuing to swing the knife around. Within moments the playground has cleared entirely, people running either into the school or into the road where they start shouting behind the fence.

By now we've got through to the police.

'I'm sorry,' the man at the desk says, 'we've nobody here ...'

'But this is serious ...'

'I'm sorry, sir, but there's only me, and I've got to man the phone ... I'll try to get a car ...'

I'm now out in the yard, cautiously moving in the direction of the mad woman, and talking her down as though she is a plane with no engines, preparing for a crash-landing. 'Come on,' I'm saying. 'Put that thing down, now ... Someone might get hurt ... There now ...'

The poor woman is bemused, unsure of what she's doing, and she stares at me as if preparing to flee, or possibly even to attack. I keep my distance, but step by step she walks over to me – all like something out of a second-rate movie – finally handing over the knife; and I take her arm and lead her into the big hall. There I sit her down and the secretary makes her a cup of tea. The police haven't arrived and so we call for an ambulance which comes quickly and takes her away. Apparently there has been a long-standing family feud. This lady was one of a number of relations in a lunatic situation where children, aunts, uncles, everyone had been regularly throwing stones at each other's windows, until finally she'd cracked and come up to the school, maybe on some vague revenge mission. It was sadly just a dramatic attempt to get someone to understand her problem.

23

Naughty Children

The burgeoning spring is heating the adolescent blood. There's the constant threat in the area of all-out war between rival secondary school gangs, prompting regular police patrols, complete with vans and horses, as the children are leaving their schools in the afternoon.

Even primary-school children can do outrageous things, from stealing to bullying – one boy severely beat up a girl after school and landed her in hospital. And general nastiness, implacable defiance and rudeness, and dangerous or crazy behaviour are not unknown. One girl set a boy's woolly on fire. Twenty girls formed a thieving consortium and robbed a local shop of much of its stock; they then traded the goods on a school blackmarket.

Girls are particularly shrewd at bullying, threatening to post 'terrible' notes through someone's letterbox addressed to the victim's father if protection money isn't paid. A group of boys surrounded a female student teacher at the bus stop and pulled her skirt above her head. One boy hit a particularly vain man in the stomach, a tutor from a college who was demonstrating to his student 'how to teach'. He had made the mistake of putting his hands on Conrad's shoulder. 'Important,' he said, 'to be firm with them.' He backed out of the classroom in agony and did no more demonstrating. Three boys locked themselves in a classroom during lunchtime and wouldn't come out: we had to smash the glass in the door to reach them. Fights in assembly, in classrooms, in the playground were common enough, with children pushing, banging, punching, scratching or even biting each other once an argument had started. Stealing was a persistent problem: from cloakrooms, from shops, even from teachers and the secretary. All the cooks' weekly wages were stolen one Friday. I eventually retrieved them from under a loose brick in a wall in Murdoch Road, for in this case, as in many others, it wasn't too difficult to pin down the perpetrator.

Another boy came in with a hundred pounds in fivers which he dished out like lollipops to all his friends. His granny had given it him: all the family's food money for the week. The mother shook her head in despair. I suggested that she should tackle granny rather than the boy, but this was apparently unthinkable. I had a go at granny myself and she nodded, smiling patiently. After my speech about being sensible with money, she said, 'but he's a lovely boy, isn't he.' This was the very same boy who had eaten a large toilet ring a few weeks before, thinking it was a polo mint, and when he had turned green and moaned in school with stomach ache, we had rushed him off to hospital.

Other parents took to bringing their children to me to deal with. 'She kicked a hole in the living-room door,' announced the mother of a girl, showing me the battery of bruises up her legs. Another mother admitted that she barricaded herself in her bedroom every night by pushing the wardrobe across the door, after her son had attacked her in bed with a knife. A father brought his son to me for disrupting an airline flight from India, pinching things off other passengers and running up and down the aisles.

Just as we are about to perform our first school play, when the audience of parents have seated themselves in the big hall and the children are getting into their costumes, the two leading characters, both boys, begin a fight during which one produces a knife with which he threatens the other. The children, half of them in costume, and some in make-up, scream at the two marauding boys in white cotton togas leaping over the desks. I'm in a highly stressed state as director of the play. Prima donna-ish and liable to go berserk, I put them across my knee and spank both of them, without pausing to discuss the matter – breaking all my own rules – and I then send them onto the stage ten minutes later, tears still in their eyes. To their eternal credit, they start the play in great style without a hint of a sulk or hesitation. The incident melts away as fast as it happens; indeed it's almost as though it never happened, and the play, a meditation on Tolstoy's *Ivan the Fool*, ends with a huge dramatic *coup de théâtre* when Dawn, a lovely, tall, athletic black girl, playing the part of the Devil, leaps from a huge tower we've built out of stage blocks from such a height that she makes the audience shout out with surprise.

After the play's been such a success – an important success, for this is the first big performance we've done for the parents, and there was a great turn-out – the boys who were *so loyal* make me, momentarily, feel terrible. I want to apologize to them. At least I might have listened to what they had to say first. I should have kept calm. It was a terrible example of impulsive behaviour by *me*, of exactly how not to deal with children. What kind of an example was this? I do apologize in the end, the next day, telling them how great they were in the play; but they look at me in a puzzled way, not, I think, understanding what I'm on about, why I'm bringing this up again, since it all happened *yesterday.* They appreciate that bringing knives to school was a serious matter. They are mainly relieved that I haven't told their mums and dads, who in fact were in the audience at the time. We shake hands and part friends.

Dealing with such a range of incidents is not easy. Disapproval must not lead to things getting out of proportion.

Bad behaviour can't go unrecognized but whatever you had to say, whatever action you took, a line must be drawn in the sand underneath it, and the child must be recognized once more as an equal, forgiven member of the civil community. Punishment is, as I have come to realize – since I am so often in the firing line – a human, interactive phenomenon that requires great sensitivity, skilled judgement and intuition, and a lot of stops to play on. I always try, in the end, to speak to, and perhaps eventually praise, a chastized child.

Clearly in such a mélange of offences, some were much more serious than others. There were some heart-stopping moments. One boy, Adam, played racing cars with the TV stand on the way to the toilet when the TV became detached and crashed to the floor, just missing him. There were frequent instances of children climbing on the roof, an offence which was automatically punished. I envisaged a day when in court I'd have to show how much effort I'd made to ensure that children did not climb on the roof. One night a boy fell, crashing through one of the glass roof-windows, and cut a great swathe through his skull: he was rushed to hospital by ambulance. It was a miracle that he wasn't killed – and that the caretaker's wife happened to be around at the time.

I was worried, too, about fire. The land at the back of the Soho Road shops was a favourite place for bonfires. The Rastafarians were occasionally torching parked cars. Wild boys from other schools were burning down playground equipment. There was a local practice for them to throw fireworks, especially bangers, at each other. I was aware how naughtiness merged into extreme danger without children realizing it.

On the other hand, naughty children are a fact of life; and in some ways to be naughty is a healthy way of asserting yourself against the world, of building up independence and self-confidence.

There are some school regimes so total, so ferocious and so uncompromising in their demands that they allow no space for a child to manoeuvre. Most children find such illiberality as unreasonable as they find excessive permissiveness unsettling. In fact, most normal children learn to become self-aware about the game of naughtiness, its risks and its limitations. For rougher boys and girls this is more like rugby, assertive and physical. For the cooler temperaments, more detached and more middle-class, the game is more like cricket, and breaking the rules becomes a more deliberate business.

The child knows the game, and its rules, and naturally assumes that there will be proper referees with consistent and comprehensible penalties. The average youngster has antennae for fairness and appropriateness in such matters. Punishment is a commonsensical fact of life, a condition of the game, and with help children are well able to adjudicate for themselves in such matters. Respect comes from allowing the children some leeway to play the game without interference.

Dealing with events quickly has the considerable advantage of being time-efficient. The aim is the aim of good refereeing: to keep the game flowing, and to be as good-humoured and conflict-resolving as possible. It's also to be fair and tough in making judicial decisions. Most important of all, it is to try to give the child *insight*.

'So what do you think I should do?' is the question many children have to face. They usually want the incident involved to be marked down and then forgotten.

This is a test for them of self-perception. I sometimes use a driving analogy to explain things. 'This is an example of poor driving. You're steering badly. You've gone and crashed the car.' The child understands, and, though I'm by no means beyond punishing some of them, I recognize that such understanding is almost enough, almost sufficient in itself.

Except in really serious cases I involved parents as far as the child wanted them involved. Even that was negotiable. The time would come, from the mid 1980s onwards, when parents in schools everywhere would be expected to take fuller responsibility for their children's behaviour at school, the teachers increasingly becoming go-betweens. By that point national data for suspended pupils showed that suspensions and exclusions were four times more frequent than they had been ten years earlier, with parents being summoned to school far more frequently.

There is a down side to this. The child who is trying to escape from home, to assert a natural independence, is sometimes troubled when parents are brought into a dispute. Most normal children rank involving parents as a top-of-the-range punishment. There is a danger of some parents overreacting wildly, quite out of proportion to the offence. One mother, confronting her miscreant child in my room, picked up a huge piece of wood to threaten her with, and I leapt on her to restrain her while the child hid behind a cupboard. Others simply avoid any responsibility altogether. What kind of punishment is it when suspension (say) is no more than a holiday in the park?

It is all as much a test of the teacher as of the child. There are many hazards, such as the real danger of overreacting to what the child has done, and becoming over-emotional and over-punitive, and getting everything out of perspective.

Teachers – indeed, almost anybody – can fall victim, when angry enough, to a paranoia that splits the world into good and evil, black and white, mirroring, as it happens, the more disturbed behaviour of the children. A righteous anger can suddenly sweep down and block out all commonsense. Sometimes I could feel it inside myself. I also knew that it was there in the Handsworth community.

One day an Afro-Caribbean boy, known by the children as Big Pete, threatened a teacher with a baseball bat in a PE lesson. The teacher, genuinely scared, said that he had swung the bat deliberately intending to hit her, and luckily missed.

'You've got to expel him,' she demanded, supported by some other staff.

'Really?'

Divided by the issue, the staff got up a head of steam. What was it in these situations that brought out that greatest of personal assets, good judgement?

'What'll happen if you expel him?' one teacher argued. 'His mother can't manage him at home. He has no father. It's a very insecure family. She finds it hard enough as it is: she'll be broken-hearted. What good's it going to do?'

'But children should not be allowed to get away with such appalling behaviour.'

'How many children are going to copy him?'

'That's not the point.'

'He's a bright boy; he lost his temper. Aren't you getting it out of proportion?'

'It's the principle of the thing.'

'It's the *boy's* needs that matter, not any principle.'

'What about the *teacher's* needs: what do you think we feel?'

'We are here to put our own feelings second to our responsibility for the feelings of the children.'

'The children will expect him to be punished.'

'To be punished but not to be expelled.'

'But what he did was outrageous – completely out of order.'

'For him it was one misguided moment; he lost his temper; the teacher went and confronted him – he's a boy who finds it hard to hold himself together ... We have a responsibility to him ...'

'Are you suggesting it's her fault, for heaven's sake ...?'

'Maybe she mishandled it.'

'Oh, come on. Even if she did, that doesn't justify what happened.'

'He's a child, we're adults. The perspectives are different.'

'It's about moral standards. We have a responsibility to ourselves ...'

'You think the other children are going to copy him?'

'Possibly. There's some kind of example being set here.'

'The question is whether we are willing to assess each individual case on its merits. What you don't do is overreact.'

'Or underreact. I mean, this is really serious.'

'It doesn't happen every day, does it? It's a one-off. He hasn't done this before, has he?'

'No, and we shouldn't give him the chance to do it again. We have a responsibility to protect the staff.'

As for Big Pete, here was a boy of high intelligence who was morose and depressed at what he'd done. There was no excuse for his behaviour, he didn't understand why he'd behaved the way he had, except that the teacher had riled him, got under his skin (as he put it himself). He apologized to the teacher, and he meant it, but she refused to listen, turning her head away. He had not only frightened her; he had broken into a fragile emotional world like smashing a glass, showing her vulnerability, her lack of control. Children are not supposed to behave like that. And even teachers who believed that punishment was wrong in principle were now advocating the educational equivalent of capital punishment: get rid of the child at all costs. In the end, I took the matter into my own hands, and I punished the boy myself. It was to the staff's considerable credit that they accepted this judgement without doing more than disagreeing.

As it happened, I met Big Pete almost twenty years later. He had got into the grammar school which had done well with him, despite a few ups and downs. A great hand had descended on my shoulder as I was standing listening to a band in Cannon Hill Park. 'Hi, sir,' said the huge figure, with an attractive Lenny Henry smile. He was successful, had a good job, and had settled down. His old mother was rightly proud of him. I didn't like to mention the incident that had so nearly thrown all this away. We shook hands warmly before parting, and, as we looked at each other, I guessed that Peter remembered everything.

24
Truants

Every school has its own variety of backsliders and truants. There is the child who sets out from school with good intentions but finds, as he wanders Tom Sawyer-wise along the road, that the sun is out, the park is within spitting distance. Meet up with a friend, an older brother, a child from another school, and suddenly the world is your oyster. Then there is the child, a rarer breed, who deliberately defies all conventions and plans to stay away from school for the day. An elaborate plot is constructed which begins with deceit. He sets off for school in school uniform, and kisses mother at the door. It concludes when he returns home at the usual time and talks at length about the excitements of the school day. Such pretence can, in theory, be carried on indefinitely, but the maestros of the technique mix their absences with days when they attend, offering teachers extensive excuses about colds and flu, and about having to go to the airport to see important relatives off and so on. An even rarer breed are children who are frightened to go to school, usually because of bullying: such children are usually found out rapidly because they eventually crack under the strain of lying and avoidance; they stop eating or display a range of emotional characteristics that alert parents to the problem.

The attractions of a free holiday, especially in the summer months, are obvious. Young children progress from their first experience in the park, where they play with other local recalcitrants for an hour or two, and then, bored, discover new places to go. In the city, the City Centre is a big attraction, with shops and streets for them to explore, the only drawback being their lack of funds. This leads many children to steal on their illegal trips out, and from time to time I find myself travelling round the city to pick up, or detain, pupils whose poor ability at nicking sweets in shops will lead in due course either to their giving up stealing, or else to their arrest by the police.

There is a Just William impudence to some of these children. Ranjeet, the son of an elderly bald-headed man with a gammy leg, would hare up the road, running away from his irate, stick-waving father, who had no hope of catching him. Once in India on holiday with his family, Ranjeet ran away in earnest, caught a bus a hundred miles north and got employment in a hotel as a crockery collector and washer-up. With the money he earned, he travelled about, and he returned to Delhi at exactly the right moment to rejoin his family. The parents, used to such eccentricities, no doubt chastized him in some way, but in any event he caught the plane back to England and arrived in the best of health. At sixteen he left school to set up his own business.

Some years later, and now in his early twenties, he returned to school rolling up to a parents' evening to ask me whether I'd like to view his smart new Mercedes sports car sitting in the school drive.

'Whachu wanna be a teacher for, mon?' he asked, patting his hand gently on the gleaming car bonnet.

The downside of absence without leave – apart, of course, from the fact that you miss schooling – is its hazards. The City Centre can be a dangerous place for children out on their own during the day. Josette took herself off with a friend and was caught being picked up by men in the Birmingham Bullring Market area. She was lucky. The police had a patrol of plain-clothes women in the area, and she was brought back to school. Her mother was sent for, and patrolled round the room waving her arms about and cursing the day that the girl was born. Josette, who was an attractive eleven-year-old, stood and pouted, not looking her way. 'You look at my eyes, child,' her mother shouted: 'you hear?' Josette stared down at her shoes. Then, with a turn on her heels, mother picked up her bag and announced she was off. 'I'll leave her to you,' she said; 'I wash my hands of her.'

The school had a success with Josette. We counselled her. *You know how dangerous this behaviour is? You want to throw yourself away?* She was, I knew, in her way a proud child, a leader amongst her friends; and the key to getting her on our side was her exceptional ability at badminton. She was soon to become the under-thirteen city badminton champion. The day would also come when finding herself insecure in her secondary school – where there was no provision, can you believe it, for the younger children to play badminton – she would run away from *that* school back to us and turn up quietly and politely at our door. 'I want to come back here,' she said. To me she would listen. 'You must go back,' I replied, and it took me a long time to persuade her. I came to the conclusion that she just wanted someone, maybe anyone, to listen to her. In time she settled down, and as she got older she returned to her badminton with considerable success.

I had a white van, which the children dubbed the ice-cream van, and, equipped with a pair of powerful binoculars, I roamed the streets from time to time, surveying the park especially. My presence in the area became well known, and it was probably rather a joke. But at least I gained the reputation of being on the track of truants and if they were spotted they were in trouble.

There was one particularly troublesome boy who I was convinced was hiding in his house while his mother was out for the day. I went round in the white van with Edward to Mrs Santer's house to see if he was lurking at home, or at least to tell his mum, if she was there, that her son was not in school. I parked outside the house and left Ed while I checked out the house. I knocked on the door and Mrs Santer was there, pleased to see me. 'Oh goodness,' she said, 'do come inside.'

There's soft music playing in the front room, and the curtains are partly closed.

'Won't be a tick,' she says and disappears; and when she comes back I survey a slender, beaming woman in a shortish black dress and high-heeled shoes coming towards me. She goes to the windows and draws the curtains, turning down the music and switching on the standard lamp. Only when she comes to canoodle on the sofa beside me, do I fully appreciate what is going on. I bristle, sit upright, stare at her and say, 'Mrs Santer, you do know I'm the head of Antony's school ...'

'Oh my God,' she says, squirming away from me and standing up; 'Christ Almighty,' and she puts her hands to her face laughing. 'Fucking hell.' She pauses, and apologizes profusely. 'Thought you were someone else,' she says, putting the light back on and positively assaulting the record-player to turn the sound off. Then she re-opens the curtains, sits on another chair and says, 'It's our Antony again, isn't it?'

Outside in the road, Ed observes the closing and opening of the curtains with astonishment, and when I finally come flustered out of the house, he asks, slyly.

'Was it OK?'

'Oh, come on,' I said driving away a bit too fast.

Long holidays abroad were much the greatest cause of absenteeism. A small, stocky smiling and unshaven father comes to see me to ask if he can take his two children on holiday.

'Oh, I should think that will be all right – how long for?'

'Only about a year.'

'Doesn't that sound a bit long for a holiday?'

He looks mystified.

'Does it? We're going to India.'

'Are they going to school in India?'

'No. They don't like Indian school. It beats them too much. They stay with grandmother.'

'It's too long,' I protest. 'We're very full. I can't keep their places here for all that time.'

'Six months then.'

It was like selling a carpet.

'Weeks.'

'Weeks? Only?'

'That's right. I can manage six weeks.'

He blows his cheeks out and shakes his head.

'OK,' he says, 'if you say.'

On the way out he turns round and suddenly says, 'They can't lose their place. You know they love you round here.'

This more or less silences me and moderates what might have seemed an irritable tone. Only after he's gone do I start to wonder whether the children will really come back in six weeks' time.

25

Emotional Survival

A small number of children are persistently worrying. These are not conventionally naughty children; they are struggling for emotional survival. I calculate that there are about two dozen of them across the school with serious emotional and behavioural problems, and in addition a much larger number who are vulnerable, easily led to commit fairly outrageous offences, immature children who get caught up in the culture of the group.

Dealing with them means sometimes being tough, asserting yourself, and taking over part of the role of the father. Most of them suffer from poor or absent fathering. Sharp, clear discipline for some children is like providing an outer shell, a boundary, making them feel safe. They need in the end to discover what it's like to become free, to be able to make decisions of their own. They need to be guided through careful management of their feelings towards an ability to make good judgements in a tough environment.

Discipline on its own is never enough, and it's important that a whole community of much more easy-going, maturing children shouldn't find themselves oppressed by a regime that has been set up for the purposes of managing a small minority. The problem of the *appropriateness* of disciplinary regimes in schools with such a diversity of problems remains, for me, a central one.

Often these vulnerable children are impulsive, reacting rather than acting, with little or no ability to pause and think about their behaviour. They frequently feel weak, and so they pretend to look super-strong. It makes them feel better about themselves if they are friends to the unscrupulous and, as they see it, the brave. Some of the most violent, disturbed children are therefore perversely turned into heroes.

Those two dozen or so children at the core of the problem would have difficulties that persisted whatever action you took as a teacher. Some of them persistently steal – often incompetently – as a cry for help. Some are wildly volatile as though they have hypersensitive skins; touched or offended, they explode into an uncontrollable temper, and I sometimes find myself having to sit on them, holding them tight until they cool off. They struggle and curse and hurl things about, screaming and often sweating profusely, in hurricanes of rage. One boy came within an ace of taking my head off by throwing a heavy piece of prize pottery (made by another more peaceful child) at me, missing me by an inch or two, and cracking the window instead.

Most children calm down after twenty minutes or so, although once or twice, at the point when the hysterics seem uncontainable, I call for an ambulance and have the child taken to hospital. He is now becoming a danger to himself, and I'm getting exhausted and stressed out. One child is so bad he's kept in hospital overnight.

Once their foul tempers have subsided the children will often stand or sit in morose silence, exhausted, shocked at their own bizarre behaviour. Often they will apologize. Or they will distract themselves with some activity, unable to deal with the pain. I try – I really do try – not to lose my temper. But occasionally I myself explode in a kind of controlled fury, when unpredictable things may happen.

One boy, Jason, had violently attacked a girl, almost breaking her arm. It was his second or even third violent offence. This time I crack, furious with him. The boy comes into my room effing and blinding, screaming at the top of his voice, and I whirl myself up into a temper tantrum, at first poised uneasily between real and pretend. The boy is scared, as well as no doubt surprised at this adult descent into childishness, and bit by bit as the shouting goes on between us, I become aware of the strange phenomenon of the boy getting quieter and quieter until he stands quite still and silent, watching his headteacher's histrionic performance. Finally, my heart pounding, my fingers gripped tense, my head shaking, my blood pressure rising, I run out of steam. And of words. We stare at each other in total silence.

'Are you all right sir?' says the boy.

I am astonished. It seems that the boy is genuinely concerned.

It's as though I've taken him into myself and ingested all his feelings. We've exchanged roles, I'm now the child, and Jason the concerned adult. I stand there shaking, almost in tears. A teacher comes in and quietly takes the boy away.

There were other children as well who needed special support, a quality of support that I felt the school was not able to provide. One little girl had witnessed her mother's suicide: she had found her hanging from the bedroom window, a noose round her neck. She was living now with a neighbour who had since adopted her, and she had become withdrawn. The child, such children, were offered no provision, no professional counselling or support. Nationally, children's mental health is a disturbingly low priority. Adults are treated differently, often more sensitively and with greater respect.

These were not naughty children, or at least not *just* naughty children. They had a range of difficulties that made demands that were quite out of the ordinary.

So what do you do with them? We could of course have expelled them, as some schools did; but expulsion merely threw the problem onto someone else's shoulders. One twelve-year-old boy at a local school was expelled for pinching the bottom of a woman teacher: it was a life-changing experience for him. His schooling fell apart and he ended up in one of the numerous local street gangs, edging towards criminalization. His mother (he had no father) fought a huge battle to keep him in school, even involving the local MP, but she lost and finally gave up in despair. Such a disaster for such a boy was a community disaster too.

We had a duty to keep children in school at all costs, but that is not possible without excellent support and provision: it can't be done on the cheap. The dilemma was whether to struggle on with them, or to move them out for others to worry about. I'd taken a few of these 'lost causes' from other schools; but I asked myself, even while I felt it was in principle the right thing to do, if it could be justified.

It was an issue that was hard to resolve: it would run and run. We knew that 90% of prisoners at, say, the local prison, Winson Green, had records of problems that ran right back into their early childhood: learning difficulties, emotional abuse, disorientating families, insecure and chequered schooling careers. However, there was no national will to face the nature of the evidence and to provide commonsensical, properly resourced solutions. We needed to start to develop effective strategies for prevention, for picking up problems early and tackling them with all the powers at our command. In the past the strategy had too often been to sit on a problem and wait and see; to leave it to the teachers; to hang on until the child got older and more obviously unmanageable, and so to miss the boat. It was obvious that we had to give more thought to these children as early as possible, well before age burned up their life chances. I wanted to set up a unit of some kind, giving specialist provision within the school to support children at risk. It was one more item on my list of ambitions.

26

James

The school's educational psychologist was a particularly bright and personable young man. I'd argue hammer and tongs with James about the virtues of such things as structured-learning programmes, behavioural reading strategies, such as the American Distar scheme, and the general virtues of reward and punishment regimes. Behaviourism, whilst intellectually in fashion in some quarters, was seen as a scientific alternative to some of the 'liberal-humanitarian' practices then in vogue in the 'educational establishment'. It was a philosophy premised on the notion that human behaviour can be shaped by a step-by-step use of learning targets, reinforced where necessary by rewards and punishments. James certainly felt that some of the things he saw happening in schools were sloppy and unsystematic – a view that was not easily dismissed.

I had my doubts about an excessive use of behaviourist approaches, which could all too easily become naive and mechanical; but James would point out that I was myself often distinctly behaviourist in my approach to discipline in the school, aiming, as I did, at a rational use of rewards and punishments. Didn't I emphasize the importance of being rewarding and positive with the children? Didn't I want to encourage them to be confident about themselves, praising them whenever possible, and telling them how good they were?

'What's this but behaviourism?' he argued.

'As a general principle, perhaps, but pure behaviourism of the kind you're describing asks us to go much further. You give children rewards on a moment to moment basis, centred on very specific targets. For example, you expect to extend the general principle into close controls and monitoring of individuals. I'm not sure it's practical. Or necessary. Or come to that, morally right.'

'So what's your working theory?'

The question throws me. A working theory? Do I need one? I struggle to answer it, whilst at the same time feeling that this mode of interrogation is valuable. It makes me *think*. Heads of schools are often drawn into the whirl of life so intensely that they forget to find time to think. It's a professional hazard.

'Parenting,' I say, 'good parenting.'

'That's not a theory,' James protests; 'tell me more.'

It sends me back to the drawing board. Am I claiming that a generally intuitive approach to managing children is sufficient to underpin the world of my practice?

'Well,' I say, 'the key text seems to be the Cleese and Skinner book on parenting.'[11]

One day I resurrect it and quote from it.

That was, James would insist, insufficient. Just talking about 'a good parenting relationship' is simply not enough. Which good parents are we thinking of? What *is* this good parenting that the common law espouses?

'Behaviourism is a rational and scientific approach to the management of behaviour and learning.'

'You don't think that it can become oppressive?'

I was later to mount the argument that, with some of the most disturbed children, behaviourist techniques, however well planned, simply did not work when they were used as an exclusive approach to management. For the moment, I had to fall back on instinct or what I liked to call commonsense.

'You don't think that, carried to an extreme, behaviourist

philosophy resembles capitalism, a world in which everything depends on exchanges? Isn't it in danger of eliminating a part of the person, the world of feelings?'

This rather annoyed James, who had strong socialist beliefs and was troubled by being seen as a promoter of capitalism.

'Part of what we are about,' I said, warming up to the argument, 'is to make children happy. Especially,' I added, 'children with emotional problems who are self-evidently unhappy.'

'How do you define happiness?' said James sharply. Years later I was reminded of this by the famously contemptuous remark of Eric Forth, Minister of Education, when he described primary education as 'all happiness and painting'.

'Happiness,' said James, 'is only meaningful in relation to observed behaviour. It means nothing to me as an objective unless you can analyse and describe it in some sequential and developmental sense as a set of behaviours moving from what you might describe as *less* happy to *more* happy.'

Our conversation became a reference point for my rethinking of some of the things we were doing in school. Was James right? It was certainly true that in some half-articulated and broad-brush sense we were deploying behaviourist theory in managing the children. They behave because there is pressure on them to behave, with penalties if they do not. Their performance is tested and their work is marked, and sometimes graded. There is a long tradition of child management both in the home and in the school, which in this wider sense is clearly behaviourist. But how far should it go? And to what extent is it just one strand in a more complicated story of relationships and those mysterious, shadowy spheres of culture, imagination and emotional hinterland. What role was there for a therapeutic approach to working with children's feelings?

What did the teachers think? By now I had a staff with the brains and ability to focus on such issues and understand them. There were some, for example, who thought marking children's writing was a particularly intrusive and invariably pointless exercise. How often did children take any notice at all of the teacher's comments? I didn't agree with this. In my own teaching, I aimed at regular marking and even grading of work.

'It helps to motivate,' I argued.

'It puts them down. How would you feel having red ink all over your work?'

'It shouldn't be all over. It should be kept in perspective. Don't children learn through feed-back, and by interrogating their mistakes?'

'Over-assessment makes them less fluent in their writing, and it dampens their enthusiasm.'

I agreed – up to a point. It was true that the children were settling down better and having more fun these days because the staff were much more positive about them. There was, to put it in James' language, a lot more rewarding going on.

My critics continued.

'You should acknowledge to the children that you have carefully read their work, but the traditional business of grading and marking in detail is surely discouraging. And you say they should interrogate their mistakes, but do they really take any notice of what you've written? Isn't it better if they can learn how to scrutinize their own work?'

There were, I admitted, arguments on both sides. The issue was put to the staff as a whole and most came up with a view that ran somewhere down the middle. Marking had a value, but we should watch out that it didn't become a put-down. Children should take notice of marking, and they should redraft or respond to the teacher's comments. It should set up the basis for some kind of dialogue with the children; it should be a form of communication, of conversation, which as with all conversation had to be conducted with sensitivity.

So that was the conclusion of the debate, which ended

with a broadly agreed policy. Some, we knew, would be inclined to continue their existing practice regardless of anything agreed. But this was an issue for another occasion.

However, we are now in deep waters. Is structured, academic learning the crucial priority? How important is it that the child is happy and emotionally well adjusted? If you think that 'happiness' is all important and you concentrate on it as a primary consideration, then you are likely to create a different style of classroom and treat the children differently from the way you would if you think academic achievement is the absolute priority. Those who prioritize learning will put more pressure on the children; will focus more on discipline and order. They will command more and if necessary upset children to make them work harder. Those who focus on the children's feelings tend to be more liberal in the way they manage the pupils, and slower to intervene, giving more leeway to their behaviour, and allowing more generous movement about the class, and time for children to do their own thing. And there is perhaps a subtle cultural difference between these two stereotypical positions: as between a masculine/paternal and feminine/maternal perspective. Commonsense suggests that both are important and I stuck to my view that behaviourism or any other theoretical 'ism' provided nothing like a complete solution to the intricate dilemmas of moment-to-moment interactions with children.

27

Marcus

Our educational psychologists evidently take the view that what is not seen cannot properly be believed. So they listen carefully to what the teacher and (sometimes) the parent has to say and then make up their own minds by watching the child in action.

The teacher can say what she likes about the child, but unless what she says is actually seen to happen, then it's open to dispute, not to say denial. This can have the advantage of delaying diagnosis and avoiding costly outside support and the laborious procedure of giving the child a 'statement of special educational needs'.

Whilst admitting that teachers' management styles can, and do, make a difference, many of us in the school found all this naive, even absurd. Many children who proved extremely difficult for the class teacher to manage were perfectly able to sit obligingly quiet, beavering away at their desks, sucking their pencils, whilst being observed by the psychologist as he sat obtrusively on a tiny chair in the corner of the room, taking his notes. Invariably, the psychologist's subsequent advice to the teacher was to be more rigorous in managing them, and use some type of behavioural reward system. This was sometimes useful and paid dividends if, for example, you wanted to get a grip on small, irritating misdemeanours and persuade one of them to sit for ten minutes on a chair without falling off; but much depended on the level of problem the child posed. And sometimes the advice was given to highly skilled teachers who knew what they were talking about, and actually delayed a detailed investigation and diagnosis of a child's needs. We began to see the whole business as an exercise in procrastination, a special needs policy on the cheap, designed to leave us to carry the can.

Marcus had had a turbulent time at another school. He was a handsome nine-year-old, from a children's home, with a track record of running away. He had a ferocious temper and would sometimes lie on the floor and scream until we managed to talk him out of his foul mood.

More of a problem was his habit of wandering off, out of the classroom, out of the school, on a whim, especially if he was thwarted in any way. He took to disappearing from his children's home and camping for the night on the streets, with the police regularly trying to track him down. The next day he'd invariably turn up at school on time, in school uniform, as though nothing had happened. There was no way he was going to tell anyone where he'd been. It was, if nothing else, a vote of confidence in the school. He liked his teacher, who had the patience and skill to manage him.

He was a smart lad with a winning smile, but very demanding on time. He needed a good deal of extra support, as these children often do, beyond the limited help you can give a child in a class of thirty youngsters. But the problem was that he did not have a statement of special educational needs. Such 'statementing' requires assessment and time-consuming procedures that involve the psychologist. Without statementing there was no possibility of any extra provision. Schools in such a situation were expected to take the wholly inappropriate view that it was merely a matter of a naughty child who, with a bit of reward and punishment, would soon toe the line.

It was certainly the view Mr Jolly, the psychologist, took of Marcus. Mr Jolly, along with many of his colleagues, suffered from what we came to call *empiricist's block*. Every time that he came to visit Marcus and observed the boy from the studious corner of the classroom, Marcus behaved impeccably, in the way I've described. His work was good. He could read and write well, which was something of a miracle considering his lack of schooling. This was a period when there was, understandably, great sensitivity in categorizing youngsters, and especially black youngsters, as 'problems'. Black children were much more likely to be suspended from school than those from other racial and cultural groups, which was suspicious. Many were suspended as a result of the inability of white teachers to contain immature behaviour; there was a lot of overreacting. But Marcus's teacher was black, and a solidly commonsense person of high intelligence. She was dealing with Marcus day in and day out, and she insisted that Marcus was not just a naughty boy. Marcus was crying out for help. He needed a great deal more than we were able to offer. The children's home was, for him, a disaster, the school a haven of peace and good humour.

Mr Jolly decided that he was a naughty boy: perfectly normal, but environmentally stressed. There was no need to statement him. On three occasions he was observed for twenty minutes and was only off task for a relatively short time. Alarming accounts of explosive behaviour and reports of his walkabouts were of limited interest. What is not seen cannot be believed. The relationship between the teacher and Mr Jolly began to break down. In the end, Mr Jolly agreed to interview the boy again on one of his visits.

The second interview took place in the staff-room, which was an attic room at the top of a flight of stairs. By all accounts it started well. But then things started to go wrong.

'Read this, Marcus,' said Mr Jolly pleasantly.

'No,' said Marcus.

'I want you to.'

'I ain't going to. What you going to do about it?'

Mr Jolly persisted.

'Fat bastard,' said the boy and headed for the door. Mr Jolly blocked off the door and Marcus shifted his tack to the window.

'Leave that window alone,' said Mr Jolly, alarmed. He had a problem that, here alone with this boy, he couldn't leave him for safety reasons, but it was clear that he was going to need help. He leapt forward and grappled with the boy to try and stop him climbing though the window.

But Marcus was up to fighting. He was good at it. Better at it, as a matter of fact, than plumpish Mr Jolly. And after a few pushes and punches Marcus was out of the window and fleeing across the roof like Oliver Twist in the David Lean movie. Mr Jolly now panicked and ran downstairs calling out for help, red-faced and sweating, his tie awry.

But Marcus was down the drainpipe in the twinkling of an eye, and up and away.

'How's it going?' said the teacher, with the tiniest hint of amusement, as he rushed towards her.

'He's gone.'

'Don't tell me you've lost him,' she said.

'That boy,' said Mr Jolly mopping his brow, 'has got *such problems*.'

28

The New Building

For some time the school has been on the priority list for a new building. There's a large plot of land next to the Grammar School, on the side of Dawson Road opposite the existing school, which from now on we are to call the Old Building. The plans are for a complete new Junior School to house the seven-to-eleven-year-olds; and the separate Infant School will take over the Old Building which currently houses both schools. There is thus the opportunity to expand the nursery and to demolish the terrapins on the Old School campus that take up so much playground space. There is, at present, a national Labour Government which coincides with a Labour Local Authority in the city – a brief and unusual period for Birmingham, which for decades has typically see-sawed from one party to the other. This moment of Labour dominance raises our hopes.

We have heard very little about how the scheme has been progressing and have not at any point been consulted. News has filtered through like intermittent and unreliable weather forecasts. I should have been much better prepared, of course; I should have anticipated what might happen. I should have recalled, for example, the recent business of the painting of the school fence.

One day two men turn up and start painting the outside railings that surround the school in blue. I'm astonished.

'What on earth do you think you're doing?'

'We are,' says the painter, pausing in his task, 'painting the railings.'

'I didn't know anything about this.'

'Who are you?' inquires the painter.

'Blue,' I say feeling the question didn't deserve an answer. 'Do we have to have it blue? It'll look like we're Thornhill Road.'

'Thornhill Road?'

'The Police Station.'

The man considers this.

'There are lots of blue schools.'

'Is that the only colour?'

'Green – you can have it green.'

'Is that it?'

'Green or blue.'

'Fine – green.'

The painter pauses to consider this.

'It's already green.'

'It's a tradition,' I say. 'We've always been green. We're very conservative. Generations of green. Is that all right, then?'

'Hold on,' says the painter. 'It's not so simple.'

'Why not?'

'My instructions are to paint it blue.'

'From whom?'

'Engineers' department.'

'I'm the head of the school,' I say; 'I want it green.'

The painter shakes his head at such a maverick attitude, eyeing me with considerable suspicion.

'I'm afraid you'll have to get in touch with Engineers – Building Maintenance Division, Mr Plunkett. Anyway, I've got all this blue paint ... I've started now.' He stares at me. 'You'd better get a move on.'

'It's only undercoat.'

The painter shook his head.

'You talk to Mr Plunkett.'

Which I do, easing Plunkett round with as much persuasive charm as I can muster over the phone, arguing for a seismic shift from blue to green, on grounds of school preference, tradition, and, more vaguely, community sensitivity.

'You've got to realize things blow up round here – just like that – you wouldn't want to feel responsible would you ...? I'll put it in writing if you like ... The fact is that people are much happier with green ...'

As I say, this should have been a warning. I had heard on the grapevine that the new school, planned, as I assumed, to be a complete school for the current number of 430 children, was clearly going to be much too small: a hall plus eight classrooms, and able to accommodate only 240 maximum. Each classroom would be thirty square metres, one square metre per child, assuming a class of thirty. This was the minimum Department of Education specifications, the building being a Mark 4 version of an excellent single-storey design that had been pared down year on year to create the cheapest and most basic of provision. The large piece of derelict land on which it was to be sited was to be chopped in two, leaving a playground space of minimal size. A social services building was to be put on the other half. There was car-parking at the forecourt of the school that was sufficient for eight cars, presumably for the eight staff who were to teach the eight classes.

But we already had fourteen real classes in the school most of them numbering over thirty, and overall numbers were rising.

The new hall was to double up as a dining-hall, putting it effectively out of action from midday to two o'clock in the afternoon; and dinners were to be cooked in a whole new set of kitchens – as large as a classroom – thus duplicating the existing kitchen with its much better facilities and the separate dining-rooms in the Old Building.

This was more than a slap in the face. It was a crisis of confidence. It made me stare suddenly into the greater world of politics. A host of issues spun in my head. It was well known that primary education was, financially speaking, something of an afterthought. Not so many years later, next to the New Building, the Grammar School was to build a Science Laboratory, which was larger and more expensive than my entire new school.

The critical financial issue that lay buried beneath all this was that the older the child was, the more money you got. Could no one see that this was the most bone-headed of policies for a government which was seeking equity of provision for its citizens? Follow the life-cycle of a child aged three to twenty-one: work out the public educational provision per child for each year, and it requires no great intelligence to realize that the longer you are educated and the cleverer you are, the more money you get. The vast majority of children in higher education are from the middle-classes. The children of the inner city, the working-class – socio-economic strata levels four and five – have substantially less money spent on their education in their lifetime, and yet are precisely the group who need the money most. The school was currently receiving an extra 'inner-city' allowance which worked out at a penny per child per day. And we were to get a school building the size of a water-closet. Oh, you can hear the voices calling: 'but they're only little children.'

The quality of educational life in the New Building promised to be dismally disappointing. The Junior School would be permanently split in two. A large part of the school would have to stay in the Old Building. There would be very little space gain for the Infants once the terrapins were removed: in fact at least two of the terrapins, the temporary classrooms, would have to remain. The Infants and the Juniors would overlap in the Old Building causing logistical problems of space and resource location. The cost of running the two buildings would be much higher than that of running one.

Letters between myself and the Authority began to flow, in which the powers-that-be expressed surprise and regret that I wasn't over the moon about my fine new school. I argued that in a socio-economically deprived area such as this there was an obligation, most assuredly for a socialist government, to achieve the highest possible quality of environmental provision for the children. Next to home, the school was the place where children spent the most impressionable part of their lives. Didn't the Authority realize how much Finland, for example, spent on its new primary schools? The projected school was a scandalous underprovision in an underprovided area, and its planning reflected a scant regard for the needs and importance of young children. It was an underprovision for who knows how many generations of children.

I grew more heated as the letters and phone calls passed to and fro. There was the further critical issue of my – that is the staff's – sense of powerlessness in this situation. On the surface, it seemed that a headteacher in the 1970s and early 1980s had considerable powers to manage his or her own affairs. There was no statutory curriculum or heavy inspectorial network. But it was easy to forget that there was the monumental constraint of financial allocation and the grey commandants of the Local Authority, its officials with various statutory powers and responsibilities peering over your shoulder. You were not allowed to spend more than £100 without the approval of inspectors. The overall allowance which the school had freedom to spend amounted to 4.5 pence per day per child. When it came to the allocation of funding for a new building, this was plainly the territory of the Local Authority: its officers, architects, local politicians and advisers. They knew what was best for you and – stop worrying – they'd let you know once it had all been sorted out. This was a period when the Local Authority was at the apogee – as it would turn out – of its power and influence. The implementation in 1974 of the Maud recommendations had led to a great expansion of Local Authorities, with the advisory service in Birmingham, for instance, enlarging from a mere nine rather patrician inspectors in 1968 to more than sixty advisors and inspectors by the end of the decade.[12] Patronage was rife. If you knew the right person, you could double your capitation allowance (the money spent on equipment for the children) at a stroke. There were huge inequalities between Local Authorities, and Birmingham was a low spender on education and getting lower as money was filtered off into other city projects.

My exchanges with the Authority on the subject of the New Building became more animated and vitriolic. Didn't the fools realize what they were doing? Was there no one there with any commonsense? I tried contacting the architects to catch sight of the plans, and they fobbed me off with what I'd already been told – that they were instructed on no account to communicate with the school.

One day I set off on the number 74 bus to the City Centre to challenge the Deputy Chief Education Officer, on whose desk this affair has now landed. As though signalling my impatience and agitation, I accidentally kick a large black lady when I get on, and she stares at me angrily, bending down to rub her leg, and so delaying the bus with its queue of passengers.

When I arrive at the Office in Margaret Street, I find myself waiting for thirty minutes outside the office of the Deputy Chief Officer, a vast room on the second floor, near to where I'd been interviewed for the headship ages ago, as it now seemed. When I'm finally invited inside, and led in by his secretary who has already apologized for not offering me a cup of tea, the young be-suited Deputy Chief Officer is amiability itself.

'David,' he croons. 'It's so good of you to come ...'

I'm duly seated in a comfortable chair facing the super-large desk, a protective barrier, a mark of power and separation. I note that it is clear of all papers except a single blue folder. At the Deputy's side is a junior officer who is supposed to take notes, and I now begin to put my case for and against the various options, pointing out with animation my sense of alarm and irritation at being excluded from the process of development for what is after all my own school ...

'*Our* school,' the Deputy Chief corrects me with a smile.

'Of course,' I say sharply. 'But I thought we would want the best for the children, wouldn't we? *You* do, don't you? We're in the same business, aren't we? – as you say – but you must surely accept that I have a special interest as I'm there every day of the week battling with things ... I mean, have you ever *been* to the school?'

Ah no, this school he has not yet visited; but he has every intention of doing so, and as a matter of fact would appreciate an invitation.

I'm not to be distracted.

'This is a decision that will affect generations of children ... We – you – have a responsibility to ensure they have the best new building possible ... Have you, for example, looked at the size of the classrooms: I mean the amount of room for each child? You know the last school built to this model is substantially larger on a per capita basis? Have you considered its location? It's in an extraordinarily vulnerable dark side road. Do you know the crime rate for this area? But the worse thing is that you seemed to be unaware, when you came up with this, that the school is substantially bigger than the building you have budgeted for. This will mean that you've planned for a split-site school for the next generation of children, which will mean that the teachers will have to continually shunt the children back and forth across the road. Only the Old School hall will be big enough to hold everyone for assembly. You've planned for two kitchens. Have you analysed the cost of this? Have you asked whether it's necessary, given that we have two existing purpose-built dining-halls in the Old Building?'

'Ah,' says the Deputy Chief, thoughtfully, resting his elbows on his great desk. 'Let's look at the plans.'

And he unfolds the plans for the new school across the desk in front of him and invites me to peruse them, as though they're the crown jewels; as though once I've seen the plans – for this was the first sight that I've had of them – I will be crying with joy.

As it was the plans confirmed everything I had said. The project was, for all its fancy drawing, *minimalist*. It was apparent that this was a job on the cheap: the smallest, least well-equipped, least spacious, least costly solution possible. There were no corridors. Classes were open-plan; children would get in and out of the building from outside doors to the playground. The only link between the two blocks was through the playground, which itself was tiny. There was little space for car-parking so that the existing problem that cars took up half of the children's playground space was not addressed. Better provision was given to the kitchen than to any space occupied by the children.

I pick all this up, and continue my harangue; and as the interview continues, I become increasingly hostile and aggressive, while the Deputy and his colleague become defensive, soothing and – in my view – slippery. They come up with a new tack and a new A4 sheet with figures on it.

'These are,' says the Assistant Officer, 'projections.'

'Of what?' I say shortly.

'Demographic projections of population change in the Handsworth area over the next ten years.'

'Are they reliable?'

'Of course. At least, they're our best guess.'

'And?'

'And they show declining numbers year on year. We can predict therefore that the numbers at the school are likely to decline.'

'To what?'

'We envisage in due course a two-form entry school.'

'Ah,' I say, leaning back. 'So why the need for a new school. The Old Building can amply accommodate a two-form entry school.'

'But you surely can't be saying that we should turn down a new building when the DES has approved it?'

'Why not?'

The Deputy is confident here, and manifestly amused at my political innocence. Did I seriously think that the local politicians would turn down government money for improved provision in an area like Handsworth? Oh *come on* ...'

'So,' I say, 'when we have a new building ...'

'Which will accommodate the whole two-form entry Junior School ...'

'What will you do with all the unused accommodation in the Old Building?'

'The infants can spread their wings. We can demolish all the terrapins.'

'Spread their wings? They'll have enough room to fly a Boeing.'

'It's ten years ahead. There's a lot of water to go under the bridge. The new building will give us the chance to look at a range of options. You're not suggesting we should turn it down?'

'I am.'

'I'm afraid it's not an option.'

'Then you must spend the proper amount of money to build a school worth having. What you're currently planning is an annexe.'

'I'm afraid that there again, our hands are tied. These are Government provisions. We work to their specifications.'

'Have they looked at the site? Have you taken them through the issues?'

'They've looked at the plans.'

'That's not what I asked.'

'They've given the green light for the plans as we've put

them forward, and they've expected us to make some cutbacks on the scheme where reasonable ...'

'This is a Labour administration in Birmingham under a Labour Government at Westminster. I don't believe that between you you can't get this right ...'

The Deputy smiled.

'I think we've got it right ... or at least, put it this way: as right as we're going to get it.'

I shrug my shoulders in despair.

'I'm sorry you're not with us on this one,' says the Deputy, 'but I'm sure you realize that we really do believe, given the unavoidable limitations, that we're doing the best thing possible in the circumstances.'

'You believe,' I say abrasively; 'but you've asked no one who actually works at the school. In my view this whole thing's been codged together from a very great distance without any proper grasp either of the issues, or of the logistics of the site or the area.'

The Deputy's eyes glint.

'I think you underestimate us, Mr Winkley,' and he rustles his papers, stands up tall and handsome, like a Prince of Wales, and ushers me to the door with the utmost courtesy.

29

The Councillor

Our meeting led to a variety of people actually visiting the site to take a look at what the fuss was about. One or two councillors passed through. The Chief Inspector came to the school with two advisory minions in tow, saw the irrationality of it all but had no further constructive proposals to make – or was perhaps by now powerless to influence events.

The Council changed over to the Tories in May 1977, but there was no change to the plans, although no move had yet been made to develop the site. I continued my flow of complaining letters, wondering whether the new political regime might take a fresh look at them.

A member of the Education Committee came to discuss the matter with our ever more disgruntled staff who were now beginning to realize the full implications of the New Plan.

She sat with them to listen to their arguments, displaying an endearing thinness of understanding. Her great concern, the bit she latched onto, was about the needlework, as she had learnt from one of the classroom assistants that there would be considerable difficulty transporting the sewing-machine, a splendid old shiny black, very heavy Singer ('oh, those are *marvellous* machines: last for ever, don't they') back and forth across the road.

'We'll need a trolley,' said Beryl, forthright as ever; 'I'm not carrying it, and you can't expect the children to lumber a thing as heavy as that ... It weighs a ton ...'

'I know,' said the Councillor sympathetically. 'Really,' she added, animated; 'it really is too bad.'

I laid on lunch for her, and we were joined by the Chief Inspector, an extremely tall geographer, who always wore heavy black shoes as if signalling that he was at any moment going to head off on a long trek across the mountains. The three of us sat together in my small room round a table that had been specially laid with a red, chequered tablecloth which Bernie the cook had unearthed from somewhere. The Councillor reflected back all she had heard, and above all her concerns about the needlework, which she felt was very important in a school like this one.

'It must be so difficult for you, Mr Winkley. I do so admire the way that people like you keep going.'

She smiled. She had slightly bluey hair, and took pride in her appearance, and she reminded me curiously of my old Auntie Kate who lived in a rather splendid house in Sutton

Coldfield, raising funds for the Conservatives by holding summer strawberry tea-parties on Uncle Jack's immaculate lawn. They would none of them know that Uncle Jack took his first step towards his considerable wealth by acquiring premises on the Soho Road in the heart of Handsworth in the late 1930s and stacking up as much barrel-oil as he could muster in a warehouse at the back, which he subsequently sold with no questions asked at immense profits during the war. It occurred to me that this good lady might well have known my aunt before her death in the 1960s. But I held no hope of her doing anything about the new school fiasco: it was obvious she was just as accommodating and effusively pleasant as she was hopelessly incapable of grasping any of the issues.

Over the fish and salad she talked about her recent holiday in South Africa.

'I have a friend, you know, who is an obstetrician out there, and he says that coloured children have relatively small brains and thick skulls.'

She looked at me sympathetically.

'Do you have a lot of learning problems here?'

The Chief Inspector's fork quivered in the air; he was momentarily as speechless as I was myself. He was a good man, excellent in his job, mature and sensible, and genuinely bothered about the teachers he supervised. He was also rather serious, even solemn, taking life as a series of principled steps each one of which required grave consideration. I imagined walking with him would be a cautious, meticulously thought-out business, with no danger of falling down crevasses. And here he was, suddenly faced with an unexpected thousand-foot drop.

While I was completely lost for words, my colleague took control of himself, and put his fork down, icily calm now.

'I'm afraid, Councillor, your South African friend is wrong.'

'Oh,' she said, puzzled. 'You think so?'

'There are no physical differences between blacks and

whites, apart from skin colour, and there are no differences in intelligence.'

It was clear, straightforward, incontrovertible.

'If anything,' I said, plunging in regardless, part of me wondering whether this was the final nail in the coffin for my new school, 'the black children here are the highest achievers.'

The good lady detected the shiver of hostility. She reconsidered her fish. 'I'm sure you're right,' she said, smiling at the Chief Inspector. 'One lives and learns.'

'It's very nice fish,' she added distractedly.

None of this made any difference to the outcome. Over the next six months the small, inadequate annexe of a building, this substitute for a real school, was built. And at the last, the money ran out, as perhaps it was all along intended to do, so that there was nothing left for 'frills', and any short cuts that could be made, would be made. There was no wall-boarding to display children's work anywhere, no burglar-alarm, a cheaper roof than had been specified, and no money for new furniture. As a quid pro quo, perhaps in a last effort to keep me quiet, they agreed to build a tiny corridor between the two halves of the building so that children could walk from one block of classes to another without going out into the rain. They also agreed to pay for soundproof folding-screens to cut off the classrooms when required. It was my, and the staff's, one very minor contribution to the enterprise.

Old furniture had to be taken up from the cellar, and there were deliveries from storage depots across the city. Ancient chairs with metal frames arrived in dribs and drabs, and soon started to chafe holes in the new carpets.

The building had no exterior lighting and it was set in the darkest part of Handsworth: down a side road with little traffic, well away from housing, and backing onto the rear of warehouses and shops that were little changed from the days when my Uncle Jack used to operate round here. I had by now decided that the best plan was to call this the Upper School and for it to house two year groups of the oldest children, which would provide for two spare classrooms for specialist teaching activity. The kitchen was left vacant and I was already trying to think up subversive plans to prevent it going ahead. At lunchtime the children would troop across the road to the existing kitchens and dining-rooms just as they had always done. Cars continued to need to be parked in the Old Building playground since they got broken into if they were left in the road. New supervisory staff had to be appointed. I now found myself endlessly crossing and re-crossing the road.

The roof was constantly leaking because children from the neighbourhood climbed all over it in the evenings, puncturing holes in its vulnerable surface. One little girl put a tiny umbrella up in assembly one day, to everyone's amazement.

'Excuse me, Claudia,' I say, 'what *are* you doing?'

'I have to sit here every day, sir,' she says, 'and when it rains it always drips on my head.'

There was nowhere to put up children's art-work, or writing, and teachers vainly tried to sellotape bits and pieces onto bare walls, or nail them onto the woodwork. The back playground had no fence, and there was a right of way for people to walk across the playground from the main shopping centre on the Soho Road back to Grove Lane, so that all through the day there was a regular troop of people moving across the yard. At the back of the school, there was a tiny road called Baker Street with a few houses that were due for demolition. In one of them, the very end one next to the school yard, there was a squat of young Rastafarians, twenty or more of them living in what was a three-bedroomed closed-down house. From time to time they invaded the playground and the school, threatening the teachers – sometimes with baseball bats – and shouting abuse at the children and walking off with equipment. I tried to keep the many external doors locked all the time, but it was a virtual impossibility with so many children moving in and out of the building.

The first break-in took place within the first month and set an ominous trend. I had a second little study in the New School, which doubled as a storeroom. During the first week of occupation, tape-recorders, a TV set, cameras and even the phone were stolen, my papers being strewn all over the floor.

I wrote my letter of resignation.

> You have left me in this ridiculous, impossible situation, in which the difficulties of running an already difficult school have been hugely compounded by this totally inadequate building. This is your responsibility and now it's up you leave me and the staff to get on with it. I know you despair of people like me whingeing – as I guess you call it – but you've managed to totally disillusion someone who I think was, and is, deeply committed to trying to make something of this school. I agreed to stay here for two years, which I've now done, and I've had enough. I wish to resign my position here from the end of this term, which should give you time to appoint someone else.

I took my resignation letter as far as the postbox, wanting to post this particular letter personally, and stood there for a while on a cold day in early spring, poised to push it, along with my fate, into the slot. Instead, I walked on and at the first wastepaper-bin shredded it. I could see a child over the way eyeing me curiously, maybe a child from another school, not someone I recognized. It was, I fear, gesture politics, and maybe the child saw through me: this was an angry debate I was having with myself, wildly out of perspective.

The truth was that the school was still in place and stood unmoved on the corner of Grove Lane. And now there was an extension, which gave us more space, more possibilities, whichever way you looked at it. And the school was not, in any case, merely buildings. What of the hundreds of souls inside? Moreover, lots of things had been going well before this business with the new building blew up. Rather than wasting my time pratting about writing letters, I'd do better to restate my case, to look again at what we wanted to achieve, at the thousand and one things that were still left to do, and encourage my ever-improving staff to keep going.

I had, however, sent off for details of a job somewhere else, all the same. It was, when it came to it, a close-run thing.

30

The Unit

I was now looking at the bright side. We did have more space, especially if we could get the Authority to abandon the idea of the new kitchens, which would create a useful room, and allow full use of the school hall, which otherwise would have to be used from midday to early afternoon for school dinners.

It struck me that there was a real possibility of our being able to install a unit to support the children with more serious behavioural difficulties. My plan was to set up a specialist base in the new kitchen area. I outlined this in a letter of 21st May 1978:

> Dear Sir,
>
> Added to the absurdity of building a school half the right size is the added nonsense of building a second kitchen. The school does not need a second kitchen as it already has kitchens of its own. Do you expect us to operate two separate lots of kitchens? And if we did, where would the children eat as no provision has been made for a dining area. In the hall? So the hall would be out of action for 20% of the day to be used for preparing the meals. Where are the dining-tables to be kept as no storage has

> been accounted for? The whole idea is absurd. It will be easier, cheaper and more sensible to walk the children (all 200 of them) down the road to the purpose-built dining accommodation that we already have. There are more important concerns for the school, notably the fact that lunch hours are highly stressful, as the more difficult children frequently get out of hand. Why can't I turn the kitchens into a support unit for children in difficulty?

There was no reply, but I was used to this. So I wrote to the new Conservative Chairman of the Education Committee, not particularly hopefully. It was a great surprise when I got a phone-call suggesting a visit on site.

The Chairman turns up accompanied by an architect, a secretary and two Local Authority officers. A small bald-headed man in a suit, covered by a brown mackintosh, he shakes hands, and I take him along to the new kitchen area.

'What's that?' he says, staring at the enormous stainless-steel duct projecting from the middle of the ceiling.

'An exhaust fan,' replies the architect who stands with a clip-board and a piece of paper. We all stare at the duct.

'What's that?' says the Chairman, surveying a pile of unopened boxes.

'Cookers. Not yet unwrapped. Not yet connected.'

'Ah. And you don't need them?'

'No,' I say.

'Not at all?'

'No, not at all.'

'Amazing,' he says, with a faint sigh. It suggests a hint of sympathy, the ghost of a chance. The Chairman grunts, and trawls round the room looking in every corner, and his minions follow him. 'Ghastly colour,' he remarks.

'I know,' I say. 'You don't get much of a choice. Pink or green.'

'Amazing,' he repeats.

'It's like the fences,' I say, 'They have to be green or blue.'

'Is that right? So you chose green.'

'You noticed? We thought blue might have made it look like a police station.'

'Not a great idea.'

'Nope.'

'Might have reduced the local crime rate,' the Chairman smiles. 'It needs reducing.'

'Bit unlikely,' I reply.

'Anyhow,' says the Chairman, non-committally. 'Thanks for the tour. We'll be back in touch.'

On the way out, he suddenly pulls me aside and whispers in my ear.

'It looks like a pig's ear to me,' he says. 'Bloody architects, think money grows on trees.'

I had pointed out, as clearly as I could, all the money the Authority would be saving by not duplicating kitchen staff and equipment.

'You think you could survive in here?' he asks. 'It's a bit small.'

'Sure, as long as that thing in the roof came out. All we'd need for a unit is a bit of furniture ... In any case it's as big as a classroom.'

'Never.'

'You haven't seen the classrooms.'

The Chairman is shaking his head.

'This unit ...' So far he'd only thought of the savings made by abandoning the kitchen project. 'Haven't properly got my mind round that. Write to me about it.'

'I already have.'

'More detail,' he says. 'Make out a case. OK?' He smiles, and out in the car park, as we shake hands, I detect the faintest sign of a wink.

So it was that the Unit got established. I managed to persuade the Authority to find money from its community budget to support a part-time teacher to work with a small group of our most highly disturbed youngsters; and bit by bit over the next few years the Unit provision evolved.

We worked from the start in a commonsensical, pragmatic way. The 'Unit children' were not to be isolated, and all of them had a mainstream ordinary class place. The time they spent in the Unit was planned according to their particular needs. One criterion for deciding whether or not a child was progressing was the amount of time they successfully managed to spend in their ordinary class. It was one of the first 'integrated units' of its kind in the country and, over the years, it began to attract a good deal of attention.

The main approach was to support the children through play, close supervision and counselling to try to give them insight. Educational psychologists gave us useful support in designing approaches to anger management, and criteria for admission and success criteria. Gradually, we began to take children from other schools, for many years on the most meagre of resources, with the school sacrificing half a teacher as a quid pro quo for the LEA who funded the other half – allowing us to create a full-time head of Unit post. The Unit steadily expanded and became a city-wide resource. It had two full-time staff and two special-needs assistants, one of whom was a trained child-counsellor.

None of this was easy, and we did not sense that the many visitors from inside and outside our own LEA understood the full implications of the work we were doing. These children were very difficult, and the strain on the staff working with them was exceptional. The senior management team, particularly myself and my deputy, were heavily involved in behavioural support. We worked to the principle that the children must conform to the basic disciplinary expectations of the school as a whole, even though all of us (including the rest of the children) realized that allowances had to be made for these unusually troubled children. There was the added problem that the children were hard to place in secondary school, since there was no comparable secondary provision. Nonetheless, many of the Unit children did well and we all benefited from developing our expertise in managing difficult children.

The teaching staff in the Unit offered a great deal to the mainstream staff in supporting the school's special-needs pupils, and in generally formulating behaviour policies. This was the up-side: the down-side was the stress children could constantly induce, suddenly losing their tempers, throwing things about, becoming abusive and unpredictable, and needing close supervision throughout the day. For each class we had a rescue plan if a Unit child became unmanageably difficult, with me stepping in as the last resort if the violence became completely uncontainable. Just occasionally, even I couldn't manage, when I became worried about the problem of restraining physically violent pupils, and I'd bring in parents as an emergency, although they invariably couldn't control them either. In extremis, we called for an ambulance. One pair of ambulance drivers got so fed up with a particularly hysterical and violent child who was attacking his mother with punches and kicks and X-certificate language that they carried him bodily into the ambulance and strapped him down, before taking him off to hospital.

There were regular problems with the Local Authority special-needs department. They were increasingly anxious for us to take any child, however difficult, who came their way, and when we couldn't manage them, they refused to give us any proper support. Social workers and educational workers alike too often seemed to fail to understand the level of day-to-day skill involved in managing these children; the extraordinary expertise the teachers were building up; and the nature of the stresses involved.

Violent children are not like disabled children. Emotional volatility is deeply threatening, sometimes dangerous. Some of the parents of the children were themselves highly disturbed, or even crazy. One father had bought his child everything he wanted on demand, including hundred-pound pairs of fashion trainers. A formidably large French grandmother continually told us that the French did things better, fencing the children in and beating them when necessary. English schools were altogether *too zoft*. She nonetheless agreed to come and sort out her grandson when necessary. One mother, refusing to accept that her son was any problem at all, turned to abuse the teachers for the slightest correction. Another almost had a nervous breakdown at the thought of a yellow card being given to her child to monitor his daily behaviour. A drug-addled pair despised us for not using the cane on their obstreperous youth. ('We have no problem with him,' the mother said contemptuously.) But the boy was clearly deeply disturbed.

I only lost my cool completely on one occasion. It was when a fix between social services, the educational psychologist and the Local Authority resulted in their insisting that one boy was 'perfectly manageable' and ought to be in a normal class. There was no way they were going to back us suspending him, which was what we were reluctantly, and somewhat desperately, proposing. The boy was at a children's home where I discovered the care-workers were convinced that he'd tried on more than one occasion to drown younger children (but the social worker had refused to listen). We tried him with our most experienced teachers and they all found him deeply worrying and frightening to the other children, which was generally not the case with the Unit children. The medical report from the child-psychiatrist supported us. But the social worker had a bee in his bonnet and wasn't having any. To the LEA's dismay I suspended him, and he spent his time roaming round the area on his bike, threatening other children. They then moved him and refused from then on to give us any further information about him. He was, we discovered, taken out to a country residential school, where he had a disturbed, chequered career. What annoyed us all so much was the dismissive contempt with which our teachers, for all their efforts, had been treated.

Many of the children clearly had serious psychiatric problems, and yet they only came to us superficially assessed. Many needed long-term therapy and even medical support. When this additional support was available the children often did much better. Some children's problems seemed intractable, though. There was a feeling that too many of them came to us too late and that we should be working more intensively with children at a much younger age, preferably before they were six. But there was no national or local policy to identify such children, let alone support them. On the contrary, it seemed to us that there was a strategy of delay, which was linked to inadequate resources. Once we'd received a child, we were expected to keep him (usually him), and there were increasing difficulties for us as the years went on in developing the principle that we wanted to work with children we could potentially integrate fully, girls as well as boys, who had a variety of conditions, including autism, extreme shyness and withdrawal. The Unit, like any other workable institution, needed balance. The last thing you wanted was twelve very violent, disruptive boys in one place.

But despite all these difficulties, we managed to create a highly professional resource which developed over the years and helped many children across the city. It had a record of making very rare exclusions, and a commitment from the various teachers and assistants who worked there that was worthy of high-level recognition. A major proportion of our Unit intake were from white families, and it was one of the encouraging aspects of the experiment that it was extremely uncommon for a family – often from a white council estate, with a record of racist attitudes – to express concern about bringing their child into all-black and Asian Handsworth, and to a school with few white pupils.

However great the difficulties, not least that of finding staff with the exceptional professional skills needed, we were deeply proud of the Unit. In one way or another we kept it going in that kitchen area through the skill and dedication of the Heads of Unit, Nina, Gill and Muriel, together with their back-up staff of specialist assistants, for the next twenty years.

31
Theatre

A new school hall also brought us new possibilities. From the first I had a personal interest in what could be done with children's theatre. Most years the school managed to stage a major production which I often directed myself. I had evolved a technique which combined the virtues of children improvising with the discipline and polish of a finished performance. I'd start by coming up with an idea – the story, the narrative: children of Junior-School age were well able to grasp the subtleties of a story, and the moral ambiguities and complexities which lay beneath the surface of a storyline.

It was important to choose a story for its resonance, and one that was not patronizing to them. There should be scope for lots of children to be involved, with music, dancing and the like being part of it. The play would have a highly polished trunk with extending branches being provided by the school's Indian-dance team, or samba drumming, or brass players, or a choir, or a contemporary-dance team. Other children could work on scenery or manage the lighting, and in no time you had a full-scale theatre company, which often involved a hundred children or more.

The new school hall was ideal for this. It could – if we provided curtaining – be blacked out. We could add lighting boards and spotlights and stereo sound. Classrooms could be made into changing rooms. The only drawback was that the hall was a third the size of the old Victorian hall.

Once the story was chosen, the casting of the main characters was critical. During the year, all the children in the school had a chance to perform mini-plays at their Friday assemblies, and everyone was on the watch for new talents. The core cast would finally emerge after a painful series of auditions (children here were invariably wildly keen to act, the school being full, it seemed, of performers), and a script consisting of a story outline broken up into, say, twenty scenes or sections would be handed out. All the core cast knew the story, and had an idea of how the characters should talk to each other. It was now up to them to work over the material, and improvise against a rough blueprint.

I would watch fascinated to see how the scenes would work out. A lot of time was spent playing about with the problem of character development, ideas constantly being thrown up, used or rejected. Through this process the children seemed to evolve a feeling for character from the inside, and perform much more naturally and confidently.

They would sit around and continually comment, and offer criticism, put in new ideas. Finally there would come a point when the scene started to harden up, and a script of sorts was produced which would be more or less the basis of the finished version. Twenty or so scenes would form the outline of the final play. There never was a final version, as this greatly encouraged improvisational skills, and I could rarely remember any performance running exactly to expectations. There was the feel of jazz about our approach: characters would suddenly invent new lines, or run off at a tangent, and sometimes greatly extend a scene, particularly when it was funny. Extemporizations were often hugely amusing, the actors being in full flow, and playing up to the audience. The structure of the play lay in the scenes themselves, so that even if one scene was elongated, or whirled off into unknown directions, the next would bring things back on track.

My first production had been *Ivan the Fool*. In time we were to produce versions of *Troilus and Cressida* (twice) and also *A Midsummer Night's Dream*, *Treasure Island*, *The Tempest*, *West Side Story* and a variety of musicals, to all of which we gave our own original twists and touches. Other staff put on joint productions which often involved contributions from across the school – we already had some skilled teachers of music and drama – and Ann, then head of English, directed a full musical version of *The Wizard of Oz*. Slowly the new hall was developed, whenever money could be put aside, with a spotlight being installed here and there, or a simple sound system with a dimmer-board. At its best, the great Spring or Summer Show became an event in which most of the older children could be involved in one way or another. It developed into one of the most memorable of the school's achievements.

There was always a tremendous buzz around these productions. As well as the hundred or more children who were taking part, the costumes, make-up, scenery, staging and stage-blocks, lighting and so on involved many teachers and classroom assistants, and many hours of work after school. We were strong at contemporary and jazz dance, and also had specialist African and Indian dance groups, and we were lucky to have teachers and classroom assistants with real expertise who could work with children in clubs after school to build up a very high standard of performance.

Wherever possible, we involved the children themselves. They would eventually handle all the lighting and stage management for the show itself. Design for a production varied from next to nothing to an elaborate backcloth and constructions. As the hall would hold an audience of two hundred at most, we tended to favour a performance in the round, the audience being spread on three sides of a stage which was often elevated with stage-blocks. In one of our *Troilus and Cressida* versions the teachers built a huge wooden horse as a *coup de théâtre* at the end, with a complicated lighting system that illuminated the beast – especially its eyes – in startling ways. It caused gasps of astonishment on the night.

Invariably the evening performances were heavily oversubscribed and they were made complicated by the fact that some parents found it very hard to arrive on time. It was always a mug's job managing the front-door entrance. Once or twice we were hijacked by parents demanding entry at the door even though the hall was already heaving, and all the tickets had been sold. By the end of the show there were people standing in every inch of space round the edge that could be occupied. Babies were a particular hazard, howling in inappropriate places. And as the performance proceeded, with the lack of air in the hall, the intense heat of the spotlights and the cramped-up audience, the temperature would rise to a point where one mum described it like this: 'My God, it's like India in hot season;' and programmes would flap as people fanned themselves. In the end we installed Indian-style fans, borrowed from local homes, which would buzz away during the show.

The windows were, of course, open but they were heavily covered with blackout curtaining. If we opened the emergency exit doors which were like French windows taking you out to the side of the school, consisting of a weedy few square yards of ground leading to the main school playground, there was the danger of our being invaded by the local teenage troublemakers.

The local boys would sometimes throw showers of bricks and stones over the fence at the cast as they took a breath of air in the playground before the performance, their make-up on and attired in costumes. Appeals to the boys' conscience and good humour, plus an invitation, when there was room, to come inside and watch the show, dealt with most of them. But some would still hang around, throw more stones, climb onto the roof or try to get into the hall during the performance through the open exit door. In despair I would eventually call the police to chase them off.

Directing a show for children brings the kinds of stomach-churning tension that real-life professionals experience. An extraordinary intensity builds up, which is partly the result of the hundreds of hours of hard work that is involved, but partly – and particularly perhaps with children – due to the unpredictability of it all. I wanted to prove something: that plays with young children do not have to be wooden pastiches of the real, adult thing, but can make even the most sophisticated theatre-goer laugh and cry, like 'real theatre'. There's also the issue that by and large our children do not go to the theatre, although we arrange trips out for them, and there's something exciting in bringing the theatre to them, and giving them the chance to understand what a powerful and important medium it is.

There were some remarkable moments. I had a tiny Afro-Caribbean boy, a seven-year-old, playing Trinculo, who the moment he walked on stage was a natural comedian, inventing lines with an eye-rolling facility, tossing ideas and jokes around as they came into his head, turning seamlessly – in the middle of the scene – to comment to the audience, who by then were convulsed with laughter. Farrhat, our Ariel that year, memorized chunks of Shakespeare's lines and could move from Shakespeare's language into contemporary lingo and back with bewitching facility. Ita, as Maria in *West Side Story*, had some of the audience in tears by the end of the play. The Lion in *A Midsummer Night's Dream* was a tiny boy whose main problem was getting to school on time in the evening, as his dad didn't quite seem to understand how important it was to have him there. The boy produced a Lion performance worthy of the Royal Shakespeare Company, endearingly and brilliantly funny. Less intended, that night, was the refusal of our Titania (a true primadonna) to have anything at all to do with our Bottom, a happy-go-lucky Bottom-like Muslim boy, after his magical transformation into the lovable ass. The love scenes were scarcely what was intended. That performance was also marked by my directorial explosion at one of the actors (a spoilt little boy) refusing to turn up as he wanted to stay in and watch *Neighbours* on the TV. He suffered next day from a corporate hostility from children and teachers alike that must have taken him by surprise. He was the only child in any performance over the years – and this included many boys and girls who had an additional obligation to attend the Mosque – who let us down.

But most striking of all perhaps, a real find, was Amritraj who played Cassandra amongst other roles over the years, and was maybe the most talented performer we ever had, with her clarity and conviction of speech and her hypnotic ability to hold an audience entranced.

The underlying themes of these plays were as serious and relevant to children as adults, dealing with social and emotional issues that they were able to grasp. They could handle issues of war, insensitivity, insecurity, cruelty. They had a pretty fair, highly involved, understanding of the gang warfare in *West Side Story*. They could grasp the subtle ins and outs of relationships between the young and the old, and had a very strong sense of comic opportunities. Our Pandarus was wonderfully pompous, our Achilles effete and devious, our Prospero wise and oddly charismatic.

Troilus and Cressida, *A Midsummer Night's Dream*, *The Tempest* threw us the challenge of presenting theatrically some of the issues of arranged marriages in a community where arranged marriage was still, for many, the cultural norm. 'Marriage' is a key theme in all these plays, involving tensions between fathers and daughters – a point which was not lost on some of our girls – and I wondered sometimes what the parents were thinking as they watched the issues being played out with real children on the stage in front of them.

The children invariably rose to the occasion. It was as though all their, and our, energies flowed into this one great corporate act, a huge explosion of fun and display, which always managed to catch the imagination of the audience. Gradually that audience came to include a wide range of academics, other teachers and headteachers, writers and artists, senior officers from the LEA and elsewhere, local community leaders, the press. It's an experience for the children that digs deep, stays in the memory, and creates moments of high intensity. It is as if we had done something together that transcended us as individuals, and had made and *felt* something which, while seemingly ephemeral, truly and inexplicably mattered.

32
Space

The new building was by this point fully operational, with some two hundred of the older children milling about, and those two classrooms kept for extra teaching facilities. We had room for some specialist group-teaching, a resource room, maybe even a library. The downside was that the school was now split into two great, separated hunks: there was a new strict rule that no children should ever cross from one building to the other by themselves. The road running between the buildings was a favourite for local joy-riders, who hared their ancient BMWs and Saabs along at crazy speeds, scattering anyone in their path. On one occasion, one of them almost ploughed into a crocodile of our children going across the road at lunchtime.

There was little space for each individual child in the new classrooms, far less than in the Victorian Old Building. However, we shouldn't have complained: we now had an extra hall for our school plays and also our lively new Unit in the 'kitchens' ... The classrooms were at least *light*. Their big windows exposed a lot of sky and you could at least *think* about space. A modicum of space is surely required for you to move, to think, to explore. To reflect.

Space, we know, has implications for time. Just as there was little space for children to move in their tightly cloistered environment, how much time did they have in their lives to allow them to play with thoughts, to explore ideas that might occur to them? How much space – by which I mean relaxed time – do we need to allow ideas to ferment?

Once again I watch a class in progress. What is happening inside those minds, what bursts of distraction? The children are well behaved, engaged, interested, but they are not asking questions. Tightly controlled, they listen and write, and perform manageable tasks. Is this activity expanding their minds? If so, in what way? I realize that the children are often distracted: the quirky provocative matters that attract their attention are often nothing to do with the lesson. The colour of their friend's pen; what they're going to do at break; odd things they can talk about as they work on the mainstream task. While the class activity can seem to run along tramlines, their minds are actually whipping about following all manner of alternative thoughts and enquiries.

Some children sit looking vague, thoughtless. These are the ones who seem to have no room to move at all within their own heads. They accept, they enjoy drifting and being filled up like buckets. They have no internal linguistic life to explore. When they read, they take in what is there but they don't furnish the rooms they inhabit.

We had one boy called Matthew whose father was a fearsome Old Testament figure with a large beard and a fine command of rolling, abstract language. He commanded – not to say, commandeered – the boy's whole life, disciplined him like a soldier, dressed him immaculately, demanded absolute submission, insisting on perfect behaviour at all times, with the consequence that Matthew boiled inside like a kettle. The boy was rigidly well behaved except when you weren't watching him – when he went berserk. The terrible constraints imposed on him seriously damaged his learning, although there was no doubt that he was potentially a very able pupil.

Many highly able children, by contrast, seem able to find space in their minds to build ever-widening networks of increasingly complex connections and interconnections. They have the ability to roam about with ideas, their curiosity leading them to link the outside world with the world of the classroom, and ruminate on their own experiences. They read capaciously and, where necessary, apply a riveting scepticism. They have large minds, internal mansions of endless investigation. How much, I ask myself, does having sufficient space in their school, in their classrooms, or at home, matter to them?

Is it possible, as the decade comes to a close, that education may be increasingly in the business of closing down minds via ever-tighter definitions of purpose? Are we in danger of developing, and perhaps institutionalizing, a culture of telling other people what to do, giving teachers and children less space and opportunity to think for themselves? As we move to a general election in 1979, the jury is out, politicians and inspectors bracing themselves to tighten up the loose-limbed, decentralized education service, and prepare for a future of much greater central control.

One of the great educational quarrels of history was between Plato, speaking through Socrates, who thought philosophy – thinking – the path to true knowledge, and the despised Isocrates with his rival educational system based on the teaching of rhetoric. Isocrates stood up for the service of authority, of pedagogy; his inheritance lies with those who promulgate educational systems that set out to tighten things up, to determine rigorously what to teach and how to teach it. The Isocrateses of the world connect learning with political power and look to political programmes that exhort and systematize. They value discipline at all levels: they approve of the public image of the uniform and the ordered learning environment, with children firmly under the direction of the teacher. As we now reach the end of the 1970s, we can detect a new interest in such matters in public and political debate, and an increasing sense of urgency.

Pedagogy can be all too easily measured by its usefulness in relation to the values of social control. It's all too easy to encourage teaching methods that undervalue the need to create space for individual minds to shape, argue, discover or decide for themselves. We can conveniently over-emphasize utilitarian virtues in order to legitimize claims for much improved government funding for education.

One key question for an educational world in which a National Curriculum, together with other reforms, is being prepared behind the scenes, will be how far maps can replace journeys. Surely the engagement of the teacher's mind with the child's mind is the real journey, the one that matters? Pedagogy is from the Greek *pais* and *agoge*, and meaning the *leading* of the child; education is the *drawing out* of the talents of the individual to create a fulfilled personality. Better curriculum maps will certainly help define and guide our teaching: they are the teacher's essential tour guide. But in the end it will always be the teacher who draws out, and creates, and there is no substitute for the quality of the teacher's mind.

In this period of uncertainty, therefore, as we begin to settle down in our new, overcrowded school, with a fresh political regime looming on the horizon, it occurs to me that we should not forget that the tradition of Isocratean pedagogy – perhaps soon to be revitalized – has little interest in creating intellectual or physical space, and at worst starts to look like Matthew's father.

33

The Next Step

It is 1979 and we are making real progress. This is now quite definitely the school that I want my own children to attend. There's a weekly evening club in the Old Building for children, which we run from 6.00 to 8.00 p.m. on Wednesdays. In the New Building we have twice-weekly evening classes, run by the excellent Mr Mohan, employed by Further

Education, which attracted a regular hundred and fifty or so people – for classes ranging from learning basic English to yoga and music lessons. We have scouts and guides at the school, and I've managed to find money for a part-time community worker. The Unit is in full flow, and home-school visiting well on the way. Problems with attendance, which is still not good enough, are at least spotlighted.

We have an annual art exhibition, assessed by a professional artist, or by the LEA's art adviser, to which every child is expected to make a contribution. We have a variety of community events in the school, and a local photographer, Vanley Burke, has launched his career with an exhibition in the Upper School which attracts wide attention. We have introduced ability-setting in maths and English in the Upper School for part of the week, to give extra support for the particularly advanced children, as well as for the slower movers.

For me there's a new sense of focus and purpose. The plans are coming to fruition. The staff is high quality and working as a team. The place is beginning to hum. I want to believe that Grove is becoming a focal point for this part of Handsworth. It strikes me that these days the primary school in some respects is like the Victorian Church, the gathering point, the soul of the community. The school seems so buoyant, whilst the huge old St Peter's Church next door crumbles away, locked up and deserted.

Schools evolve in cycles: I guess that five to seven years is roughly the time-span for each of them. Eventually, some dozen teachers will become heads and deputies elsewhere – a sure sign that this is a career-building school and has attracted some of the brightest teachers around. I am also aware of the research evidence that as the seven-year cycle ends, headteachers can easily start to become too comfortable and settled, and lose that sharp edge that drives a school forward. I am soon to have a break for a year, allowing Edward, my deputy, to run the school in preparation for the headship he is certain to get before long. But I realize, too, that as teachers leave and change, the school will in some sense start afresh.

1979 was the year that the Conservative Government came to power. During the mid-1970s a number of economic shocks had impacted on the developed world, and inflation had been further accelerated by spectacular increases in oil prices. By that point the UK had large borrowings from the International Monetary Fund and inflation was spiralling upwards through excessive salary rises and a general economic downturn, which brought ever-tightening public-spending budgets. Gloomy economic news coincided with a vociferous call for educational reform that was driven by right-wing critics of permissiveness and low standards, and surprisingly climaxed in a speech at Ruskin College by the Labour Prime Minister, Jim Callaghan, on 18th October 1978. Keith Joseph's early criticisms were clearly reaching the arterial bloodstream of the system. Teachers had just received their biggest pay rise in history, but were now being accused of neglecting the entrepreneurial attitudes that were needed to resuscitate our flagging industrial base.

Keith Joseph, soon to become Secretary of State for Education, put out his stall:

> 'The blind, unplanned, uncoordinated wisdom of the market,' he said, 'is overwhelmingly superior to the well-researched, rational, systematic, statistically respectable plans of governments.'[13]

It had largely passed me by that education, and the curriculum in particular, was moving slowly but surely out of the professional arena and into the political one, with profound consequences for schools; and that what we should be doing was to develop a much greater awareness of what was happening at Elizabeth House, where the Department of Education was then based.

Even now officials at the DES were secretly producing what came to be known as 'the yellow book' refuting:

> any argument that no one except the teachers has any right to a say in what goes on in schools.[14]

Teachers in the early 1980s largely ignored such signals of change to come. It was the Local Authorities and their inspectors and finance officers who controlled and constrained schools. In so far as I had any insight into the rumblings of the outer world, I felt it was the LEA which was holding us back, the LEA against which the battle lines needed to be drawn.

The LEAs were as diverse as they were inconsistent. Inspectors and advisers were in the business of 'control', but they were also cautious about telling teachers what to do. It was an odd state of affairs and it was at precisely this moment that the DES was flexing its muscles to dramatically change the balance of power in favour of central control at Westminster.

There were also signs that the profession itself was changing, to the extent that professional views were being expressed by its divided unions.

Terry Casey, the leader of the National Association of Schoolmasters, a stocky person who would have fitted in perfectly in the movie *On the Waterfront*, was a key figure in developing the bruising negotiating style of this particular union, which opened a new page in teacher-salary negotiations by arguing that teachers are only paid 'for normal school hours'. Everything else was classified as 'goodwill' – and thus was devised the tactic of 'withdrawal of goodwill', which meant stopping doing anything but teaching. Other unions were quick to follow up on this bright idea. The *Times Educational Supplement*, in a perceptive editorial, warned about the dangers of playing this game.

> What would do most harm to the cause of education would be for the public to become cynical about teachers.[15]

And meanwhile, picking up the right-wing agenda, Rhodes Boyson, darling of the Keith Joseph camp, and later to become an Education Minister in the Thatcher Government, argued for a National Curriculum; for centrally controlled school inspectors, with systematic inspection for all schools; for national tests at the ages of seven, eleven and fifteen; for close checks on attendance figures; for teachers to be subject to formal assessment, with their salaries linked to performance; for all children to be provided with 'a common strand of basic knowledge'; and for a massive extension of parental choice, including the use of vouchers which a parent could use to purchase a place in the school of their choice. All of which was almost universally seen as extremist, and slightly dotty.[16]

My attention was focused on our own Local Authority, which now ruled that 'community evening activities' must be centralized in secondary schools, thus at one stroke closing down Mr Mohan's Further Education Centre, and the scouts, guides and children's evening club, all of which were funded by Further Education. The school's long-term plans to become a fully-fledged community-education centre were delivered an almost fatal blow. None of this endeared me to the Local Authority, which I felt was being excessively high-handed. I thought it failed to understand the importance of acknowledging and strengthening the confidence of the local community. It failed, moreover, to appreciate the importance of the primary school as a focal point for the families in a community. Secondary education was the flagship; it had more money and prestige, and its larger, grander buildings seemed to offer more opportunity for big-scale projects.

But these changes at least had the virtue of making us become more politically aware, and realize that there was a political world out there with the power to change our lives radically, if the circumstances suited it.

Summer

The 1980s

34
The Trip

The summer months provide pleasurable distractions. You can go out of school more, and visit the park which is at its best. It is when we have our annual sponsored walk: the entire school walks ten times round the Handsworth park lake, and finishes up with iced lollipops for the children and bacon sandwiches for the teachers. One young boy, thinking the duckweed is grass, walks straight into the water, and I take him home still covered in weed, looking like the Green Hulk. Another picks some flowers in the park garden to give his teacher, which is not likely to endear him to the park-keeper. But in general it's a great event with hundreds of happy children slowly and contentedly ambling around the lake.

We often take the children camping to our School Hostel, which was built some years before by myself and a group of teachers. The Hostel was twenty miles out of the city, set on a high woody ridge surrounded by magnificent north Warwickshire countryside and overlooking the rolling fields of Leicestershire. It was not far from the farming town of Atherstone, near the Dugdale coal mine, which was soon to be closed down.

It was a bungalow with sleeping accommodation for forty children, and it was used by our school and about twenty others. It had a curious history. One day driving down the old Roman Chester Road through Erdington, Birmingham, I had spotted teams of builders dismantling old second-world-war prefabricated council houses, meccano-type buildings, based on a concrete-slab construction and screwed together in sections. In a mad moment I had bought three of them on the spot for £125 each, and had them delivered on giant lorries to the Atherstone site. A local Sutton architect gave his time to design us a building based on the interlinking of the three prefabs with a reconstructed interior, and a new roof and foundations. Atherstone farmers organized planning permission; a United Nations work camp constructed the sewage and electrical arrangements and helped with laying the foundations. A long march from Birmingham City Centre all the way to Atherstone raised enough money to get us started.

Once the building was up, we began taking children out there from Birmingham, and we eventually set up a consortium of schools to manage the venture, my mum and dad being hugely instrumental in helping to raise money for it year on year and managing the Hostel accounts. Five thousand or more young children visited the Hostel annually. It gave us a lot of pleasure, and for the many teachers who contributed their own time in abundance, it was a great deal of hard work.

It was from the beginning entirely the initiative of the teachers, with no financial support coming from the Local Authority; and it was by now entirely funded as an independent trust run by the teachers.

All the children in the school visited the Hostel from time to time. Sometimes a whole class would go during the day for nature expeditions, geographical surveying and art activities. Sometimes they stayed overnight, often for the weekend, playing games, going on environmental study-walks, rambling through the fields and woods, visiting the farms with their animals, and finishing with bonfires and exciting expeditions in the dark. There were ridiculously late nights and ghost stories might be told when the children were tucked up in bed.

Then the staff would have a quiet time with a beer or two, sitting by the dying embers of the bonfire, and talking things over. Not long after the 1979 General Election we discussed light-heartedly the implications of Tory rule under the unlikely Mrs Thatcher. Despite all our residual doubts about the LEA, we still thought that local political power would be enough to keep the DES, at the centre, at arm's length.

In any case, the resourcing of the primary schools already seemed to have reached a low-point, and could surely get no worse.

Our reasons for being in the job and trying to make something of the school certainly wouldn't be changed much by political musical-chairs at Westminster under a woman who had after all been a one-time fairly low-key, cautiously conservative Secretary of State for Education under Edward Heath.

It was important for our children to get out of Handsworth from time to time, since many of them rarely left the streets where they lived. Trips, even to the City Centre, helped widen their horizons, and sharpen their awareness of the world. Surprisingly, it was some of the most difficult and intractable children who got the most out of the experience.

The occasional trip goes wrong. One fine summer's day a teacher takes her class to the science museum in the centre of town. She lines the children in pairs at the bus stop, ready to come home. When the double-decker bus arrives, she makes the fatal mistake – as a young inexperienced teacher might – of getting onto the bus first to pay the fare, at which point two-thirds of the children run away. And the bus sets off.

She pulls the emergency cord in a panic and rushes off after them, by which time they're right in the distance. Eventually they come sheepishly back to the bus stop, and in school the teacher is in tears, firing off about the awfulness of the episode and the impossibility of dealing with these horrific children.

I march into the class and rage, threatening ever more dreadful penalties.

'And if I don't deal with you – what will your parents say? *What* are they going to say?'

The children freeze, alarmed at the prospect of their parents and teachers working in tandem. They understand perfectly well that their behaviour has been outrageous and also that it is difficult to find any one person to blame – usually the most effective defensive ploy. But what has happened has happened and that is that. Duly ashamed, they resign themselves to the worst. There are to be no more trips for them for a good while. For a few days they will behave immaculately for their teacher and a contrite group of them organizes a whip-round and buys her a present. It will take time to calm her down and their Great Summer Outing is at serious risk. But the incident will soon be forgotten. It's not the kind of thing that's likely to happen again.

The Great Summer Outing for the older children this year is to London. It's a hot June day with no threat of rain, and British Rail lay on carriages to accommodate all the eleven-year-olds. They set off in buses to New Street station.

It is one of those occasions when classroom assistants, and especially Beryl, come into their own. Beryl sees herself at these times as taking responsibility for practical command, ushering, directing, shepherding the children, and rushing here and there to ensure that no one's left behind. Edward, the teacher in overall charge, is a good deal more laid back: for the teachers as well as the children this is a day out to enjoy, a few hours, as far as that is possible, to relax. I go along on this trip to the metropolis, and I'm even more at ease, since for once the organizational responsibility is not fully mine.

The children arrive at the station in tee-shirts and shorts, or glamorous party dresses, some looking like young teenagers with posh hair-do's and wearing their best shoes. Everyone carries bags of sweets and crisps, and some of them have excessive amounts of money to buy presents for various members of the family. They pile onto the train, eager to get seats near the window – best of all seats by the window facing in the direction the train is travelling. Beryl, who always does everything at great speed, hurries about the platform, running on and off the train, and completing her mopping up operation. Checking that everyone's now on board and in the right carriages, she shouts at recalcitrants: *'Get on the train, you hear me? You want to be left behind. Look – the man is ready to blow his whistle – can't you see?'* At this, a fog-horn rather than a whistle, the children bustle on.

Even then there are two children left, a girl and a boy. They see Beryl coming for them and they leap onto the train, heading the wrong way down the corridor, Beryl just behind them.

'You're going the wrong way,' she bellows. 'It's *that* way – use your eyes ... get in there and sit down and don't you dare let me catch you dropping bits of crisps on the seats. People have to sit down on those seats. And no chewing-gum, do you hear?'

'Yes, miss,' say the children, joining the wrestle for seats by the window.

The train begins to move away, with Ed and myself sitting together at the far end of the carriage, where we can easily scan the children. There are more staff in the other carriages. I'm nicely settled, with my copy of *Passage to India,* as the train gathers speed on its ten-mile run to the station at Coventry, when, glancing up, I happen to ask who the two little white children are.

'I suppose they're new,' I say. 'Don't remember seeing them before.'

Ed looks puzzled. He is the year group-leader and knows all the children.

'No,' he says, 'I don't remember seeing them before either.' He leans over to Beryl.

'Who are those two?' he asks.

Beryl stares at them.

'Oh my God,' she suddenly says. *'They're not ours.'*

She rushes up to them, demanding to know their names.

'What on earth do you think you are doing here?' she cries.

'You told us ...' one starts to say, standing up for herself valiantly.

'Told you *what*?' says Beryl scornfully.

'To sit here.'

'Who are you with?'

'Mum and Dad.'

'How stupid,' says Beryl, 'How stupid can you get? Your mum and dad must be looking for you everywhere. They must be worried sick. Get back up there – you get back up there – you hear? My goodness, if you were mine ...' She looks at them darkly, 'I know what I'd do with you.'

The two children are playing cards, a game that looks distinctly like four-handed bridge, and appear to have found new friends. They are clearly reluctant to leave, not in the least bit missing their unfortunate parents. They throw Beryl a fierce stare as they give up their seats, and gather their bags, and shoot down the train with a last pitying glance at the rest of the unfortunates having to put up with that awful woman.

'Who were they?' I ask.

'I've no idea,' says Beryl crossly, 'Ridiculous children.' Then muttering under her breath, 'I blame the parents.'

London has its hazards. First Satnam, a very tall fat boy, is terrified of the Underground and stands howling at the top of the Euston escalator, refusing to move. The other children in their crocodile joyfully bounce down the escalator, a novelty to most of them, it's like descending into a magical cave with tunnels and whizzing monsters. They have strict instructions to stay together, and what with Satnam's operatic performance, there's every danger of getting separated in the crowds. I take it upon myself to persuade the boy to move.

'Move,' I say gently, thinking the child is in some way traumatized. 'We've got to get down there. It's quite safe. Look at the others.'

Satnam holds tight to the rails, refusing to budge. The rest of the children are almost out of sight.

'Move,' I say more ferociously; 'I'm telling you.'

Then, finally losing my patience, I grab the howling boy round the waist and lift him bodily onto the escalator, holding him tight until we both reach the bottom, while the crowds of travellers view me with considerable suspicion.

'There,' I keep saying, 'it's not so bad, is it?' and, sure enough, Satnam relaxes, no doubt pleased with himself at having overcome so great an emotional obstacle.

As we are setting off walking towards the Planetarium, the children chattering away in their ragged crocodiles, and impeccably behaved, a man comes from the opposite direction and spits in the face of one of the little girls, calling her – and presumably by implication her friends – *black shit*.

The children look shocked. They are stunned by this assault. Edward is within earshot, and in front of all the children he reacts instinctively, unprepared (who would be prepared for such a thing?) but furiously angry. He confronts the man head on, and all the children stop.

'You racist bastard,' says Ed, grabbing the man's shoulder and pausing as if to consider whether to punch his head in. The guy's young and looks bigger than Ed but he is by now shocked himself, not expecting this reaction out of the blue; and sensing that he might get thumped, he takes a step back and mutters some pathetic apology.

'Not to me,' says Ed, 'to that girl.'

The guy eyes the girl, mumbles something inaudible and walks swiftly away. The children stand watching, and spontaneously clap.

'Come on,' says Ed uncompromisingly, 'Get back into your pairs.' But they see him, as we all see him, as something of a hero.

The day finishes merrily with a picnic in the park. There are few other people about – no doubt they saw us coming – and there's a pool with paddle-boats. After sandwiches, the children get into the boats and take sides as in some naval conflict.

'They're getting all wet,' says Beryl.

'Let them,' says Ed. 'It's their day out.'

In the end, Ed and I and the other teachers join in, splashing from the side and the boatman comes up, good-humoured. 'Time's up,' he says, and the soaking children jump out, having had the time of their lives. They strip off in the heat and lay their clothes out on the grass; they show each other their little presents, bizarre things they've bought, and consume more vast amounts of pop and crisps, of which there seems to be a bottomless supply. It's time to go, and one of the great virtues of trains is that children are not sick on them. They travel back quietly, as they always do, some of them sleeping, exhausted after a long day.

35
The White Dog

The racist incident on the London trip might have been dismissed as a momentary aberration, a verbal assault by a nutcase. But then came the netball match.

The netball team is organized by Ann and competes regularly and highly successfully against local schools. The second match of the season, a 'friendly', is to be played at a much more middle-class school in an area of the city still largely inhabited by families of white-collar workers, on the edge of Handsworth.

The team is ferried out in cars and greeted hospitably, and taken inside for the traditional pre-match orangeade and biscuits, the host teachers being enthusiasts as much as Ann herself. There was friendly rivalry between the local teams: the standards were high, a great deal of preparation went into the game, and for the teachers as well as the children there was much pride in winning.

The weather's fresh, with bright skies and a cool wind;

the girls are smartly kitted out in their green skirts and white tops emblazoned with the school name. Some of them are tall for their years, one or two taller than the teachers, and for all their languorous appearance off court, once the game starts they have a quicksilver alertness, sharpened by their teacher's driving enthusiasm and discipline. The opposition possesses a kind of polish and protected urbanity, puppy fat covering self-assurance – these were the children of parents with ambition. Maybe they convey a faint sense of feeling superior, something in their gaze assuming they have the right to win, and also perhaps a hint of do-your-homework-every-night and must-get-to-the-grammar-school intelligence.

Already lots of children from the other school have assembled in the playground surrounding the netball court to watch the game, a neat sea of school uniforms and bright voices. A few of our children are also there, clustered in one or two little groups on the side.

The match starts smoothly. The sun creates flickering shadows; the girls are in full flow. I stand on the sideline with a handful of parents and teachers encouraging their teams. Netball always seems to me to be an odd game. The lack of physical contact and the peculiar practice of freezing players into bits of the court, give it an old-ma'am feel, as though it was originally founded on an old-fashioned view of girls as prissily unable to engage in unladylike behaviour. All the same, the game in reality has a kind of contained ferocity: girls find their own way of battering each other, frequently tussling violently for the possession of the ball, the umpires endlessly and sometimes frantically blowing whistles. Hostility between umpires, encountered occasionally, can bias you towards your own side in the unending need to offer Solomon's judgement on joint possession of the ball. But, for all this, there are some great young players here with fierceness, speed, a rapid eye for the ball and the ability to dominate by sheer personality and throwing of pinpoint accuracy.

What starts the chanting is impossible to say. But it starts soon enough when our team – who are mostly black girls – are winning.

'Black rubbish' comes the first whisper, like smoke in the wind. It catches the adults by surprise, momentarily freezing the brain as something shocking invariably does. But 'black rubbish' it definitely is and, now in the open, it begins to flare up as if caught on the breeze, and carried round the square from child to child, until this dense crop of polished pink and white young faces, with their immaculate school uniforms, a sign of order and discipline and good homes, are chanting in unison: '*black roo-bish, black roo-bish*'.

A flow of blood runs from my feet into my head. What I can't understand is why the teachers at the host school seem not to have noticed, as though nothing is happening – or if something *is* happening, it's a bit of a joke and of no importance. But I feel, as the black children must have felt, an accumulating sense of anger.

By now Ann has heard the chanting. She glances over her shoulder at me and is as decisive as ever. She stops the game in its tracks and the ball goes rolling away somewhere whilst the girls stand still, bemused. She marches off the court announcing 'that's enough girls'. Then she goes up to the games teacher and protests.

The reaction is one of puzzlement. Other teachers and a few parents gather round. But by now my attention is focused elsewhere: in another part of the playground a group of Grove boys are confronting some two or three dozen children who are surrounding them. Amongst the boys is one that I know all too well. The situation is rapidly getting out of hand. I had guessed Leroy would soon be hitting someone. He is big and has a volatile temper, and now he has every excuse for flaring up. I plunge in and tell the boys that they've got to go home immediately and make no trouble on the way, not so much as a sound, or I'm after them tomorrow.

'You understand?'

There's silence now. The girls are gathering round Ann, who's packing up the equipment. The cars are ready to take them back. The parents are muttering, one or two of them confused and embarrassed. I have to go to my car as I'm going to shuttle some of the girls back home.

But then after the cars have gone a man appears. He is one of the parents, and he has an enormous pale Alsatian dog with which he confronts the four or five boys and a couple of girls heading home.

'Which one hit my daughter?' he's yelling.

The dog is snarling.

'The one that pushed my daughter is dead,' he screams.

The boys start to run, with the dog barking and straining at the leash.

'Fucking black bastards, shit, fuck you, you fucking come down here again, he'll rip your guts out ...' The girls are terrified, and one bursts into tears. The boys are silenced, stunned at the attack. It's only later that I learn that the parent wasn't joking: he admitted that his white dog had been trained to 'go for the blacks', and keep them off his territory.

Later, of course, the head of the school, who had not been there at the match, rings me to apologize: action would be taken, he says. For sure. But the damage has been done.

36

The National Front Meeting

There's nothing we can do to prevent the National Front meeting at the school even though I have had prolonged meetings with an extremely sympathetic Local Authority. The law at that time entitled any legitimate candidate in a national or local election to hold a public meeting in a school of their choice in the constituency in which they stood. The National Front has put up a candidate in the Soho ward for the May local elections – obviously a deliberate provocation for the largely black and Asian community – and we're powerless to do anything about it.

I'm left with a bleak awareness of the divisions between the centre and margins where a cat-and-mouse game is being played out between political fanatics and vulnerable minorities who feel exposed and unprotected against this kind of invasiveness. The National Front is made up of hooligans led by devious manipulators who target the vulnerabilities and incipient paranoia that run beneath the mainstream of society.

> They're taking your jobs, attacking your children, lowering the value of your property, undermining the traditional values of the nation. These are the riff-raff from the nether reaches of the Empire, allowed in through the absurd liberality and incompetence of successive governments. Do you seriously think they're English?

Young white disaffected boys use such messages as an emotional support to build themselves up. They create a negative identity – *we are what you are not* – bolstering up immature and damaged personalities by turning against people easily identified by their race, whom they crudely describe as a different species. The middle-aged men who front the organization clothe these messages in a kind of mock moderation, trying to use the reputable language of conventional politics. They think up 'policies' with the aim of creating habits of mind, and build up an (apparently) respectable platform through which their gangsterism can slowly poison the thinking of the mainstream, and get to 'ordinary folk' out there who can appreciate their 'commonsensical down-to-earth views'. So they manoeuvre themselves from the margins to the centre, climbing on the backs of those – also on the margins – whom they demonize. For such people, the more fuss, the more public attention and press profile they can get, the better. They can always blame others for violence. Doesn't this prove their point that the blacks and the liberals are the problem?

News of the meeting, advertised, we suspect, by the Front itself, spreads like wildfire round the West Midlands. Coaches are laid on from universities as far away as Warwick for armies of protesting students to turn up in defence of anti-racism and civilized values. And turn up they do in their droves. In my view, I say to the staff, we should keep well away from the meeting. Nothing of any value should be left in the Old School hall where it's planned to take place. All doors to classrooms should be locked. It's like preparing for an earthquake. Only Roger, a determined left-winger, is going to ignore my advice.

On the Thursday night of the meeting, so many people have appeared outside the school that the police have cordoned off the area. No one is allowed inside prior to the arrival of the NF leadership, although presumably someone inside is making things ready for the arrival of the gang. It's now about seven o'clock and a crowd is gathering outside – at least a couple of hundred people, very youthful, colourful, vociferous and restive – and growing bigger by the minute. Some people start chanting and the police protect the doorways: they have a substantial contingent strategically placed round the school, including vans and horses, preparing for trouble.

The senior National Front members eventually arrive all together at twilight in a fleet of vans, like something out of a speeded-up black and white 1940s movie, and they hurry through the pathway created by the police, jeered by the crowd. The figures all look heavyweights, one or two – probably including the leader himself – middle-aged, and they all wear smartish coats and suits. There's a long restless pause and then some minutes later the public are let inside.

It seems at first to be an orderly entrance, but the meeting never gets going. Those who go in first see the hall neatly set out with a stage and a desk with three or four chairs, a microphone and even a glass of water. It might have been as anodyne an event as an annual parents' meeting. There's something grotesque about this meeting being held in a room with its walls covered with bright children's pictures. There are still people flooding into the hall when someone picks up a chair and hurls it onto the stage, which is enough for the police to pile in – just, you suspect, what they are waiting for – and they start to throw everyone out, shouting and pointing to the doors. A bald-headed guy in a dark suit and tie on the platform begins to shout, at which abuse from the crowds of youngsters flies in all directions, people bellowing at the tops of their voices and waving their fists in the air. Some people are reluctant to leave and there are a few moments of saloon-bar mayhem, with screaming and fighting, chairs being hurled, desks upturned, punches thrown; and the police clear out those who are still hanging about. The National Front gang are escorted away, surrounded by police. Roger is kicked as he leaves by a large police sergeant and is limping for days afterwards.

We turn up the next day to survey the debris. The hall is badly smashed about. Windows are broken, and glass is still everywhere, although the caretaker has been working overtime to clear the place up. Parts of the children's display work is in tatters; there are ugly holes in the walls as though someone's been hitting the plaster with hammers; the piano has a swastika engraved on it with a knife.

The children come to school as usual to witness their broken and battered building, and they're understandably subdued. I suspect that, like the rest of us, they feel that they have themselves been in some way abused. In assembly I express my dismay and apologize to the children, who can scarcely be expected to understand the politics behind all this, and I promise them that the hall will be put right soon. They stare silently at me. Are they convinced? It is at such moments that you learn the importance of trust, the feeling that we and they are in the same boat, on the same side, and full of the same indignation.

37
Race Issues

Writers from the black community were now not merely questioning openly the general and obvious signs of racism and its impact on the minority communities, but raising more fundamental questions about inappropriate 'permissive' schooling, teachers with low expectations, and disproportionate underachievement by black youngsters, especially boys. There was a call for black self-help groups based on American models to be set up, linked to the charisma of Malcolm X and black-power movements. Saturday schools were springing up, mostly for children of West Indian (progressively retitled Afro-Caribbean) backgrounds. 'Immigrant' was out; multi-culturalism was in. Some communities, notably Muslims, were beginning to demand their own schools. There was a heated public argument about the School's Council project, *Education for a Multi-racial Society*, since the first section was heavily watered down prior to publication as people were frightened of being 'too hard-hitting'. The articulate parents were beginning to speak out:

> How can alienated working class black youth in Britain be rescued from semi-literacy, despondency, ennui, unemployment and eventual crime?[17]

The American influence in all this was strong. The writings of Maureen Stone,[18] a black academic commentator, paralleled a movement to the right in the USA, a fundamentalist shift to the externals of control, with emphasis on such things as school-uniform, the radical revision of reading programmes to emphasize phonics, corporal punishment, old-fashioned drills and routines, times-tables testing and Standard Attainment Tasks. President Carter was firmly in the back-to-basics camp. We were to see an increasing tendency for the UK to look across the Atlantic in search of ways to tackle what were perceived as similar problems of low achievement and poor discipline.

Dinah, a black welfare-worker in Handsworth, put the argument starkly:

> Lots of black kids ... don't want all this liberal shit about reasonable discussion and talking things over. They can't handle it and they get scared and lonely. They want to be told to do this and that, then and there, or else ...[19]

Teachers were frequently accused of patronizing black and Asian children, stereotyping them in much the same way that working-class white children had been stereotyped in the past. The Select Committee on Race Relations had in 1973 made recommendations for improved teacher-training, proposing that more teachers of English as a Second Language should be made available. Two major reports in 1981, the Rampton Report and that of the Parliamentary Home Affairs Committee, expressed disquiet at 'the overwhelming picture of the failure of teacher-training institutions to prepare teachers for their role in a multi-racial society'. Seminars on multi-culturalism began to proliferate. There was a flow of theories about curriculum as cultural transmission, leading to various tinkerings with history, religious education, and geography programmes 'to reflect' the needs of ethnic-minority pupils. These ideas rarely penetrated into 'white' schools.

The general debate seemed simplistic, failing to take into account the complex meanings of 'culture' in places like Handsworth where youngsters were caught between the traditional values of their own cultures and the pluralism of an increasingly multi-cultural society – disseminated through the ever-growing influence of the mass media. There was a sense in which the communities themselves were trying, not very successfully, to protect themselves against what they saw as the excessively liberal, unstable values of the Western world. Television in particular was influencing the thinking of the younger generation, undermining their home traditions. Many local families had very different – and often stricter – views about parenting from those of the host community. 'We didn't come here to spoil the children,' as one Muslim parent said on 'Panorama'. The assumption that Western-style permissiveness necessarily produced more contented, stable children was, as many of our parents saw it, deeply flawed.

38
Harambee

A flood of reports and publications about race and racism reached its climax with the belated publication of the Swann Report.[20] This encapsulated most of current thinking, and presented particular challenges to the schools, which were seen to be the key organizations in improving social relationships.

The Swann Committee had been set up in 1979 to investigate the education of children from ethnic minority groups and covered every conceivable aspect of education in the context of race, English as a second language, underachievement, and so on. It reported finally in 1985, by which time it was well out of date. Much of what it said had been said before and was arguably self-evident. It rightly highlighted the importance of increasing the numbers of black and Asian teachers, and demanded as a matter of urgency the development of anti-racist policies in schools. But many of us found the overall package disappointing: it failed to match the complexity of the issues. It was certainly one of the first Government-sponsored reports to identify schools as the key formative social force in improving the lives of underprivileged pupils, and signalled a new political interest in bringing schools nearer to the centre of social policy – where they were to be ruthlessly spotlighted, pinned down and dissected over the next few years. But to those of us spending our daily lives at the grassroots, the complicating contexts of poverty, of parenting, of health and of housing were insufficiently explored.

I ploughed my way through this fat green volume and came to the conclusion that it was well intentioned but toothless. It failed to address the social malaise of insecure families facing all the problems of disorientation and pluralism in a rapidly changing social culture. It served little purpose beyond summarizing a mass of existing material, and for a short while raising the level of the debate. It failed to communicate a feel for the real world that I experienced every day on the streets of Handsworth. It upset both the brighter teachers, who found it naive, and the local activists who found it soft-centred and out of touch.

Swann, along with other Government communications, was certainly viewed with scepticism by the activists of Harambee. This was much the most articulate of the various black groups in the area and, as I have said, the one that tried hardest to support the local black community. Their centre was a shop a couple of hundred yards from the school on Grove Lane. The lads – they were mostly lads – who ran the shop were predominantly students, many of them law-students. They used the school at weekends to run alternative 'Saturday Schools', something which I grudgingly allowed, although I was doubtful about the legality of the 'all black' requirement for entry and I was well aware that the teaching – what there was of it – was very different from that of the rather prim and proper supplementary local black Saturday schools with their strong Church connections, desks, formal teaching and use of the spanking paddle.

The Harambee School was more the product of 1960s and Black Power freedom movements, which were run by bright students with their own utopian vision.

The student-teachers had difficulty controlling their lively young protégés, and from time to time found themselves forced into forms of discipline that they would in other circumstances have considered to be the typical weapons of oppressive imperialism. Occasionally they forgot to rub the classroom boards clean and left behind evidence of the lessons they were endeavouring to teach about Marxism, and in particular, it seemed, Maoism. They set up what might be best described as a first shot at a 'childline', encouraging youngsters to report back to them anything that they thought to be racist in the way that white teachers dealt with them.

The element of indoctrination concerned me sufficiently for me to decide to talk it over with officers and councillors; and at one point I became really angry and wrote to the press. This led to a correspondence with the black activists who (probably rightly) saw me as overreacting. The fact was that the Saturday School, though in some ways ahead of its time, turned out to have very little effect on the children. Few of the youngsters seemed to take much notice of what they were being taught, and in any case their parents were far from persuaded of the virtues of Marxist revolutionary thinking.

I was to find out that Harambee kept a secret file on me in their headquarters in Hall Road. They publicly maintained a generally hostile stance on the school, seeing me as a local bastion of white middle-class power in the heart of 'their' community. They had a particular dislike of the caretaker whom they targeted as racist largely because we complained about the mess they left at weekends and their unpredictable timekeeping, which drove the caretaker to distraction. On the other hand, it was difficult for them to ignore the fact that the school had by now quite a number of black and Asian teachers who were making a crucial contribution to its success and were notable not only for their intelligence but for their commonsense.

The truth was that since the late 1970s I had developed a soft spot for Harambee, particularly after the help they had given me in the alarming business of dealing with violent families. What's more, I liked some of the young activists who had the guts to fight for causes I had – though they might not have realized it – always believed in. On their side, there was a grudging admission that the local families rather liked the school, and the children were, maybe to their surprise, coming out to defend their teachers. The one thing I guess that Harambee now accepted was that I was no fly-by-night.

Despite our occasional public spats, and my continuing suspicion of the Saturday School, the philosophical gap between us was not the yawning abyss that they imagined. Harambee had the considerable virtue of trying to do something for the community in a way that truly represented local people.

One of their number starts to visit the school regularly. An enormous young man, six foot six in height, immensely commanding, he wanders slowly across the playground and, if children are out there, he grabs them and interrogates them and asks why they aren't fighting.

Then he ambles like a gunslinger down the corridors dressed in a handsome black-leather trench coat, black-leather gloves, dark glasses, immaculately groomed. His approach to capitalist hegemony and institutional racism is to bypass conventions of all kinds; he is impatient with the apparatus of white bureaucracy and the oppressions of authorities – especially secretaries, receptionists, bartenders. Here is a guy who expects instant service: everyone in the outfit must drop tools in order to notice him. He has a kind of 1980s Clint Eastwood persona that always carries with it the undercurrent of violence. There's no knocking on doors; he simply walks in, and towers his huge frame right over you.

He seems to have taken an especial shine to me and comes

and parks himself for long periods of time in my room wanting to talk about philosophy or women – his attitude to whom is *macho* in the extreme – or politics, and especially the state of socialism. He wants to give me the lowdown on the local scene. He likes to talk books, and he occasionally steals books from the central library which he donates to me in plastic carrier bags. When I protest, he shakes his head with astonishment: 'All learning is free, man.' So I find myself taking them back to the library, nervously leaving the bags on the best concealed tables or shelves.

His stories are extraordinary. He relates at length the tale of his guerrilla jungle-warfare training programme for a group of Handsworth children – who were taken to Africa on a Local Authority grant. He slags off many of his colleagues and one day, shaking his head miserably, he takes off his coat, his jacket and his shirt to reveal heavy bandaging round his torso – this he unwraps to show me his gunshot wounds. One of them had shot him, and it was only by a stroke of luck that he had escaped being killed.

Another time, he comes in with a little boy, clutching the child by the collar and dangling him like some cat rescued from a river.

'For Christ's sake put him down – who is he?'

'I want this kid in this school ...'

'There's no room – we're full ... where's he from?'

'He's at this special school, man, his mum don't like it; these black kids get put in these places for no good reason ...'

The child stares around puzzled. He is perhaps autistic, and certainly not in tune with what is going on. He doesn't respond to questioning, doesn't know which school he was at.

'Give me the details,' I say; 'I'll look into it.'

So he deposits the boy outside on a wall with explicit instructions to him not to move (and people tended to take notice of his instructions), while I track the boy's school down in Wales – it was a boarding school into which he had marched and kidnapped the boy. The police were after him, as were social services.

But our friend has a way of getting round authority of all kinds: the police and social services seem to lean over to accommodate him. 'Ask his mum,' he would say, but his mum would in no way defy this big guy who had told her to stick up for her son.

Social services agree in the end that the boy can go to a local school, and as we are genuinely over-full, I persuade a headteacher colleague up the road to take him. The boy turns out to be a sweet enough lad, quiet and unmalicious though extremely backward educationally, and certainly in need of specialist support. It's inevitable that he will return in due course to some form of special schooling and as soon as our friend's interest in the case subsided, he was in fact happily moved without any fuss to a local special school.

Then one day, finally thrown out by Harambee and recovered from his gunshot wounds, our friend disappears for a few months to Winson Green prison, where he disrupts the establishment by demanding all the rights of a black Muslim, including getting up at dawn to face the east for prayers. His time in Handsworth over, he heads off in the end to London to apply his new-found interest in schools down there. New opportunities, and a new name: he promotes himself handsomely to 'doctor'.

39

The Riots 1981

One afternoon in 1981 the message comes through that the local lads are in a mood, planning trouble. They are converging on the streets round about the school. The police contact us to recommend that we get the children home as quickly as possible. The news that something is afoot sweeps through the school like wildfire. Already there are gangs of boys roaming up and down Grove Lane. They are settling on the kerbs of pavements and seated on walls, baseball bats in hand, anticipating trouble. Some of the children are frightened, others excited: no doubt one or two would have liked to join in. Some of the younger ones are fetched by their parents who've heard the news, and groups of them are escorted back to their homes by teachers. They march off in little groups through the lines of youths, running the gauntlet. But the local boys are not interested in children. They have no particular sense of what they intend to do, but are caught up in some vague way by the atmosphere of excitement. For them these are the preliminaries to some possible war, its purpose, its motivation puzzlingly obscure.

Beyond the anticipated war-zone, its nucleus being the school itself, the police are already gathering their forces, including black vans and heavy mob hit-squads. Officers have been rapidly drafted in from well beyond Handsworth. They stand by at a distance, and are mostly invisible. Everyone is waiting for darkness to fall. The only noticeable sound is the battering of the hammers of shopkeepers boarding up windows in their shops. The youths squatting on each side of the road stare morosely across at each other. Their baseball bats rest in their laps or are propped up against walls. The children have been told to stay in their houses but a few – a very few – are already wandering about, occasionally hustled away by an adult.

As it turns out, miraculously the school is left largely untouched. One or two windows are stoved in, but there's no break-in and no torching of the building. A few fires are lit in the back playground, but this is small beer compared with what happened around the school itself. When darkness came, the violence started: cars were upturned and set on fire and shops bashed up, and there was a running war between the boys and the police, as the reinforcements came pouring in.

Late in the evening Ossie, our assistant caretaker, is ambling nowhere in particular. He is a young Rasta lad I took on with the encouragement of Maureen Jones, our delightful new head of the Infant School, because we liked his smartness, his open-faced good humour and enthusiasm. Ossie has initiative, and has set up dance groups at the local community centre for kids in the area. His long dreadlocks combine with a sunny temperament and a smiling face. He finds reading difficult, and I suspect he's a bit dyslexic; but he takes reading lessons with some dedication from Mrs Jones who cares about such things. He gets on pretty well with everyone except Ashton the caretaker, a much older man from a different tradition, a Pentecostal who was born in St Kitts. Ossie was born in Birmingham and has views on the world that are a mile and a half away from Ashton's and they quarrel frequently.

The one thing that he is not, for all the ferocity of his appearance – the Ethiopian woolly hat, the long hair, the street gear, all superficially concealing the gentle handsomeness of his features – is violent or criminal. I'll stake my life on that. He's an easy-going, easy-living guy with a strangely buoyant view of the world, always seeming faintly surprised that it is the way it is.

Ossie is confronted on the Soho Road by two police officers who enquire what he's up to. It's a quiet moment. The street is largely deserted. Most of the troubles are over by now, although the roads are still cordoned off and heavily patrolled. There are bricks, litter, smashed glass, everywhere. But most of the lads have gone, vamoosed into their homes, or right out of the area, for a high proportion of the troublemakers were not from Handsworth at all, but had bussed themselves in at the rumour of trouble. They might have been running to visit a fairground or a gig, the happening place with the reputation.

Two more officers arrive and the place is bristling with

police, many of them patrolling in pairs on foot on both sides of the road. It's at this point that the dispute begins. Ossie, so they later claim, pushes one of the policemen, which constitutes an assault; at which point all four pounce on him and drag him off. He's denied bail by the magistrates, along with a few dozen more young people who are arrested at the same time for various offences in different parts of the city, and taken to Winson Green prison. I visit him there, having waited for ages in a queue of friends and parents. I'm allowed to bring in one orange and a few grapes, and Ossie protests in his quiet way that he's done nothing. He's bemused: 'what's this all about, man?' And I believe he's innocent. Ossie definitely isn't violent. It would be completely out of character.

The trials in the magistrate's court are held swiftly enough. There is a lot to get through: national attention is now focused on the Handsworth troubles, and press representatives are roaming around Handsworth. Ossie comes into the court with his girlfriend, who brings with her a huge illustrated Bible, which it takes two people to carry into the courtroom. The police sit at the back behind myself and Maureen Jones, and mutter in quiet voices at intervals throughout the procedure, making the foulest racist comments imaginable. They turn out to be West Bromwich police, and not the more skilled and community-conscious Handsworth crowd.

Simon, the Vicar of St Peter's, Springhill, who has a close association with the school and often works with some of the Unit children, gives Ossie an articulate, thoughtful character-reference on behalf of the school. Mrs Jones and I had also written to the magistrates who had their lengthy reports in front of them. The police go through their evidence and the magistrates are left to make their judgements. They are fair and sensible, although they seem to be from a different social planet. I have a strong sense that even with a powerful effort of the imagination they could not understand the lives these youngsters lead in Handsworth. The magistrates' room for manoeuvre, given a guilty verdict, is limited. They are being scrutinized by the press. There's a general sense that people are appalled by the riot. They need to be seen to be upholding the law courageously, asserting judicial and moral discipline against gangster behaviour. It would seem they have no option, for all Oswald's denials, but to believe the police.

Ossie's defence is that he was walking home, just leaving his girlfriend, and had no reason to cause trouble – and would he in any case be so foolish as to take on *four* policemen? The girlfriend's testimony is that Ossie had not even been rude to the officers, but merely tried to explain what he was doing. The police argue that she couldn't have heard since she was out of earshot.

It's almost inevitable that he's found guilty, and the issue is now merely whether or not this is an imprisonable offence. It is without a doubt the testimonies that have been given and perhaps Ossie's own dignified and gentle behaviour in the court that saves the day, and he's dismissed with a hefty fine, which he has no hope of paying but is soon sorted out with a whip-round from his various friends and mentors.

Later Lord Scarman's Report on the riots marked out the problems vividly, describing the tensions, the difficulties of policing, the endemic sense of unfairness and racism. It warned that unless urgent changes were made there were likely to be recurrences. Handsworth was now on the national map, linked with Toxteth in Liverpool and Brixton in London as a lawless place, bad and dangerous. The press gave Handsworth the greatest prominence, portraying it as the very symbol of racial dissatisfaction, a place that was un-English, and troubling.

As they return to school, most of them, the day after the 1981 riots, the children are sober. They are curiously quiet about the affair, once more puzzled, offended, damaged. It is as if there's been a terrible bust-up at home, beyond their control, and they have been unreasonably punished. As the press pour scorn on Handsworth as a killer of a place, the children are calmer and quieter than they have ever been.

40

The Riots 1985

Four years later there is a Festival in Handsworth Park, with live music and stalls – a fairground atmosphere. By the evening the hundreds of youngsters are tired after a long funky day. It's been a time on air with the little kids dreaming and flying balloons, and eating hotdogs and spun sugar-candy and the older ones roaming with their friends, grazing round the various sideshows, tapping to the ear-splitting bands, soaking up the rap music which rages out all day long, and forcing the old folk in the roads nearby to shut their windows and turn their TVs up.

There's no good reason to go home. It's a night for the streets, for a drink or two, some ganga. There is a good mood for a while, with the drumming and cheerful baloney, and the cops' presence round the park being made discreet. It's an OK way of patrolling on a Saturday afternoon, with nothing much more than a pickpocket or two.

There has been a long history of problems in the Villa Cross pub which is undisputed Rasta territory and a major centre for ganga dealing. At the beginning of June that year, nineteen regulars had been arrested and £2000 worth of ganga collected. But it's easy to get this out of perspective. Much more significant, though not widely known, was that another drug squad team had found some £100,000 worth of heroin in a house not far from Thornhill Road police station, hidden under the bed of one of our children.

But Villa Cross has become the focal point of deep hostility, the point where all the anger and resentment of the youngsters in the area seems to gather and ferment. The local unemployed boys sit in the road drinking bottles of beer or Lucozade, throwing hostile stares and abuse at passers-by. It's long been a no-go area for whites and many of the local black community are also hostile to them. Many of the Rastas have a misogynistic view of women, capturing rather than seducing some of the younger girls, beating them into submission and passing them from man to man. But a Pentecostal girl, if a member of the Church, would be rescued by Church attenders, and a posse of men would invade the Rasta squats in violent rescue operations. As a result, their girls are now usually left alone.

We have our own Rasta encampment: the twenty or so youngsters in dreadlocks, heavy with ganga, living in a closed-down house in Baker Street on the edge of the school playground. The school fences are continually being battered down and there's a public freeway across the playground to the shops on the Soho Road. Old ladies can regularly be seen trundling past the classrooms and climbing unsteadily through the holes in the (supposedly) high-security metal fence.

From time to time the Rastas ramble into the playground, too; sometimes they are armed with baseball bats, and threaten the teachers and the children. Though no one is ever actually attacked, the experience is unnerving, and we make cautious complaints to the police, fully aware that a wrong move might push us into out-and-out war. The police handling of situations is rarely predictable, and we know perfectly well we may be left on our own. It would have been no great surprise to me to come back one day to find the school a smouldering pile of black ash. But it never happens, and wherever possible we try to avoid confrontation. Sometimes at night the local teenagers come round here in gangs, prowling past the Rasta house, scared and admiring, although Rastas will usually have nothing to do with them.

The morning after the Handsworth Festival, an Asian shopkeeper is stabbed outside the bank in Villa Road. Late that afternoon an officer gives a parking ticket to a black driver: the vehicle is untaxed and the driver is arrested on suspicion of being unqualified. More police arrive and accusations reach the street lads. A fight starts. Eleven officers are reported injured; seven police vehicles are damaged, two arrests are made. It's getting out of hand. By 7.40 that evening Villa Cross Hall is on fire and fire-officers are warned by the boys not to tackle the blaze. Hundreds of police are drafted in, wide-scale looting starts, the whole area is cordoned off with police barriers, more buildings are ablaze, and the Indian man who runs the post office is killed inside his own shop. News of a full-scale riot, one of the worst in British history, spreads rapidly across the world press.

The following morning Gilroy our excellent new deputy – Edward has recently been appointed head of his own school – arrives at the school to be greeted by a crowd of excited children.

'Sir, sir, saw you on TV.'

Gilroy looks puzzled.

'How d'you mean?'

'In the riots.'

'*What?* Say again ...'

'We saw you there, in the riots.'

Lots of the children have seen him, which causes Gil a problem, since he was not there.

It's a stroke of luck that someone has a video of last night's Central News, and, sure enough, there's a brief clip of Gilroy in a tracksuit, running, that is cut into other scenes of the police barricades and the general mayhem. Gil can identify the clip: it's a film of him jogging through Handsworth Park some weeks earlier, taken presumably (for what reason no one knew) with a long-distance lens by a camera team. Because the police cordon was so tight, it had proved impossible for the teams to get close enough to film yesterday and so Central TV had obviously incorporated old cuttings into its early-evening broadcast.

We ring Central TV who hotly deny the accusation of broadcasting phoney evidence, until we face them with the video. The city solicitor becomes involved and we give every impression that we're going to sue them. Discussion steadily rises through the ranks up to the highest level. If Gilroy had persisted, maybe taking it to the Independent Broadcasting Authority or even to court, he might well have obtained damages. As it is, they're lucky that they're dealing with such an amiable man, and in the end he accepts a contrite apology from Central – an admission that they behaved wholly irresponsibly. It's enough for Gilroy. In any case, the children see his TV appearance as an achievement.

41
Joshua

Resistant to the standard explanations for the riots of poverty, unemployment and young people's disaffection and sense of injustice, the Government argued that the reason for them lay purely and simply in the dark side of human nature. Douglas Hurd refined this view in the subsequent debate in the House of Commons on 23rd October 1985. He noted 'the excitement of forming and belonging to a mob, the evident excitement of violence leading to the fearsome crimes that we have seen reported ...' Hence 'to explain all those things in terms of deprivation and suffering is to ignore some basic and ugly facts about human nature.'

Some blamed the media, linking the riots to the TV broadcasting of programmes about earlier disorders in South Africa. Giles Shaw, MP, Minister of State from the Home Office, cited discipline, which 'has long since ebbed from millions of homes and it has been dragged from thousands of schools.' Others put forward a conspiracy theory: the whole thing had been engineered by extremists and malcontents. Norman Tebbit, the Conservative Chairman, was more brutal: it was, he said, just plain wickedness.

Gerald Kaufman countered sharply by asking why, if the disorders were just crimes and were not related to economic and social conditions, did they not occur in the Home Secretary's constituency of Witney in Oxfordshire?

It was an irony that in some respects race relations had been steadily improving over the years in Handsworth. Birmingham as a whole was one of the more receptive parts of the country to taking in immigrant and ethnic minority groups – maybe reflecting a long tradition of movement into the city since the late nineteenth century from the north, Ireland, Wales, and more recently from East European countries, such as Poland. There was, moreover, energetic disapproval from the mainstream of black and Asian opinion for the youths who had been seen as being largely responsible for starting the riots, although there was also a general suspicion that the police had badly mishandled the situation.

It's as easy to stereotype the police as anyone else. There were real differences between the Handsworth police, who were often more aware of local issues, and forces drafted in from the City Centre or West Bromwich. The local residents would identify individual officers in the Handsworth force with approval, particularly some community-beat officers who had got to know people as people.

By now the local community was strongly supporting the school, partly because the parents were coming to trust us, and partly because we were more in favour, too, with Harambee. The breakthrough had come through our relationship with Joshua.

Joshua is an intelligent Birmingham University student from Rhodesia, a Mugabe supporter, one of some three hundred students who came over here during the Rhodesia struggle. We invite Josh, who has regular contact with Harambee, to do some teaching in the school: to tell the children about Africa and how life was for people out there. I tell Josh that he can say what he feels is appropriate, trusting him not to patronize the children with propaganda. My only condition is that children of all races and backgrounds should come to his sessions.

Josh is a success. He has lively complex messages for them about life in Africa. He tells them about African schools where, he says, children see school as a great privilege:

> Over here some of you kids are spoiled, you know? You throw away your chances ... In schools in Africa children really want to learn: learning is the most important thing in their lives. Those who are well educated are those who will do best, and the children know it. The children are, you know, much better behaved in Africa. I tell you I've been shocked by the behaviour of some of the black kids round here ... They're throwing their chances away ...

It's a valuable message for some of the boys, who admire, or ought to admire, Josh for his charisma and high intelligence.

We already have – we have always had – some fine black teachers, as both Josh and Harambee can see for themselves. But our openness to the kinds of race and background issues that Josh starts to discuss may have surprised them. The final breakthrough comes when with the very considerable help of my wife, who is a doctor, we arrange to bring Joshua's father, a schools' inspector, over from Africa for a heart operation, to be done by a surgeon in Coventry. The operation is a success, and Joshua becomes a friend. This has the deeper effect of binding us to the youngsters of Harambee, and gives us new links with the young black community.

At the same time, we strengthen our ties with the Handsworth Law Centre. We have Shaheen, another dynamic home/school liaison teacher, who was brought up in Senegal and has excellent links with the Handsworth community; and Big Dave, a giant who works for a local housing trust, does us the enormous favour of sorting out the local Rasta encampment, succeeding in what seemed like half an hour where the police had failed for months. He simply went in and instructed the boys to lay off the school, and the trouble miraculously ceased. Soon they were to move away and the properties were bulldozed.

An acre of land at the back of the school was divided between our school and the next-door grant-maintained Grammar School. The Grammar School simply moved their fences and took their land. But we were instructed to wait for Local Authority permission, which never came, and a long Jarndice-and-Jarndice style legal affair loomed, the land remaining untouched and undeveloped for the next fifteen years. We engaged in endless incomprehensible battles with the Local Authority to get them to release it. We had nothing like enough playground space for the number of children in the school – our space was roughly half the statutory recommended amount – and we were in urgent need of the extra land. However, there seemed to be little we could do unless we broke the law and got an independent contractor to shift our own fences, and then awaited the consequences.

The riots were over, and the community was licking its wounds. From our perspective, there were lessons being learned, and ever-deepening links binding the various organizations that supported and maintained the pride of the local people were being formed. The old warmth was still there and it was spreading. It was starting to show itself in the more relaxed, improved, less aggressive and less unpredictable behaviour of the children. It was as though the riots had unwittingly driven some kind of poison out of the system.

They had, of course, been a desperate blow to the whole of Handsworth. But this was the past, and these were people with the pride and determination to pick themselves up out of the gutter. There was a future for them to look forward to, as we kept telling the children. Maybe they were beginning to believe it.

42

Teacher Action

I would sometimes walk away down Grove Lane to Mr Ashraf's vegetable shop, where you could encounter parents popping in to pick up rice, or bunches of coriander, or his excellent oranges. They always seemed reassuringly pleased to meet me. Today was bright and sunny, and at school now, as in the shop, there was a cheerfulness in the air, a measure of light-heartedness and good humour. A lot of things were going on, maths fun days, plays, trips; and there was lively teaching by teachers who enjoyed the job and liked the children.

But schools, like politics, are vulnerable to events. George Eliot once wrote that 'there is no private life that has not been determined by a wider public life.'[21] It seemed that the Government was priming itself to prove the point.

Following on from the débâcle with the miners in the early 1980s, we were to have a teachers' industrial action driven by the National Union of Teachers and Terry Casey, the *On the Waterfront* man from the National Association of Schoolmasters and Women Teachers. I had been a member of both Unions at one time or another, and I was well aware of their different strengths and weaknesses. The NUT, commanding the majority of staff, was a ragbag of an organization, with a reputation for having splendid national conferences at which the London Left made a great to-do; but there was little sense of it achieving much in educational terms. The local Joint Teachers Council (the JTC) had representation from all the unions, and its reputation amongst teachers was for the conservative defending of territory. It was rare, in my experience, for any union to start or support initiatives: this wasn't their style. The purpose of the JTC was to slow things down and in some cases ensure that forward movement stopped altogether. Most Chief Officers found them a pain in the neck. Meetings were dominated by the NASWT, which was represented by a formidably able and acerbic lady who could have made a career as a QC. As a territory defender, she was uniquely impressive; and as an enemy, with an intricate understanding of the working of local politics, she commanded the field.

By 1985 the teachers were ready for a showdown with the Government over pay. Watching from the sidelines, I was never convinced that the problem was purely a matter of pay. Pay was a symptom, an excuse for an explosive expression of anger against government political initiatives in education and the Government's denigration of teachers. The underlining sense was that the Thatcher Government was cutting back resources but pretending to do otherwise, and at the same time increasing the teachers' workload. The teachers' associations seemed to think that they could succeed where the miners had failed. This monumental miscalculation was predicated on the belief that schools couldn't be sold off, closed down, or counted out in the way that proved possible with the mining industry. Further, they reasoned that they had parents on their side: they thought that parents would appreciate that this was about more than teachers' pay. It was in fact about the preservation of the state education service and an expression of anger and dissatisfaction at the way children were being treated.

The unions were quite right, although the true facts were concealed for years. Dr Simon Szreter, a historian at St John's College, Cambridge, later found that the Thatcher Government had removed some 50,000 teachers from the state sector over a period of twelve years, a reduction that was engineered under the smokescreen of a moderate demographic fall in the child population. The result was that the UK was the only country in the Western world in which pupil-teacher ratios failed to improve over that period. By the early 1990s, in the independent school sector, the average pupil-teacher ratio in a private school was half that in a comparable state school.[22] Eight per cent of all pupils, mostly the children of the better off, including the children of most Conservative politicians, went to schools in the private sector.

The final insult came when the Government tied teachers down to a new contract with a legal commitment to work a minimum of 1265 hours a year. Heads were to monitor these hours and could command staff, if necessary, to return to school to fulfil their 'hourage requirements'. This was the first step in a long trail of legislation to clip the wings of teachers, and to create an education command economy.

So the unions ordered their members to abandon all 'goodwill' activities. Goodwill included all those extra hours when teachers offered services to pupils 'beyond the call of duty'. It was a late flowering of the Old Unionism, the kind that Mrs Thatcher intended to break. The measure stirred teachers up in staff-rooms and caused a lot of ill feeling. One NASWT member in the school seemed to be almost exultant about the action: everything should now be done to implement it, regardless of any harm it might cause to the children. But there were plenty of teachers who were uneasy with it – and a few positively opposed, who were in danger of being seen as blacklegs. I took the view that if you are in a union you do what the union says: if you don't agree, you leave. As a member of the NUT, my line was pragmatic: wait and see.

Sport stopped everywhere. There were no out-of-school activities. Teachers began going home earlier, at 4.30 instead of 5.30 in the evening. Most damaging of all, 'voluntary cover' stopped. This especially hit the secondary schools who, because the statutory hours for supply teachers soon ran out, had to start sending children home when there was no one to teach them. Grove School was invaded by bored ex-pupils from the local secondary schools, hanging around the playgrounds, and wandering into the classrooms. I found myself employing one particularly troublesome boy to mend a fence.

Meanwhile local parents were becoming ever more annoyed, particularly with the secondary schools where, with their refusal to cover classes voluntarily for absent colleagues, the teachers steadily lost public support. The Government smelt blood and kept the pressure up. It soon became apparent that the teachers were bound to lose, and union membership began to haemorrhage. The action collapsed after a long struggle that extended over a period of months. The damage was by then irreparable. The teachers could now be beaten into submission with a tranche of law-driven initiatives. The National Curriculum and, beyond it, the crags of the Office for Standards in Education (Ofsted) loomed. There was clear water for the Government to drive home all manner of reforms that had previously been held back by old-fashioned, rather gentlemanly departmental concerns, such as that it is generally wise to try to carry the teachers with you.

Teachers across the country dug in by sticking to the letter of the law. But some noble souls tried to carry on much as before, and some after-school clubs were reinstated. Our school was far less affected than most, and from the first I made it clear I had no intention of implementing, or pretending to implement, that absurd 1265-hours rule, law or no law. Some headteachers, under instruction, had taken to keeping detailed records of each hour spent by each teacher, and cataloguing the annual total for staff-meetings, parents' evenings and the like.

The school managed to keep its record in badminton. The teachers continued out of loyalty to take the children to the Hostel on muddy and uncomfortable camping trips. Only one or two dragged their feet. But the damage across the country was considerable. Teachers began to work fewer hours. They had discovered some of the benefits of not feeling permanently exhausted. Voluntary games across the country were gravely damaged. The local football league which sported thirty-six teams – which had played every Saturday morning and involved hundreds of children – and had been running for more than twenty years, ground to a halt. Football now was low-key on occasional evenings. Cricket virtually collapsed for the next five years and never regained its previous status. The loss was a loss of voluntarism. It marked a sea-change in professional attitudes: a decisive, unhappy moment in the history of the profession.

I had never focused sufficiently sharply on the importance of voluntarism – that spirited, almost careless commitment of *time* that is a requirement of success in the public sector. I had never appreciated just how much commitment is needed from all concerned, from teachers and doctors to secretaries and classroom assistants, and everyone else, if *competence* is to shift into *excellence*. There was uncomfortable evidence, I read, that:

> private school teachers feel more efficacious than state school teachers. Unlike their public counterparts they do not believe their success is beyond their control, and they do not feel it is a waste of time to do their best. Overall they are much more satisfied with their jobs. It is no wonder then that private school teachers have better attendance records or that they tend to work for less money. Private school teachers are trading economic compensation and formal job security for superior working conditions, professional autonomy, and personal fulfilment. Public (state) school teachers are doing precisely the opposite. In short private schools do tend to look more like teams.[23]

The argument was unsettling:

> Teachers in private schools have better relationships with prin-

> cipals, are more integrally involved in decision making, interact more frequently and productively with their colleagues and feel more positively about their jobs and their organization. The principals also rate them more highly as teachers. They have more freedom, more autonomy ...

One evening, it so happened, I had a phone call from a senior teacher at King Edward's School, one of the most prestigious independent schools in the country. Here there were bright, highly intelligent, selected pupils, many of whom went to Oxbridge or other top-rate universities. Here there was a bottomless well of resources with wonderful teaching facilities. Here it would be possible to focus on the job and get something worthwhile done.

'I know this is an odd request,' said the voice over the phone, 'but how'd you feel about coming to teach here – what could we do to persuade you to come?' There was a long pause. 'I know this is a long shot, but I thought it worth having a go, just in case ...'

43
The Breakfast

For all the difficulties the Government and unions have been creating, for all the local troubles, there's still the culture of the school itself to hold onto. Its vibrancy, its sense of fun, its ambience, going far beyond academic achievement, its space and brightness, the atmosphere inside, seem these days to express something. When outsiders with no particular axes to grind come to visit us they begin to search for ways to describe these impressions: electricity in the air, buoyancy, pleasure.

How important is this? It certainly provided security for

some children who had little of it at home; and we were, I think, making an impact – hopefully a memorable impact – on the children in their most formative years. But ought schools to be about security and lasting memories? Does it matter what a school is like – perhaps dull, oppressive, even unpleasant – if it produces academic results?

Were we being soft on children, high on inventiveness (whatever that is), low on demand, the school embracing a lazy fondness of the kind promoted, said the critics, by Lady Plowden's report. Or does the quality of the moment-to-moment interactions between children and adults, and the richness of the early environment play an important part in developing the children's thinking and self-confidence? Such notions as play and creativity, space and time, a culture of civility, are surely important.

Eric Midwinter argued that at its best the good primary school is the most civilized of micro-societies.[24] I watch the teachers in action and consider this. Civility is, indeed, one thing that distinguishes many of them, in the way they instantly reassure the children the moment they enter the classroom, or look at them, warm, calm, sympathetic, whilst all the time seeming to lead them on to show them something new: 'come and look at this'; admiring: 'that's really very good, isn't it', suggesting 'maybe you could have a go at this ...'; persuading the child to improve something he's done, modifying his first thoughts – taking risks – 'come on, have a go'; asking questions, 'is that right?'; and making demands, 'you can do better than that can't you?'; and every so often chastizing, 'that's not right, that's not good.' The conversations between the teachers such as Judith, Verna, Cheryl, Sue and the children flow backwards and forwards. Their classrooms have the buzz of novelty, of interesting things happening. Vivienne's absolute reliability is like a rock, founded, I think, on 'old values'. Her civility brings a kind of refined intelligence in relationships, an easiness of gesture, a subtlety of judgement.

On the other hand, a proportion of the children, many of

whom seem to come into school academically disadvantaged, are showing persistent underachievement. Our own database has now gathered a vast amount of evidence of the children's performance term by term, and registers what seems to be a law whereby the more able the child at the point of admission, the faster he or she will accelerate. Lower-ability children improve, but they improve more slowly. So, as the years go by, we see a remorseless widening of the gap between the most able and the least able, which becomes a chasm by the time the children are eleven years old. Roughly a quarter of them cause concern. We can make a significant impact on some, but there remains a proportion whose learning strategies and achievements are poor. In this respect, ours is the story of many schools in the inner cities, not only of this country but of the USA and the Western world. Paris, I discover, is like London in having some 30% of its pupils seriously underachieving in language and maths, although the French – unlike the current English government – do not advertise their problems, or blame the teachers.

One day I'm at a conference in Cumbria staying overnight in a nice hotel with good friends who gather once in a while to study primary education. I have an early breakfast overlooking the calm waters of Windermere. I'm joined by Duncan Graham, Director of the National Curriculum Council, a powerful Scotsman with definite views about pretty well everything and the full panoply of modern management skills.

Duncan looks across at me with a guffaw and says, 'Winkley? Ah yes, that fearful old Plowden romantic.'

It is a great opening gambit at breakfast.

'Less of the old,' I say.

But the remark lingers.

Later Duncan was to invite me to visit his new Valhalla in York where he had pressed the DES to build the billion-pound empire that was to become the National Curriculum

Council. It was from here that the forthcoming National Curriculum was to be masterminded, implemented and dispatched to every school in the country in a thousand vans. Clearly he saw me as an old-fashioned, entrenched romantic, beating an ancient battered drum.

Is he right? It is certainly doubtful whether the word 'romantic' would spring to mind with the school staff. It's true that I aspire to be inventive and innovative, but then why can't life in a school be exploratory? As a matter of fact, I see myself as something of a survivor. Almost everyone else I know with my kind of background has left the job. Many of them taught for a year or two and then moved into advisory work or administration, rising regularly (preferably every couple of years) from one position to the next. Having been through some periods of professional trauma, I have now concentrated my mind on the school and I am sticking to it. If I had thought I was getting nowhere, just marking time, I would have thrown in the towel.

I make the fatal mistake of tackling Duncan Graham head on, taking the accusation much too seriously when all along he is only teasing. I begin to bluster on about how Plowden came about, the new view of childhood, how it started with the Haddow Report in 1931, quoting – pretentiously as it seems later – G. K. Chesterton's remark that the chief danger of cultural and intellectual life is a standardization using a low standard.

G. K. Chesterton over the bacon at breakfast: it is all too much, and Duncan is entirely unconvinced, with good reason. He is after all overseeing the greatest thrust towards school standardization in the history of English education. Again, just for a moment, I feel that beneath the surface of his teasing there is some element of true belief. It is as though he is dressing me up in some long floral dress, recreating in his mind's eye the stereotypical lady – Lady Plowden, dancing over the daisies in some nostalgic Old World – and on the way ruining the children.

This was very likely unfair to Duncan, who many years

previously was himself the head of a Scottish primary school. But the remark did hang in the air, and I carried it around with me for a long time to come. It became symptomatic of a certain kind of managerial behaviour. Duncan could josh me about my deeper beliefs and values that might or might not underpin my life's work at school, but I felt – somehow – that I couldn't josh him back. I was unable to caricature aggressive management styles, or the kind of people who had abandoned the professional front-line but still claimed to have all the answers. It was a troubling power-relationship. Here was a model modern manager, exuding the confidence of power, promulgating rigorous beliefs and determined to 'make waves', and in the face of such an onslaught I felt distinctly underpowered.

The true irony was that there was also something of this managerialism in *me*, a restlessness, a fierce desire to make things happen, a kind of intellectual ruthlessness. There was always a danger of it leading to insensitivity, the underrating of what teachers do in their remorseless daily work in classrooms, and to a kind of impatience: 'oh, why for Christ's sake can't they – we – do it better?' Just as, for the tiers of educational managers, the headteachers and the schools they run are seen as frustrating, antediluvian in attitude, and too often 'fail to deliver' right down the line.

44
Curriculum

What few people realized outside the school was that by now we had what was effectively a national curriculum of our own – which turned out to be a precursor of the real thing. We had had regular long morning maths and language sessions for many years. We'd worked particularly hard at devising ways of improving the children's writing skills in particular, linking up our writing programme with a national Schools Council project on writing. There would be time in the morning for a break of, say, forty-five minutes for a music or PE lesson but otherwise it would be devoted to the heavyweight stuff in maths and language that lay at the core of the curriculum. The only exception to this was short periods of the year when we devoted the whole day to intensive work in one particular subject – perhaps art or music – in preparation for a 'completion date', a demonstration, a performance, a display.

The afternoons would be given over to other areas of the curriculum, which we divided into humanities (history, geography, RE), the arts (music, dance, the visual arts) and the sciences (science and technology). PE and outdoor pursuits rested uneasily for a while under the humanities umbrella, but were eventually given a PE and outdoor slot of their own.

The development of each of these spheres was in the hands of what we called a 'Faculty'. Each Faculty had a knowledgeable chair, who would usually be a departmental head, and at least one teacher who was there as much to learn as to contribute. Every teacher in the school was a member of at least two Faculties, but they could attend as many as they liked.

The Faculty's job was to create outlines for the work of each of the year groups. The Faculties produced the motorway maps; the year-group teams turned these into practical working units with A roads and B roads. One aim was to get over the horror of children repeating the same 'thematic' work year after year, sometimes without the teachers being aware of it.

One dispirited HMI told me his son's junior school had 'done' canals for four years running without anyone (apart from his son) seeming to notice. Then there was the important issue, which Duncan Graham's National Curriculum was later to address, of the need to build one year on another in a systematic and meaningful way, so that children's skills and understanding *progressed.*

We encountered many of the issues that were later to hit the real National Curriculum. How do we make best use of the limited time we have available for each of the subject components? Do we work most effectively in a secondary-school style with thirty- or forty-minute weekly slots: good for building competences? Or do we work intensively and in depth for a sustained period of time: better for developing thinking in depth and engendering enthusiasm?

It becomes clear that however splendid our master plans, the devil is in the detail. What does an individual teacher make of a particular item that has been identified as important by the Faculty? How well is it going to be interpreted in action, given the undeniable fact that teachers vary greatly in ability and experience in any particular subject?

There were always those who would argue that the best teaching was linked to the *enthusiasm*, even the eccentricities, of the individual teacher. If he or she knew everything there was to know about the Russian Revolution or folk-dancing or the life-cycle of the marsupial, why didn't they teach it, as it was bound to be communicated to the child with enthusiasm? There were plenty of arguments against this individualistic approach, which was still not uncommon in schools at that time. It was too ad hoc, and without systematic follow-up year on year. However inventive you were in developing cross-curriculum literary, historical, scientific and artistic components through your 'projects', the enthusiasm generated too often turned into dull work that didn't connect well with the child's own interests, culture or evolving skills. But when it *worked* – that was something different. I retained the view that there was a place somewhere for eccentricity, experiment and risk. I accepted that some of the most exciting work was only tenuously linked to any formal, central planning.

But as a general approach to developing the texture of

work across the school, eccentricity would not do. Not only do we need to know what has happened before; we need to know what will happen next. The liveliest learning for young children has a strong sense of narrative. Ideally, the first new experience in a section of a curriculum programme should have the explosive force of the opening of a story, pregnant with possibilities. We should then build on this grand overture by sustaining the pupils' interest, drawing them ever more personally into the development of the narrative. The story needs to lead somewhere, so that the pupil not only sees the point of it, but gets some sense of the achievement of reaching the end of a section of the journey. So a sequence of lessons ought to give a feeling of completion, maybe signalled by a completed project, a piece of writing, a folder, a theatrical performance, a small published manuscript, even a challenging test of competence. ('What have I learnt doing this? Was it worth the effort?') The whole programme will have its ups and downs, its moments of difficulty as well as its triumphs. There will be times when the children are investigating; others when they're listening or practising. Information-giving, the developing of the necessary knowledge base, should combine with discussion, thinking, trying something out for yourself. And you must never quite lose the sense of discovery, of the unexpected. This is not easy: the children need to feel confident that they can get through to the end.[25]

We were some way along the road to achieving at least part of this. We had a full programme in place in every subject, subjects being spread across the year in regular sessions (as with PE and music) and some completed through intensive work over a six-week period. And in certain cases we had a grand climax when work was publicly celebrated. There was the art exhibition; music reached its climax in a winter festival, a two-day event during which all the children performed at some point or other. Drama was a mixture of weekly Friday performances in assembly for the whole school and, of course, the annual theatrical 'event'.

This approach raised all manner of new issues. How much time could be spent on such a wide range of curriculum, given that we were already spending an hour and a half a day on maths (except on Friday) and an hour on language work, with specific programmes for skill-building, such as intensive spelling sessions first thing in the morning, plus more writing and reading linked with humanities subjects? It meant being clear about when lessons and combinations of lessons (projects or topics under the banner of traditional subjects, such as history or geography) began and ended. We came to realize how little time there was in the school day; how quickly your five and a half hours, just 25% of the child's waking life, ran out.

These were precisely the issues that were to surface with the implementation of the National Curriculum. We gave some help to John Beighton, once a Birmingham Inspector, now a senior officer with the National Curriculum Council, in writing one of the most interesting documents which the NCC was to produce on 'The Whole School Curriculum', and which discussed the complexities of shaping the various subjects into something meaningful for the children, and looked at links between subjects and the issue of timing. A subsequent national survey of 'time spent' on different subjects followed, a misguided initiative that produced little of useful interest, outside what was already known, i.e. that there were considerable differences between the amount of time schools spent on different things. As it happened, we turned out to have one of the longest working weeks in England, which was not necessarily something to be proud of as I was not convinced that there was a direct connection between time spent and quality of outcome, although common sense suggested that there was a minimum time input below which children's learning would be significantly disadvantaged.

There was now a convincing rhythm to the day, the week, the term and the year, a planned cyclical shape to the children's learning, a purposeful structure. But it was only a beginning. The important question was how well the 'stories', the planned narratives that lay at the core of the curriculum, were made to unfold in the classroom. How good was the teaching? How strong were the components at year-group level? Our first project in history, for example, was for the seven-year-olds, with a focus on palaeontology, the beginnings of things, the world as it was before the arrival of man, plus a great deal about the early development of life, leading up to stone-age man. There was lots of writing, film, art, drawing, and there were many visits to the science museums. Was the success of this component to be judged by the enthusiasm of the children? Was it to be found in the historical quality of their work as opposed to its literary or artistic character? Or in the sheer razzmatazz of the 'component', the fact that the children enjoyed it? What was the rationale for choosing it for seven-year-olds as opposed to the thousand and one other things that might have constituted the history curriculum? Could we find a more appropriate and relevant project for this age group?

To assess that and other aspects of the full programme, I invited in a team of external consultants to look closely at what we were about and to produce a written report for staff and governors. We had a university historian, a science specialist and other specialist assessors in maths and in English, which we divided into reading and writing. We had no money at our disposal to pay for all this help, and these people gave us their time for free, looking at the children's work, watching lessons, assessing the programme as a whole.

A distinguished local GP, Laurie Pike, carried out a detailed analysis of the school health programme and wrote a paper on it for the staff. Dr Pike happened to be watching teaching in progress at the same time as we had a flying visit from a Junior Conservative Minister of Education. The Minister was a solicitor-turned-politician, who was interested, I suspected, in prep-school-type neatness. On his tour of the school he suddenly did what no visitor has done before or since – he asked a child to open his desk for him to look inside. It was a miracle that this particular child was immaculately tidy, and the Minister purred with pleasure, looked at me and congratulated me on having such well-disciplined pupils. I smiled at the children, and the children – knowing exactly the name of the game – smiled back. Dr Pike then happened to wander past, wearing his old mac, and carrying a black bag.

'Oh,' I called, 'Dr Pike, come and meet the Minister.'

The Minister shook hands enthusiastically with Dr Pike and told him about a Government Health Education Committee for which the Government had high hopes.

'Important stuff,' said the Minister, 'waiting to see what it has to say.'

After listening politely to a long narration from him, Dr Pike remarked:

'That's very interesting, Minister. I am, of course, the chair ...'

'The chair?'

'Of your committee.'

With a smile, the good Dr Pike picked up his bag and ambled off.

The consultants' reviews were detailed and technical. Some comments took us back to the drawing board. Was palaeontology *history*? Strictly speaking, it was not. Wasn't our health programme too academic, when what was needed was good straightforward information about the prevention of disease, eating, smoking, the bringing up of children? Was our RE more a study of externals without addressing the deeper issues of spirituality? Did RE evolve and develop sufficiently as the four-year plans (ages seven to eleven) unfolded? Did science build up skills and a continuing knowledge base? The art programme was varied and imaginative and some of the outcomes were fabulous; but again – our consultant asked – did it develop and flower as fully as it might, and make increasing demands as the children grew older? And was the quality of the various components as they were delivered in the classroom sufficiently secure: wasn't there an unacceptable unevenness of quality? How could we know?

We were learning to become more obsessive about detail. It was not just the motorways, nor even always the A and B roads that mattered; it was the mile upon mile of country lanes, the moment-to-moment way the teacher put the lesson across. I found that once the great enterprise of definition and shaping the curriculum began, you wanted to know more about how it was working out in detail – and to be sure it really was happening in the way you intended. There were two consequences. The first was that we began to record, to catalogue, to write things down. The second was that we needed to control, to try to make sure that teachers were really committed to, and able to, deliver the 'pieces' of the curriculum that made up the overall design.

The matter of recording evolved slowly. In the end we attempted to computerize all the pieces in order to have the full curriculum picture at our fingertips. The ideal solution was to evaluate each piece, say, each sequence of six lessons on a particular subject, by getting the children and the teachers to assess their success on a five-point scale. If the plan produced results which were below par, we'd throw it out and put something in its place. In the early 1980s I wrote an article about this, calling it *the Lego curriculum* which imagined the whole curriculum as a series of different coloured pieces, each piece with a shape and integrity of its own, assessed, trialled, tested, and well resourced, well prepared, the colour being associated with a particular subject. If a piece turned out to be a dud it would be thrown out and replaced in the way I've mentioned. There would be hundreds of these pieces and teachers could construct their own shapes using combinations of them, sometimes linking colours if the overall shape of the construction seemed to allow it. One great virtue of a scheme of this kind was that there could be particular pieces for children of special ability

– differentiated pieces that allowed further exploration or the development of advanced skills.

By developing a computer-based curriculum database we could identify what children were doing and the quality of the components, and map out and quality-control the whole programme. In due course children might even design pieces of their own to suit their own needs and interests. A grander and more improbable vision might be of a component bank to which teachers in many schools might contribute and which they could access according to the constructions – that is the strategic design of the programmes – they wished to build. As a matter of fact, all this could potentially be accommodated within the confines of the real National Curriculum when it finally came out.

The merit of our curriculum, rough-edged though it was, was that it worked. It allowed an element of elasticity. It was controlled by the teachers whose only commitment was to give the programme a run for its money, to the best of their ability. There were spaces during the week for different and more personal slots. We had now modified our health curriculum for children to develop life-skills, to think about food, diet, how to bring up children, sex education. The art programme covered a range of experiences, including three-dimensional construction and work with clay. On Friday afternoons we developed a semi-specialist programme of options where children rotated around different teachers who pursued their own passion or a particular specialist skill in art, dance, technology, science, music. Two sixth-formers from the grammar school came over to work with six of our children and a pile of technical Lego and Fischer-technik. One of the boys had a flair for getting children to produce astonishing constructions without doing things for them. Alas, after university he went on to work not in teaching but on atomic submarines.

We realized that the fulfilment of so ambitious a programme would take years, and perfection was not what it was really about. For the one thing you discover about curriculum planning is that it must constantly *evolve.* Completion, setting in stone, would be the death of the thought, energy and continuous reassessment that kept it alive. Life was the issue: was the experience *alive* for the children? Did it mean something to them? Did they think it was worthwhile? Did they enjoy it? The answer was that they did – like the curate's egg – in parts. Much depended on the individual teacher: in the end, however good the Faculty and year-group plans, it was the teacher's flair that mattered most.

But a huge variety of work, some of it impressive, was beginning to pour out. We started to display the children's own work around the school to show it off at its best, another skill which some teachers have and others don't have. Our curriculum was in place and working, and there was a steadily growing interest in what the school was doing. And people were coming from far and near to see it.

45

The Visitors

Many of the visitors were stimulating. If you're going to stay with an intensive job like teaching it is important to be challenged, revitalized, made aware of different horizons. Some were intriguing. There was a special appeal in the young Mormons who came dressed in full Red Indian gear, and demonstrated ancient tribal dances and talked at length about the ritual significance of headdress feathers. Or the entire Australian Rugby team, who took a day off from their England tour, carrying youngsters round on their enormous backs and wearing their immaculate bottle-green outfits, brimming Aussie power and charisma, and showing genuine interest. They made a great impression on the children.

Then there was Rod Hull who brought his famous ventriloquist performance to the school, a live TV show set up in the middle of a classroom in Upper School, with the Bird Emu. This dummy-bird turns out to be much larger than I realized, a great half-alive creature with thousands of paper blue feathers that fall off from time to time and spew across the room. I'm interviewed in my room with Emu, and after what once happened to Michael Parkinson ... (grabbed by the throat and grappled to the floor, an almost career-ruining event that has entered the mythology of television), I insist that 'on no account is That Bird to touch me in any part of my anatomy ... you understand?' Rod Hull nods and laughs. Of course he understands: no problem. So the show goes on national TV, loved by the children; and Rod Hull's wife spends the afternoon roaming around the school and afterwards takes me aside and says slightly sadly: 'I love this place; I wish I could bring my own children here.'

'My own children *are* here,' I say, moved by this unexpected accolade – and how much more force it has for being so casual and from an outsider who is not here to do anything but wait for her husband.

Some of the more official delegations are very different. One day a very Senior HMI arrives to visit the school. This is a singular honour, as is emphasized by the Department of Education organizer. Our delegation arrives on a Tuesday afternoon at relatively short notice, comprising, along with our HMI, a civil servant of high rank and a bevy of other departmental specialists interested in multi-racial and community education, and ways in which challenges in these kinds of communities can be faced. This much-trumpeted visit has the Local Authority Inspectorate bringing its own set of troops from Margaret Street. It is to be a full inspection, in gold braid as it were, and in a fit of agitation (how headteachers feel the need to be in control!) I take a run around the school to track down any sign of Walkers crisp packets, and bang on at one or two teachers for their intolerably messy classrooms.

So the visitors arrive in a fleet of cars at the front of the new Upper School building, and climb out in their smart suits and upbeat smiley enthusiasm. They may have been surprised to find no children waiting at the gate to greet them. This welcoming party was something of a tradition that schools commonly laid on for VIPs and which I disliked. It just seemed inappropriate to use children, who after all had no choice in the matter, as guide dogs, as well as wasting their time. So the visitors have to come through the door on their own and search out our new, glamorous, Afro-Caribbean secretary, Marcia, who welcomes them with her usual warmth and panache.

I had no particular brief for Her Majesty's Inspectors one way or the other. They came and went from time to time and I recorded a dozen official visits between 1975 and 1985, and a handful of short unofficial ones. They were usually occasions for them to take copious notes in identikit flip-over notebooks, an uneasy mix – as it seemed to me – of journalistic investigation and police-style reporting. This would be followed by classroom visits, where they were often inspecting or researching one particular aspect of school life such as multi-cultural or behaviour policies, or the Unit, or the databases, or the teaching of mathematics.

Some of the inspection reports were now encouragingly complimentary. One noted that 'the Unit is an imaginative and outstandingly high quality provision, which genuinely integrates children into the whole school community.' The visiting HMIs had said it was an example that ought to be followed up further by other schools and authorities. The work on assessment was being closely monitored, and we were by all accounts the school with the most advanced assessment database in the country.

Many of these visitors had excellent consultancy skills which, if anything, I felt were wasted in the murky organizational pond of Her Majesty's Inspectorate. Occasionally, as with one particularly distinguished practitioner of the art of school analysis, Mark Caton, I invited them back, asking them to talk with the staff about progress, or lack of it. Mark, a one-time middle-school headteacher, was sensitive and perceptive in his analysis of class-teaching. He would lower himself as inconspicuously as possible to the level of the child, and explore what was happening with a compelling good humour and balance. I persuaded him to come to staff meetings and to discuss our strengths and weaknesses as he saw them. He had that special skill of delivering critical, thought-provoking observations while at the same time making the participants feel better about themselves. One of his remarks stayed with me. 'My impression, sometimes,' he said, 'is that the teachers are working harder than the children – you whirl around exhaustively planning and encouraging, really trying ... but you might ask yourselves sometimes if you're doing too much for them, whether they can't do more for themselves ... What matters is the quality of what's going on in their minds, not just the quality of the work you are preparing and presenting for them.'

This was the kind of comment that captured our attention. Not exactly a dagger to the heart, but certainly an engaging provocation: it drove us back to first principles, to the drawing board; it raised questions, opened up avenues for further discussion and led us to stand back and think.

Other inspectorial visitors sometimes annoyed me with their self-righteous attitudes and a know-all disdain. They offered no constructive criticism, and failed in any sense to engage us in a debate on how to move forwards. Nor did they help give the teachers and me myself a sense of confidence, a general psychological lift. If visitors leave a school feeling bad about itself – powerless, inadequate – then they are in danger of damaging that school community, or the individuals within it.

One particularly pompous Inspector entered a classroom and wandered around without introducing himself, a man with a dark pinstripe, a light-blue silk tie and glittering black shoes. No doubt he didn't want to interrupt the lesson and could pretend to himself, exotic creature though he was to the children, that he could slip into the room and move from desk to desk unseen. The teacher said nothing, and he ended up sitting by Adie, a boy whom few teachers anywhere could have managed in a class of thirty, but who was somehow held in check by this teacher's patience and good humour. The HMI did not of course know Adie who was, as it happened, dutifully working at his desk, writing with admirable care into his notebook. The HMI leaned over, took hold of the book, and pulled it towards him to examine.

'And how are you getting on, young man?' he asked.

By now, other children had stopped working to watch this particular engagement, well aware of Adie's potential. It was all the teacher could do to keep their attention, and when he realized that Adie was within arm's length of the visitor, he sidled within range, half anticipating trouble.

There was a long pause after the Inspector spoke and Adie very slowly leaned over, grabbed back his book from the hands of the intruder, put his nose close to his, eyeballed him, and then shouted loudly and deliberately, with a roll of the tongue and a street-wise lilt in his voice: 'White fuckin' trash.'

At which the visitor shuffled off to another desk, stayed but a moment, and then retreated hurriedly from the room.

This caused much amusement, which the teacher afterwards confessed he did not attempt to suppress. Adie was extremely pleased with himself, momentarily the star of the show.

But the visit today from the Senior HMI and his delegation makes an impact of a different kind. The grandees trail in and occupy my study in the New Building. There are greetings all round. Our chief guest is an HMI in his late forties, well known on the national scene, and rightly considered to be able and capable of balanced judgements. He already knew our man from the Local Authority, a dapper Welshman, whom I rather liked. Together they joke and joust and gesticulate like a pair of lads at the bar. I stand and listen. Without a by-your-leave they troop off into the school, led by the LEA delegation. I suddenly find myself left on my own. It occurs to me that this is not my school at all: I'm a kind of appendage, a minor functionary to the Government Inspector. The inspectors and the civil servants sweep graciously from room to room and eventually return, animated, talking away nineteen to the dozen about such matters as the underachievement of the ethnic minorities, the statistics on racial issues, the Swann report, one or two interesting things they've seen, how delightful the children were, the difficulties, the potential, the value of such surveillance exercises as this, as – of course – there's no substitute for seeing things for yourself. And as they talk and drink their tea, with home-made cakes cooked by the classroom assistants on the school's best china plates, I feel dispirited: *it is as though I'm not here.* At one point I leave them and wander about the school to catch a breath of air, feeling a strange sense of anxiety, of irrelevance, and when I return to my room it's as if I had never gone, my absence apparently not having been noticed. One of the teachers, Roger, in order to test the alertness of the children some years back, had climbed through the window and come in again through the front door, when he was disarmed by the extraordinary realization that the children hadn't noticed. 'Am I needed here?' I ask myself.

The merry group now announce that they must go: a hugely valuable, wonderful visit, and 'Thanks very much indeed,' says the HMI to our man from the Office. 'We're really most grateful.' He eyes me suddenly, offering me his thanks also. He shakes my hand, but I'm all too aware that at that very moment he looked away, his mind already somewhere else. And off the party goes.

I was left extraordinarily drained by this experience. All at once I felt small and powerless, a tiny cog in the vast machine of state, a blip in the evolving debate between the DES, the national centre of power, and the Local Authority. The truly important players had passed through our little school like lords commanding great estates, gathering useful trinkets from the people out there who kept things afloat. It was the first time that I'd felt that, as a teacher, I was a victim.

'Are you still here?' said one young man to me, an ex-pupil who now had his own clothes business and was doing well: 'Can't you think of anything better to do?'

The HMI and his minions had conveyed to me the idea that this was not quite the sort of job bright people should stay in. Maybe I had been here too long and ought to be thinking about my career, and move up in the world ... Our school, the smallest of the small in the flow of the wider politics of the educational world, had been moved aside like an old stone for them to see what was underneath, and, momentarily excited, these collectors had now gone, leaving the stone indifferently rolled back into place.

Only one question had been asked by our visitors that I could now recall, and it hung glowering in my mind.

> David, I expect you've got plans to move on, have you? What are you going to do next?

Their message to me was: *this is no place to stay.*

It seemed to me that all of us in the school had been somehow diminished and this generated another moment of defiance that made me all the more determined to stay. You survive these absurd events by laughing about them with the staff, shrugging them off as a joke. I was reminded of the story that when the very holy Father Vincent McNubb revived the ancient practice of kissing the foot of his host, Ronald Knox commented: 'Such a distressing experience after lunch.'

46
Reflections

'MPs Want Stale Heads Moved On', runs the headline. The small print argues that seven years is the optimum time for a school's headteacher to serve. And I am now coming towards the end of my second seven-year cycle.

There's no doubt that in the first years of headship you will have energy, alertness and freshness as you come in intending to make your mark, and set in place a map and a vision. This will be followed by a period of consolidation. All being well you will have turned the school around a few degrees, and given it a sense of purpose and life. By the end of your first seven-year cycle there should be visible achievements, the sense of a deeper, more thoughtful stability, a strong evolving culture and the self-confidence which comes from feeling that you can manage most of the difficulties of the job and harness the prevailing winds to move things in your favour.

But this takes a tremendous amount out of you. You discover as much about yourself as you do about the school. You learn how to take things in your stride, how not to overreact. You learn how to decide which matters require immediate attention. You realize that good communication is essential, but memos, instructions and directives are invariably filtered away in interpretation. What matters is setting balls – ideas – rolling that become part of a dialectic. I appreciate more and more the importance of conversation, of talking things through, and bouncing ideas off other teachers, especially those alchemists who I know are most likely to be able to turn ideas into practice.

I come to the view that one key component of a good school is the quality of its discourse: the spirit of enquiry with which we talk to each other, in the inexhaustible business of working out how we can do things better. This discourse creates an expanding, permeating network of ideas. As I've said, it's like kicking a ball from one person to another, learning how to pass, learning how to move it about creatively – not forgetting that the point of the game is to score a goal.

When we're working well, the staff team moves the ball around brilliantly. Ideas take off; they come to fruition; they are tried, tested and interrogated. At its best, the team attains a natural rhythm that raises the quality of everything we do. This seems to happen in the same way to great football teams, or theatre companies, in which after a huge amount of ground work the effort briefly falls away and a lightness of spirit takes over: an ease of performance when everything suddenly comes together at exactly the right time.

But headteachers are vulnerable. Over-control is a persistent hazard. You can aspire to get right into the heads of the staff and the pupils, so they behave the way you want them to behave. A desire to control everything can lead to the fear of subversion, an overreaction to what seems like defiance, an over-the-top insistence on order, tidiness, neatness, quietness – even silence. Obedience starts to become the point of the exercise, with everything being made orderly and ship-shape.

This is the way schools have been run historically. A measure of control and order is clearly necessary, but it can easily lead to a closing down of debate, with ideas being passed down as edicts, so that people are discouraged from valuing their own ideas. Pupils, like teachers, may become correspondingly passive and disinclined to think for themselves.

Carried to extremes such over-controlling may become a kind of madness. A head in one nearby school began to spend his days roaming round his school, picking up crisp papers or looking for lost gym-shoes. Everything, even the crisp-paper floating down the corridor, became his personal responsibility, and in the end the poor man had the inevitable breakdown.

There is an opposite danger: that is, giving up in the face of what seems to be an impossible job, and withdrawing into your room or engaging in various administrative distractions that help you avoid difficulties or decisions. You can feel overwhelmed by the seemingly impossible problems you encounter. At another school down the road, the head locked himself in his room, smashed it up and wouldn't come out. His deputy had in the end to get his wife to come to persuade him to unlock the door. In another three-storey secondary school the staff held a weekly sweepstake on who would see the head first – five pounds on the ground floor, fifteen pounds on the top (rarely won).

There are times still when I have been aware of how much stress I have myself been under, although I doubt whether the staff realizes I have been. I try to avoid such extremes, having become increasingly conscious of how vulnerable headteachers can be, as I have said. After my first seven years I took a break to research at university, and now I am allowing myself membership of one or two professional and Government committees, even though during meetings I find I'm thinking about the school most of the time.

There have also been times of real doubt when I have become anxious over what might seem relatively small things, when constraints have become exaggerated, especially constraints in resources.

Lack of resources holds back everything we do. There's never going to be enough time and intellectual space for discussion in a primary school of this kind simply because teachers have so little time out of class, and there isn't enough money to employ the cover staff we need. The classes are too large. We have far too little money for key items of equipment, such as computers and even books. It's like fighting a battle with all one's plans drawn up but with the prospect of victory, of mastery, looking increasingly unattainable.

Another problem is instability. Like it or not, schools are

constantly changing, and often necessarily. Some of the best teachers leave and others with new talents replace them. Some will take a couple of years to become part of a team: they will need training and support. Lose too many of your outstanding people and you're liable to have to take a few steps backwards. Politics plays its part, especially if the Government's political macro-vision doesn't seem to match your own. You can easily develop a defensive posture that isn't good for the kind of free-flowing game that develops naturally when things are going well. The National Curriculum turned out to be much more time-consuming than anticipated, and we were in danger of being bogged down. We try not to be forced onto the back foot, but to keep the best aspects of our own planning going, and not to allow the evolution of ideas, and the associated energy, to falter.

But perhaps the greatest problem is one of personal balance and determination. You need to be able to play on a variety of organ stops to be a head. You can be too much of any one thing: over-caring, over-considerate, over-tough, over-directive, over-administrative, over-anxious, over-indifferent, excessively exhausting in generating ideas. You can become engrossed in winning, and competitive within a limited, narrow focus, and – to change the metaphor – drive forward as though you are desperate to get out of the trenches, to gain territory.

It's easy to see your world as a battlefield. I go to a neighbouring school, and we're walking down a corridor when suddenly my headteacher colleague collars a child and thunders at him, shouting at the top of his voice. He is almost screaming. This certainly raises the adrenalin, energizes the atmosphere. It creates a fearful tension, and for a moment or two, like the silent child, I feel truly scared. This is the language, the spirit of war. The boy has, after all, been running down the corridors: 'How many times have you been told I will not have you running down the corridors?' my colleague yells. 'How many times?'

A similar thing happens to me when I too have a visitor

in tow. A boy hurtling across the lower school hall bangs into us. 'Come here,' I say, annoyed. 'Why are you running?' This is a foolish question that doesn't really require an answer. He's running because he's chasing his friend. 'Look,' I say, trying to control my temper, 'running is really dangerous. Have you ever seen a headteacher explode?' The boy picks up that this might be a joke, meant to tell him something. Maybe a veiled threat. Understandable. He shouldn't have been running. And I'm not smiling. 'Sorry,' he says, and then I smile – suggesting that maybe I was teasing him all along. But he also knows that I might have punished him, and that this was a quiet, low-key correction which was probably also a threat. But not warlike.

I've always found it difficult to shout at children. When you're embedded in the needs of an organization as demanding and complex as that of a school, you feel there's something unbalanced about such expressions of inflated energy, which can narrow your perspective. You can become insensitive and fail to ask the right questions. You can start to over-focus on what's wrong, and become negative.

What matters, by contrast, is the quality of what is happening, the quality of human engagement and, in a school, the quality of learning. It is important to worry about the fact that today Mrs X was obviously miserable and upset or that little Maxine in class 3 green was bullied, or that Miss Y's maths teaching was badly prepared. These small factors are cumulatively of great importance. It is for the leader of the team, the trainer, the manager, to consider these things. People – including children – know when you've noticed and you're bothered. Eventually such troubles, like any others, will need to be broken up into puzzles and turned into actions. You can lose a lot of sleep taking on the pains and troubles of others as well as your own vulnerability and fears. At four in the morning you lie there wrestling with your problems, trying to make sense of them. And maybe the sense you make of them will in the end become the foundations for the sense the school makes of itself.

All heads, and all those in a position of leadership, need to have personal support and advice. It should be unobtrusive, sensitive, critical but thoughtful, and help you work through problems without actually telling you what to do. My wife is the best at this. Only a few external advisers and official visitors seem to have the necessary qualities for giving it. Few outsiders quite understand what schools are like.

In a school you are trapped with your colleagues day in, day out, at very close quarters. Are there other organizations where so many people work together in so confined a space? Everyone is visibly dependent on everyone else. Our performance both individually and corporately will vary from day to day, from week to week. But we need to believe in ourselves, to know that we can rise above our limitations. It's fine to have a belief in measurement, scores, data, memos, targets, but a belief in the quality of teachers is likely to be more important. This makes leadership more like a kind of artistry where you are constantly aiming to raise the level of the game, the professionalism, the quality of performance and the maturity of the players, using imagination and empathy to travel into the unknown, and understanding that working as a team you can reach places you can't possibly reach on your own.

The seven-year decline is not inevitable. The head is only one member of the team, and if you are sufficiently aware of the dangers of the long haul, the possibility of over-control, cosiness, self-importance and the stresses that can lead to breakdown, then you can sustain a long-term professional life, constantly learning something new. With occasional breaks, a sufficiency of intellectual and emotional balance and a continuing enthusiasm, with luck your reputation with the staff and the community of parents and children will lead to yet further achievements.

Autumn

The 1990s

47
The Marketplace

Disillusionment with state education was by this point centre-stage. The disruptive union actions had given the Conservative Government the green light for radical change. The Education Secretary in the Thatcher government, Kenneth Baker, implemented a programme of reforms in the major 1986 and 1988 Education Acts. 'Reform' had become a highly loaded word, carrying a sense of threat as well as improvement. The most dramatic development was the National Curriculum, which was 'doomed to succeed,' as Stuart MacClure, the editor of the *Times Educational Supplement*, said at the time.[26] Ten years later, the grandiose Citizen Kane vision of Kenneth Baker, the National Curriculum Council's Duncan Graham, and his colleagues, would be honed down to a single volume, a modest document not dissimilar to the Scottish National Curriculum, which England and Wales could have had for free in the early 1980s, thus saving a billion pounds of public money and a forest or two.

The prevailing view was that the National Curriculum would enhance the quality of teaching at a deep level. The reality was that it would enhance the quality of teaching of those who could treat it in a balanced way and translate its ambitions into the real life of the classroom. Primary schools all over the country set out to make sense of the dozen volumes delivered for every teacher in the land by a fleet of large vans. One brave head shredded the lot, put the remains into black plastic bags and posted them, registered delivery, to the Department of Education in York Road. Various bright ideas followed with teachers now being expected to fill in time sheets recording the percentages of time they taught for every subject. It seemed to many of them that there was actually less time for them to spend on the core skills of literacy and numeracy, a problem for which teachers, in due course, would carry the blame.

Not everyone was sure that the National Curriculum was a good thing. The problem was its overweening ambition, its attempt to account for every nut and bolt, comma and dot in every subject. Ironically, this was in part the result of a desire to be responsive to various consultation exercises and to various interest groups. There was, however, an arrogance of tone in the accompanying texts which were peppered with 'oughts' and 'shoulds', 'knows' and 'understands', without any deep conceptual comprehension being evident of what 'know' and 'understand' might really mean to a practising teacher. It was also a subject-based curriculum (like ours) which gave the strong impression to many in primary schools of being put together with an insufficient awareness of the needs of young children. The consequence was that it landed like a lead weight on the schools. Many ground to a virtual halt whilst they spent hundreds of hours of after-school planning to prepare the huge and heavy machine to fly. In time the National Curriculum did improve the curriculum-planning of many schools which had given little thought to such areas as history, geography and science. But because it was so vast and so insensitively imposed in so short a time, teachers found putting it into practice very difficult. It was a classic example of the problem of centralist imposition on a community of people who were unprepared and largely unsupported in the business of turning battle-plans into effective action.

It also somehow lacked a core of meaning. It gave little idea of what we wanted an eleven-year-old to achieve after seven years of statutory schooling. Where was the sense of the needs of young citizens of the future, who had to be players in a liberal democracy, in a multi-cultural society and a global economic culture? At its heart the National Curriculum felt oddly empty.

At Grove it was potentially a distraction. We had our own school curriculum in place. We made some quiet adaptations, but we were determined not to be knocked off course.

Another strand in Conservative Government policy was derived from the theory of choice and markets for services, and focused on market competition in public education. The laws of the market suggested that increased parental choice would lead to the evolution of centres of excellence within impoverished inner-city areas. Furthermore, the removal of rigid 'catchment areas' which determined the parents' right to choose a school, would encourage the movement of children from the worst schools.

The problem was that the popular schools were already heavily over-subscribed and the Local Authorities insisted that priority was given to those pupils who lived in the immediate vicinity. The option of expanding oversubscribed schools seemed impractical. The consequence was that 'choice' often turned out not to be choice at all. In Birmingham, if you didn't get your first choice your child was assigned to any school in the city that happened to have spare places, that is, invariably the unpopular ones, to which as one parent put it to me, 'he'll go over my dead body.' Children were being sent like David Copperfield to a school far away which they'd never visited and which the grapevine suggested (sometimes unfairly) was a nightmare. Many were understandably upset and defiant.

The situation was acutely aggravated by the collapse of our main local boys' secondary school, which was named and shamed, and after a brave two-year attempt to keep it afloat, closed down. So up to 30% of all our eleven-year-olds regularly found themselves being allocated to schools in distant places with poor reputations to which they had no intention of going. This potentially explosive problem was only resolved – in part – by the reputation Grove pupils had won at a couple of excellent schools, where they seemed to have performed consistently well. So a few children were squeezed in here and there. It was also lucky that the proportion of our children making it to the selective grammar schools – there were still five of these in Birmingham – was steadily rising.

If the Government's school-choice policy was firing on only three cylinders, the new policy to devolve funding from Local Authorities to individual schools that had been introduced in the late 1980s, proved to be a genuinely radical development which gave them the freedom to spend as they saw appropriate. This highlighted – especially to governing bodies – just how insufficient funding often was.

The local management of schools (known as LMS) gave headteachers and governors the authority to spend the money that was allocated to them as they wished. In practice, there was little room for choice as most of the budget went on fixed costs, building, equipment and salaries. But the old system where expenditure was controlled by the Local Authority was gone for ever. The 1988 (and later the 1993) Act created a new category of Grant Maintained Schools, which were freed entirely from what were seen as the shackles of the Local Authority. Our Governing Body briefly discussed the option of us becoming a Grant Maintained School, and for reasons of loyalty to the LEA and to local Labour politics turned it down. In fact those schools that took the plunge during the first tranche of conversions to GM status benefited hugely from massive injections of central government funding and from a hard commercial vantage point, looking back, we might have been well advised to take a different decision.

For our school, the implementation of devolved financial management did not go smoothly. The Governors advertised for a bursar to take over the running of the school's finances. We had over a hundred applicants and chose the best person qualified. The smart young lady we appointed soon mastered the very new computerized systems, and in no time was buying suites of furniture for herself from local stores with an expertise undetected by any of us, including the professional accountant who regularly examined her computer files. The overconfidence of the criminal mind finally let her down, and she took to forging cheques with the deputy head's signature. Our deputy quickly picked up the deceit, which the bank did not. Our bursar was duly dismissed, and the last we heard of her she was running a Post Office. It is surprising how often organizations fail to ask for references.

So we became a case study for the training of employees who worked with the LMS Sims computer systems. Our next, excellent bursar had the miserable job of unpicking all the damage done by her predecessor.

The Government also wanted to improve the quality of information available to parents. Their answer was to draw up performance-league tables. Education was now all about winning. There were premium divisions of schools, and there were downright disasters which could be dramatically named and shamed with the headline-grabbing panache associated with football teams when they sacked their managers.

Now parents, and middle-class parents in particular, had a clear indication of the best place to live in order to have their children schooled away from the urban poor. The middle classes, as A. H. Halsey once remarked, translate everything into advantage. The principle that people should have maximum knowledge about their local schools, hospitals and services, had a clear priority over the interests of the professionals who had the most to lose. The outcome was unsurprisingly that the top two hundred schools were independent schools, followed by state-funded selective schools. The top LEAs were those with the richest inhabitants, and the bottom those with the poorest, with wide performance gaps in between.

Competition was all the rage. There were to be winners and losers. Examination results were the goals, and pupils the goal-scorers. The rules of the game were to be much more clearly defined and no one was able to opt out.

The political language was changing. 'Rigour' was a new word that was in fashion. 'Naming and shaming' entered the vocabulary. The game was about splitting the educational world into goodies and baddies, invoking carrot and stick, encouraging the good, punishing the bad, in the excellent cause of raising standards, expressed in the language of war – zero-tolerance, precision-targeting, zones, forward-thrusts, special measures.

To accommodate this new activity, the DES had grown exponentially over the last two decades, and it was soon to be relaunched as the Department of Education and Employment in splendid new offices in Great Smith Street, Westminster, with lobby fountains and floors of smart, circular open-plan spaces.[27]

At an education seminar in the late 1980s I had a long after-dinner conversation with Nick Stuart, Deputy Secretary at the DES under Kenneth Clarke, on the subject of school inspection. I had recently written a book on Local Authority inspection and management services showing how varied their functions and their impact could be.[28] I raised, not for the first time, the idea of making radical changes to the national inspection services. What about an inspection service, I suggested, that was wholly independent of HMI and local advisers, with its own brief and criteria? I pointed out the diversity of advisory roles both in Government and Local Authorities, the lack of clarity in roles between administration and advisory work, the overlaps between functions that often led to tension. I explained that schools were caught in the middle of all this, and their experience of advisers and inspectors at the sharp end was highly variable. I floated the possibility of a privatized consultancy and inspection service of the kind used by many industrialists. The idea would be to offer external independent support and advice that was paid for by the schools themselves. Nick listened closely, and asked a lot of questions, and we talked late into the evening.

I was certainly naive about what happens when governments throw the blistering power of funding, civil-service thinking and statutory machinery behind what on the surface sounds likes a bright idea. Our discussion anticipated the emergence of a full-scale new initiative which was to generate the final piece in the standards-assurance jigsaw: the Office for Standards in Education (Ofsted) effectively a police force to check out school performance.

Ofsted was not in principle so far off what I had proposed. But it lacked any constructive consultancy element. What emerged was nothing like the model I had had in mind, and bore no resemblance to the tried and tested field of institutional business consultancy. The new school-inspection process was bureaucratic and centralized, as well as being uneven in quality, providing what seemed very inadequate training for its array of privately employed inspectors. It was also phenomenally expensive, absorbing some £150 million of public money year on year with remarkably little independent auditing to ensure value for money.[29] Worst of all the inspection process was carried out in a spirit of negative criticism which alienated and disillusioned the teachers at a time when an imaginative consultancy and inspection service could have carried the professionals along with them positively.

Command and control was considered more important than discussion and debate. Definition of all aspects of the product was the objective with rule-book, statute-book, maps and directions being laid out graphically for implementation. Schools were now judged by one national blueprint. Each inspection assigned a number to each teacher's performance in one or two lessons. Every detail was to be inspected, and the search was on, in the spirit of the contemporary TV detective, Inspector Morse, first to find the corpse in the cupboard, and then to identify those responsible for committing the crime.

It was a classic expression of what Kruman called 'mechanical political cultures', a constitutional order designed to run with machine-like efficiency and safety.[30] The Government seemed to be trying to create a kind of educational Marks and Spencers, with regulated standards of performance across all the stores, a high customer-reputation, quality goods on show and a delivery culture that could be replicated from York to St Ives, the whole affair being run by a smart, controlling management centre.

On the surface, this mission to prod the sleeping giant of state education into new animation had many points in its favour. Children could undoubtedly achieve a great deal more, and schools were unquestionably uneven in quality. Even though many of the weakest teachers had been weeded out over the years, there were still some who should not have been there.

Our own school had in its own way anticipated many of the initiatives, as before. We had detailed information about pupil achievement and progress. We had a curriculum programme in line with the basic principles of the National Curriculum, with our own distinctive courses in history, geography, RE, and as much specialist teaching in music, drama, art and science as the school could afford. We were beginning to map out a quality-control process for the 'pieces of the curriculum' which was soon to be computerized. An inspection by Ofsted in the early 1990s suggested that we now had the most detailed database of children's academic performance of any school in the land, a fact celebrated in a Government paper on 'improving quality' that was distributed to all schools. We continued to employ outside consultants to analyse progress.

We had achieved all this without sacrificing our arts programme which gave such a high profile to music, dance, drama and the visual arts. Our behaviour-management programme built up the children's independence and self-confidence. We had highly developed strategies for discipline and mandatory homework which was regularly recorded and checked. We led the way in developing arrangements for identifying and teaching able children and children with special needs.

We had even set up something looking distinctly like literacy and numeracy hours. A new Government would eventually create a much more professional approach to what was taught in these 'hours', but essentially they would be working to principles we had defined more than fifteen years before. It had all been done in cooperation with our local community. Our remarkably cohesive and forward-looking Governing Body included, amongst others, a Sikh engineer, the deputy director of the Commission for Racial Equality and a future Governor of the BBC, a distinguished musicologist, a senior university academic, a Muslim shop-keeper, and an Afro-Carribean headteacher. They managed to get a regular two hundred parents to the 'annual meeting' – an astonishing number compared with most schools – reflecting the strength of community interest in the school.

Our teaching programme was by no means complete: parts of it were still unsatisfactory, parts required updating, completing, revising; but it was, nonetheless, way ahead of its time. Furthermore, it had been achieved with minimal resources – with a low per capita income, much lower than for Grant-Maintained and secondary schools until the arrival of a persuasive and visionary Chief Officer, Tim Brighouse, in 1993, who greatly changed Birmingham's priorities, morale and national profile.

So I felt I should support many of these Government initiatives, aimed as they were at improving poorer schools and providing much more systematic quality-control and knowledge gathering.

Why then was I reminded of the film *Twelve Angry Men* where the case against a boy alleged to have murdered his father seemed to eleven of the jurors to be watertight, and to the twelfth not proven? I felt all along, like the Henry Fonda character, that something wasn't right.

'We now know,' said the Chief Inspector of Schools, 'what

effective teaching is, and what effective leadership means. What else is there to know?' I was not so sure. Underlying all the Government's ambitions was something disturbing: a hint of intellectual self-deceit, a disinclination to face the reality of the evidence, if it seemed inconvenient.

Initiatives, even where they proved effective, tended to be abandoned as soon as they looked too expensive. One example was the Reading Recovery programme. To have tutors and teachers working with individual children who were falling behind at an early stage proved surprisingly effective, following a £3 million Government investment. But the cost of offering this Rolls Royce support to all six-year-olds who needed it was found to be prohibitive, and a promising experiment to help underachieving children died the death. There were many other examples of worthwhile pilot studies and practices being admired and supported before being rejected for lack of sustained funding.

Cheap options were, by comparison, given exaggerated acclaim. The level of resources in schools was not seen as an issue. There was a growing assumption that the teachers were rather less important than the curriculum, and that they were most effective if they were pinned down by testing and target-setting regimes. Governments ignored the fact, which was apparent to every pupil in the land, that the minds and abilities of teachers could transform any material, instruction or guideline on offer and either make it worth hearing or else kill it dead. Rigid education systems in the Pacific basin were praised to the skies, even though the countries that employed them were themselves trying to make their systems more imaginative and less centrally directed.

There were more disturbing omissions. Running under the whole edifice like a dark river was the most neglected factor of all – the depressing, intractable problem of poverty.

48
Poverty

One day I go out to look up a missing child, and knock on the door. The terraced house has a small front garden where autumn leaves have blown in, covering the weeds.

The little girl I'm searching for answers the door and stares at me, obviously distressed.

'Are you OK?' I ask.

She says nothing, standing in the doorway.

'Is your mum there?'

She shakes her head.

'You're not on your own?'

She shakes her head again.

'Can I come inside?'

I hear movements. There's someone in there, and the girl makes no attempt to stop me as I cross the doorstep and step inside into the narrow corridor that runs directly through to a back room, beyond which there is a kitchen.

In the back room I hear scuffling. I go through and there's the girl's mother *hiding under the carpet*, making a huge lump, completely invisible. She is curled up on her knees, with her head in her hands. She moans in gasps and sighs, like a tiny child. After pulling the carpet back, I pick her up and help her into a chair, the only one in the room. The girl stands and watches as though struck dumb.

We wait around while an ambulance comes with a mental-health officer. I try to console the girl as her mother is taken away – her aunty was coming to take her off to another house, and they wouldn't let her go in the ambulance. I keep telling her that she'll be able to see her mother soon. She nods, still silent, not crying. Eventually her aunty arrives and takes the girl's hand, and as everyone departs it's left to me to shut the door. It's a poor little home: I can see one large Indian-style rug, enough to cover you, a few knick-knacks, a picture and a photograph here and there, and an old TV set in the corner. I close the door quietly.

There were many people in this community who took great pride in their homes, and there was a warmth and a feeling of caring that was immediately welcoming. Many of them had to manage on very small incomes or on social security, and yet they brought up happy, well-balanced children. They were immensely likeable, and their ability to survive the local crime, the presence of a small number of anti-social families and in many cases such very low incomes was humbling to those of us who were better off.

But there were some who were on the brink of becoming an underclass. From time to time I visited other homes where there was virtually nothing: little furniture; the house was in shreds; the wallpaper was ripped off the wall; the windows were broken; there were holes in the doors. We found one recently-arrived family sitting round the sides of a room: it had no lighting or heating; there were six children and a little baby. All they had to eat was boiled rice, with the ubiquitous TV as the only sign of modern life. Any bits and pieces of self-respect were kept for the front room, which was used little for day-to-day living.

In many of the families, the children had few books and toys. Some smuggled schoolbooks out to keep under their bed. The diet of many of them was poor in a similar way, and the health indicators for the area were appalling. Many parents needed help with clothing, and we often negotiated clothing allowances for the children. As a result of my parents' questionnaire we had long ago decided on a school uniform which the school would pay for if necessary. It was not uncommon for families to live in extremely crowded accommodation, with parents and three or four children living in two small rooms. I visited one home which was like that of the old woman who lived in a shoe. A tiny child in bare feet let me in and a shout from upstairs called me into the bedroom where her mother was lying in bed with four children, who were wrapped in blankets as they couldn't afford the heating.

Break-ins were endemic and prevented people from leaving their houses unoccupied. One eleven-year-old boy went berserk when he saw two big guys trying to steal the family's TV – unsuccessfully as it happened.

'I was watching dis programme and they just switch it off,' he declared. Small though he was, he chased the burglars out of the house and up the road.

'But they run faster'n me,' he said regretfully.

Afterwards he went back to finish watching his programme.

Older sisters often kept the house going, many of them carrying far too much responsibility for their age. Some had no privacy or space for homework, and sitting quietly to read was impossible for them. Sometimes the tension between mother and children became unbearable, with huge fights ensuing. In some homes the children ran wild, climbed out of windows, kicked in the doors, came in late at night. Others couldn't sleep for the noise next door: it might be a late-night party or a screaming twenty-four-hour ghetto-blaster that drove everyone to distraction.

In one house all the windows were smashed in and during the winter they were covered with newspaper. The parents' behaviour here was extremely bizarre. The pale, subdued children found it hard to get to school. The father played cards late into the night with one of his sons and wouldn't give his wife money for food.

There were also terrible tragedies – such as mothers and children being removed to protective sanctuary against a background of violence, of families fighting families. Two mothers committed suicide; one house was burnt down, killing everyone. Other mothers were on the game. I brought a child home after a visit to our country Hostel one night and we couldn't get into the family house. The mother, a well-known prostitute, leant out of the bedroom window effing and blinding before eventually throwing the keys down.

To survive these conditions with self-respect and a modicum of cheerfulness required courage and resilience. A great many of our children somehow did manage to survive, and their overall behaviour was improving: they seemed calmer and more stable these days. Was this to do with the impact of the school or was something changing in the community? Were people, despite everything, becoming more settled, more secure? Certainly there was no sign of the children without shoes that I used to see in Nechells in the 1960s – all of them could have stepped out of the 1930s, with their little baggy shorts and thin shirts. There was no need for the bath that used to be used daily in the Gem Street School in the City Centre in the 1960s, where children were regularly washed on arrival.

Like Artful Dodgers many people today were learning how to survive by moonlighting, by living on their wits, creating alternative lifestyles; and poverty is, of course, a relative thing. Very often those who went under completely had suffered one extra indignity which had pushed them over the edge – a violent husband, a difficult child, an unwanted baby, an illness in the family, especially a mental illness. When survival was at a premium from day to day, and week to week, the normal hazards of life became major obstacles. They became immense emotional and physical challenges.

From 1980 to 1995 the gap between the rich and the poor widened. By the mid 1990s some 25% of the population was living in relative poverty. The gap between high and low educational performance was similarly wider than in any other Western nation, and poor academic results went with material poverty. Here in this Handsworth village were some of the poorest of that 25%. One in eight of the entire population had been identified as being undernourished, roughly the same number as fail educationally. The links between educational performance and health are strong: the improved educational performance of children in the years just after the First World War was closely linked to a strong emphasis on improving health and nutrition. Average life-expectancy in classy Sutton Coldfield, a few miles away, was at present six years higher than in this part of downtown Handsworth.[31]

The fashionable argument was that people can be most effectively rescued from poverty by education. Successive governments went to great pains to point out that schools really do make a difference to pupils' achievement, using evidence of the school effectiveness movement. It was argued that the problem lay not in poverty itself, but in poverty of access to good education. We certainly needed to raise expectations of children's performance in schools. But in my *Twelve Angry Men* mode I was increasingly worried by the oversimplification of an argument that led conveniently to the view that poverty was an issue that could be largely ignored. Not entirely of course, for even the most impassioned exponent of the education-can-solve-all-problems school had to admit that there was, in the end, some link between intake and academic achievement, and that there were undeniable differences between Handsworth and Sutton Coldfield.

Schools were analysed in clusters based on the proportion of pupils taking free meals, which was widely agreed to be a good simple indicator of poverty, in order to make comparisons between high- and low-achieving schools with similar intakes. There was a reluctance to take into account the full range of factors, that is the more intricate features of the evidence. Communities, the network of city 'villages', which might seem similar on the surface, were actually very different when looked at closely. Some schools were closet-selectors of higher achieving children, particularly church schools. Others had wholly different communities, ethnic balances, proportions of children with language difficulties, social insecurity and crime, movement in and out of the school, parental support. It was in reality extremely difficult to compare like with like and to be sure that the input *x* created the result *y*.

On the other hand it was all too easy for schools to argue that their pupils had a factor *x* that would *inevitably* – through the dual misfortunes of socio-economic background and genetic mischance – produce poor academic result *y*. This absurd proposition could justify a lack of effort and categorical assumptions about the inevitability of low achievement. There was a long history of teachers who expected too little of the children they taught, especially if they were from less propitious areas or from ethnic minority backgrounds.

I came to the conclusion that this whole business was riddled with the pitfalls of self-deception, of lazy assumptions and of sloppy analysis. No one had all the answers to underachievement, and whilst we could certainly be more determined in hiking up achievement, it would take serious investment and new approaches to make an impact on the children who needed it most: those disenfranchised from learning, and those in the 20% of lowest academic achievement.

For us information technology looked like one useful way of improving basic skills. But where was the money to buy the machines and the very expensive software required? We persuaded a computer company to invest in us, and they gave us twenty computers to work on intensively with children with specific learning problems. For a while they performed fine; there was a buzz of excitement from the children, and there were signs of accelerating progress. We started planning to open the school in the evenings for families to come and work with their children. All such things were possible, and would make a difference. But then it turned out the computers were clapped-out, and they broke down; and after spending an immense amount of time trying to have them mended, we gave up. We had no money to buy more of them. I once went to King Edward's School, the wealthy independent secondary school, and I saw line upon line of its hi-tech computers in various departments, including their new state-of-the-art Design Suite. One law for the rich ...

I paused outside the school one afternoon on another of my countless walks down Dawson Road from the new Upper School building to the old Lower School, and considered these matters in a faint drizzle. What had the Thatcher years brought to communities like this? Looking back, I could see the new dark-green flying cactuses round the roof of the new building – the rotating roof razor-spikes to keep vandals off the roof – and the crummy, battered surrounding land, the broken-down fences: the inheritance of years of Conservative rule. Anyone with money round here moved up and away.

The worst dishonesty was to ignore the resource implications of the evidence, especially in so far as it concerned the primary education sector. Classes in primary schools should be twenty not thirty. There should be a huge investment, especially during the early years where it would have most impact. The gap between primary and secondary school funding was as wide as ever. Education policy, for all its flummery about equality of performance and provision, was in reality geared to deliver a basic curriculum on the cheap in an inequitably funded system in which the poorest and youngest got the smallest piece of the pie.

We certainly needed a more focused determination that all children, and most especially *these* children, should have equality of access to high-grade education at all levels. But more than a little determination was required to change things at the turn of the century when a middle-class child was still twelve times more likely to enter higher education than a working-class one, and the incomes of the rich were growing three times more rapidly than those of the poor.

One day I talked to a journalist from *The Times*. She had bought private education for her three children, who were all under the age of thirteen. She said that they were all bright and being well taught, and were no doubt going to succeed all the way down the yellow-brick road to university. Her explanation for her use of the private sector was the 'poor quality' of state education.

'So,' I said, 'what you're paying for is better teaching.'

'Absolutely.'

'Nothing else?'

'How do you mean?'

'How about class-size, for instance?'

'I don't follow you.'

'How large are your children's classes?'

'The largest, I think, is twelve.'

'Ah,' I said.

And there you had it in a nutshell. There was an officially endorsed view that class-size makes no difference to teaching quality, and some research evidence to support it. Ofsted claimed more than once that class-size is unconnected to pupil achievement except in the first two years of the primary school, an argument based on its presumption that 'whole class teaching' was the foundation of all the best teaching. Gillian Shepherd, speaking for a long line of Secretaries of State for Education, consistently argued that larger class-size did not lead to poorer standards.

It was a view that in some respects made sense. Would you not prefer to have your child with a great teacher like Ann in her maths classes of thirty-six rather than with a tedious second-rater, even in classes of ten? If, as I was arguing, it is the quality of mind and personality of the teacher that is the principal determinant of quality, then what does the size of the class matter?

But reducing class-size certainly did make a difference if the teacher took full advantage of the opportunities that teaching smaller groups had to offer. Montaigne thought that the most effective teaching must logically be one-to-one. I am convinced that all the teachers who made a difference to my life did so somehow by teaching me personally, or appearing to. Yes, the size of the group makes a considerable difference. Even twenty-five children sitting in a circle in my philosophy group (which I taught for an hour each week) was quite different from thirty or more seated in a classroom. Pupils in smaller classes behave better, appear more absorbed in their work, spend more time on their tasks and interrupt less frequently. Furthermore, we know that teachers with classes of twenty-six to thirty pupils on average work three hours more per week than those with classes of under twenty-one.

Class size is manifestly not a straightforward matter. Flexibility in class-size was long ago an objective in primary education in its progressive phase. School buildings of the late 1960s and early 1970s were designed with flexible space and dividing-screens to allow for different-size teaching groups in different situations. Some of the more radical enthusiasts knocked down doors and walls in conventional school layouts, in the spirit of this particular open-plan enterprise. There were certainly times when a lecture format for large numbers of pupils was both cost-effective and fun for the children; but at the other end of the spectrum, hands-on activity, or specialist work, required much smaller groups. There were also times when teachers needed to spend time talking through issues with individuals.

The pity was that, however good our intentions, we rarely had the resources for such highly desirable flexibility; there was no way in which state primary schools could ever properly compete here with the independent sector.

49
Crime

The local gangsters became more active as night fell. During the day, they mostly hung about on street corners, idling in small groups, squatting, smoking, passing the time, with occasional gestures of abuse. There was a tiny shop opposite the school where a handful of them spent much of the day on the pinball machines or sitting out in the road throwing cheek at the Grammar School boys. Every so often they would call to me across the road, in a fairly friendly way.

Some of the boys I knew. Some had mental-health problems; some were from hopelessly dysfunctional homes, some had failed at school and got into the habit of long-term truancy. Most had had poor parenting: some of them had been virtually abandoned in crazy or neglectful families from a very young age. They were mostly between fourteen and eighteen, but often even younger, and they came from all the different racial backgrounds, reflecting the ethnic make-up of the area.

They roamed, played and made havoc on their own doorstep, as though there were invisible boundaries beyond which they were too lazy or too nervous to go. Only the older kids, in their later teens and early twenties, who were able to acquire vehicles, went in for more serious systematically planned crime. They discovered the lands of the rich, the middle-class houses and the easy business of mugging girls with golden chains in hit-and-run operations.

In some parts of the city there was an element of war between, say, the Pakistani and the Bangladeshi youngsters, but not here in this part of multi-ethnic Handsworth. What we had was thieving and violence, verbal or real, the hard boys showing contempt for most things and fear of very little. The enemies were the police and adult authority, especially that of parents and teachers, who had mostly given up on them in despair. Schools were an irrelevance to this night world, and learning a pointless enterprise. They proved themselves to nobody but their friends. For the rest of us, going about our normal business, it was surprising how, as the sun went down, the familiar buildings took on a new vulnerable aspect. Buildings such as schools, once divested of people, offered an irresistible challenge and novelty on their doorstep, and all for free. One well-known Rasta gangster walked down Grove Lane and recognized one of our classroom assistants. 'Walk down wid you,' he said; 'ain't safe down here.'

For these youngsters by and large money was not the issue. The excitement lay in new opportunities for freedom, an independent life away from home, the attraction of the tribe with its shifting culture and personalized language full of foul expletives. The boys mostly seemed to lack a sense of planning or purpose – apart from having the desire to win a video game, or to experience the thrill of gesture vandalism. The point, for them, was that there was no point.

I walked past them frequently as they lounged about smoking on the pavements or in parked cars while I went the few hundred yards between the New and Old Schools. They always seemed to me morose, or even depressed. They rarely caused much trouble during the day, and they were rarely abusive (to me at least). But at night the school – especially the new school opposite with its low roofs and big windows – regularly got beaten up; not, I think, for any personal reason but just because it was there.

These youngsters broadly fell into two groups; the disturbed, hard boys, often with serious emotional problems, and the hangers-on, who one way or another had been enticed away from normal home and school life to join their mates on the streets. Many of them had started coming home late from quite a young age. There was a mix of permissiveness and indifference in their families, many of them without fathers, and an inability or disinclination on the part of many mothers to discipline them.

Some came from homes where there had been a history of much more extreme neglect, inconsistency or brutality, as I've said. Adrian and Dean were systematically punched by their father, who after years of abusing the whole family left the house never to be seen again. Dean was a normal, likeable boy who when he was thirteen got into a knife fight, not of his own making, and was stabbed to death. Adrian had an eventful teenage gang life: he played hooky from school, got into trouble with the police and had a foul temper. But at twenty or so he got a job as a community worker and found he was rather good at it. He had a mentor who encouraged him onwards and Adrian regularly visited the school to talk to me as though I represented some kind of reassurance, a fixed point in the community; perhaps I was even a father figure for him.

Not all the problem boys were from disadvantaged homes. Gurdeep was born to a well-to-do family from the Punjab. He was a tall, goodlooking child with a thin slightly Arab face and the commanding manner of his grandmother. His father ran a family business entailing long hours of work, which left him with limited time for his children. The women often helped in the shops, except for the grandmother who had immense authority in the family.

Gurdeep was her favourite. She saw herself in him: she loved him deeply, came to all his school parents' evenings and spoilt him rotten. She attended to his every need, ran at his beck and call balking at any suggestion of discipline from the men who occasionally noticed Gurdeep's temper tantrums and felt a natural inclination to slap him. She protected him. 'You lay not one finger on the boy,' she cried one day at his mother in front of me. 'Only I understand the chick.' She cuddled and cossetted him as her own, and the mother was only permitted to deal with him under her mother-in-law's severely critical eye. Later when things went badly wrong, Gran would shake her head and blame her. 'It's his mother coming out in him,' she would say.

Gurdeep had problems at school from the word go. He was, by now, the little prince. With his fierce temper, he would lie on the floor screaming if he couldn't get his way. Academically, he learned fast, but he saw little point in working, especially when teachers pressed him to work. He could be charming and likeable, and was even popular amongst a small group of immature friends who were impressed by his confidence and élan. They loved the way he led them into trouble and faced out teachers who confronted him. He survived primary school after numerous escapades, but with little modification to his behaviour and no apparent maturing self-knowledge. Once or twice I punished him for violent temper attacks on other children, which he accepted without demur but could never properly understand. The educational psychologist who tried to work with him on anger management finally gave up in despair: he grew worse rather than better.

The family refused any further professional help. 'He's just spoilt,' his dad said. 'He does things for me,' though this was very likely because dad had now taken to wielding a slipper. Come adolescence, the boy grew tall and uncontainable. At fourteen, as happened to some of his street friends, he was finally expelled from school after numerous suspensions. By fifteen, he was on the streets and heading up a night gang. He often stayed away from home and after numerous rows and recriminations, the family gradually gave up on him. In his new life, he continued to gather others around him, and at seventeen he acquired a tall, thin, long-nosed, loppety, brown whippet which went everywhere on the streets with him.

He did mad things: he scaled walls, broke windows, set outhouses on fire, broke into the local school buildings, at first just for the thrill of it. Then, getting to know the local underworld-dealer world, he began stealing things which were passed on through the older Afro-Caribbean lads to the long-standing professional criminals.

Gurdeep scarcely knew Inderjit, who was a year or two

older than he was. Inderjit was a shy but very bizarre boy who was given substantial psychological help at school. Academically able, too, but constantly falling apart, he became increasingly impossible to cope with in class. Eventually, he was completely unmanageable with his wild mood swings, running in and out of school until he became one of the few children I excluded. Unbeknown to anyone, the father and his uncles were involved in drug dealing. One night police discovered a vast haul of the stuff under Inderjit's bed. It got worse: his mother couldn't manage him and he was finally thrown out of the home onto the streets where he camped in busted-up houses, unable to make relationships, a victim himself of street crime. It was doubtful if he ever had a true friend. He was a failure of the school – of the system.

One day he met me in the street. 'I liked you,' he said, 'you bothered about me. I loved school.' There was a long pause. Then he said, 'You gave up on me.' There were tears in his eyes, and in mine. 'I'm sorry,' I said. 'I couldn't cope with you.' He looked down. 'I know,' he said. We shook hands and parted, and I've never seen him again.

50

Breaking In

Ever since the New Building had been completed we'd had problems with burglary and vandalism. For years we had no burglar alarm and break-ins were a pushover. At night windows were frequently broken, classrooms were disrupted and trashed, children's books being thrown round like confetti, their pens stolen and their desks upturned. My room was vandalized a number of times: the cupboards were emptied and the drawers turned out. We attempted to develop a miniature nature reserve in the heart of the school and young prisoners from Winson Green constructed a small, concrete pond. But as there was easy access to it from the roof it was regularly smashed up; the fish were stolen and the water was emptied. Soon we gave it up as a lost cause and filled it in. The space became a depository for damaged tiles that had been hurled off the roof. Gaping roof-holes were frequently filled in, but the tilers became depressed as they could scarcely keep up with the destructive urge of the nightly vandals – who on one occasion stole all their equipment. Hundreds of tiles were regularly destroyed, and the ceilings of the school were poleaxed with spikes through the mostly flat roof. The holes caused rainwater to run down into the classrooms, covering the walls. The school became littered with tubs and buckets to catch the flow.

It was evident that without a burglar alarm the school was in danger of grinding to a halt, and even the LEA conceded that something had to be done. So an alarm was fitted, although in a typical cost-cutting compromise: only half of the school had one. Half the classrooms and the whole of the hall were left unalarmed. It didn't take long for the local lads to work out which parts of the school were alarmed, and break-ins of an ever more sophisticated kind continued. Moreover, the burglar alarm had a life of its own, frequently going off for no reason in the middle of the night, as well as when the more stupid of the burglars and vandals stumbled into the alarmed zone. Since the alarm was linked through to the police, the caretaker was immediately alerted and the police insisted on my presence to identify thefts. The damage was, of course, obvious. I was often dragged out of bed, at all times of the night, to check out the building. The caretaker was, meanwhile, fully employed in bringing in emergency glaziers to board up smashed doors and windows. Worse still was when he was away, and I had to turn up with bunches of keys and try to find my way through the maze of locks and alarm boxes.

Finally, the LEA agreed to fund a much more comprehensive alarm system for the New Building only (the Old Building was now being broken into as well, if sporadically). This helped somewhat, although the break-ins, false alarms, call-outs and thefts continued. Plastic windows were fitted to replace the glass; but these were regularly sprayed with graffiti paint or scratched with knives until you could scarcely see through them. In due course the plastic was in turn replaced by heavily reinforced glass – which could still be cracked, as it frequently was, by bricks being hurled at it.

On one occasion the police arrived with a dog after an alarm call-out. Two officers and the dog patrolled the building and found nothing and then as Ashton, the caretaker, was locking up, he thought of looking in a cupboard. Four teenage boys promptly fell out. The police rushed back and arrested them. I was called over to identify the missing items and made a long statement to them describing a school whistle and a couple of boxes of Berol felt-tipped pens, which the boys had picked up.

More serious was the professional team of gangsters who had worked out that there was often a gap between the time the alarm was set off and the time it was re-set. The caretaker sometimes brought in the emergency-alarm company to re-set and re-check the alarm and there could be a gap of an hour or two when it was not on after the caretaker had returned to his house down the road. A small boy would be primed to climb in through a window, or on one occasion through a hole in a smashed fire-exit door, to deliberately set the alarm off and then run away. After the grand palaver of the police arriving and inspecting the building and the caretaker locking up, everything would go quiet. In the critical interval the burglars would enter, check the alarm was off, drive a van into the playground and steal whatever they could lay their hands on.

Twice we arrived at school in September after the summer vacation to find the school had been turned upside down –

it had been seriously vandalized, with broken glass everywhere, desks upturned, locks broken. And on one bleak night all the computers, the radios and TVs, the cameras and other electrical items were stolen – some £15,000 worth of equipment. As no insurance company was prepared to insure us, we depended entirely on the Local Authority to recoup these losses, which they did – reluctantly – in dribs and drabs over the next two years. I had appealed some time ago to the children to help more in keeping an eye on the building and reporting any sign of trouble to the caretaker or their parents. In one more apologetic assembly I admitted to them that though we had to do something about the vandalism and break-ins, I wasn't sure quite where to begin without finding a great deal of money for protecting the building. After the assembly a small boy came up to me and said he remembered me saying it was a good idea to write down the number of any suspicious car they saw near the school.

'Well, I saw this van.'

'You did? Where?'

'In the playground. And I saw a man carrying a TV and he put it in the back of the van.'

'What sort of van? What did it look like?'

'Dunno – it was blue. They saw me, so I ran away.'

'You can't remember what they looked like?'

'Indians,' he said.

'You can't identify them? You didn't recognize them?'

'No. Sorry.'

He turned to go.

'But I wrote down the number of the van – like you said.'

So it was that the police traced the van and arrested the gang of men involved. There was a pipeline running all the way to Leicester, where the equipment rapidly disappeared onto the black market. But a few items were rescued and I spent an hour or two at Thornhill Road identifying them, most of them useless by now.

The school Governors were by this stage responsible for our budgets. Clearly, by the 1990s protection of the school was the top priority, after this decade of ever-escalating problems. Life was too easy for the vastly better funded Grant Maintained Grammar School next door, which could afford not only a comprehensive array of security video-cameras but round-the-clock on-site security guards. We considered using the same guards to protect our building, but it was too expensive. So the line between the two school sites remained drawn as if between two different countries, and on our battered campus the local lads were still free to roam.

Bit by bit, year by year, we spent an increasing part of the budget on security, money that would have been better spent on books and equipment. Every window and every door was seated with heavy-duty electric steel shutters. Finally, by the end of the 1990s, we had security cameras and internal twenty-four-hour video equipment at the main points of entry. The New Building, so cheapskate and inadequately planned, had turned out as expected to be a long-term security nightmare that was to waste tens of thousands of pounds of taxpayers' money and disrupted the education of the youngsters time and time again over a period of two decades.

What I have been describing were mostly nocturnal events. But occasionally there was trouble during the day. One guy the children called 'gold tooth' found his way from time to time into the Lower School (now increasingly being targeted) and walked off with equipment, including a laptop computer. He timed his entry to coincide with the moment when nursery parents came into the school to pick up their children.

One day I was taking assembly and I could tell the children weren't listening. I stopped in mid-story.

'Look,' I said, 'what's the matter with you? You're not listening ...'

Some hands went up in the air. 'Sir, sir ...' someone said.

'I'm not going to be interrupted,' I said. 'Look at me and concentrate. I'm getting fed up – you're spoiling my story ...'

But the eyes continued to wander and a brave soul continued to hold his hand in the air. Then someone even braver blurted out, 'Sir someone's stealing the TV.'

Others joined in.

'And there's a fight ... Miss McKewn's fighting the guy ...'

I could see through the window at the top of the hall-door leading to the front entrance. My secretary, Marcia, was in full flow tackling a big man with a woolly hat who was trying to get out of the building with the TV in his arms. By the time I was out of the hall – the children excited, but admirably staying put – he was out of the building and darting down the road. A teacher rescued me from the assembly, and I leapt into my white van and chased him down Grove Lane. But he knew his way about and headed down an alley. There was a safe-house somewhere round there, and he escaped.

This was all energy-depleting and demoralizing. It was very well for people in Government to bang on about standards, but they could have little idea of the day-to-day problems we were facing on the ground. These pressures were distractions from what we were here to do. I still remembered that note I had once jotted down: focus on *making a difference to the children.*

Occasionally I would still visit other schools in leafy suburbs, aware as before of just how different they were, how much more easily they could concentrate on the education of their pupils. The problems of vandalism and increasingly those of violence that we faced, had created a changed world. Our children, who continued to go happily about their business, deserved better.

51
Danger

After dark there was a real sense of danger – scary things happened which unsettled everybody.

One day a young man finds his way into the building at five o'clock in the evening. It is pitch-black outside and he slips in through a door that is normally locked, as a cleaner is leaving. He stands with his black woolly hat, his dark glasses, his heavy jacket staring down an empty hall. A teacher happens at that exact moment to come out of her classroom, and when she sees the boy she freezes, as she describes it afterwards, 'like a fox caught in the lights.' When he produces a knife, she remains remarkably calm, moving back slowly. The boy laughs, waving the knife about. 'I'm goina kill someone in this place,' he says. 'You'll fucking find out,' and he begins to move towards her. She guesses he wants something to steal, but there isn't much on offer in the hall. The new Bose speakers are too high in the roof, the hi-fi is encased in a heavy-duty burglar-free iron-box unit, sunk into the wall. The TV and video are down the corridor locked away. But there is maybe something for him in the classroom, the one with the door open.

She keeps her head, and tries to keep calm.

'Fuck you,' he says in the end, quivering, uncertain which way to go – and walks out. As it is, he ambles to the door as though any second he might change his mind, and then runs out across the yard, while she moves swiftly to the office to raise the alarm. By the time the police arrives, he's disappeared.

About four o'clock on a cold November day the children are milling outside after school, some playing football, but most of them on their way home. There's rain in the air. Then some of them see this guy on the roof with a gun in his hand. Looking down from his position on the New Building it must seem like a Breughel painting, the bright-coated gaggles of children rambling noisily, cheerfully out of the building and down the road, a handful of parents dotted here and there. Then you notice a helicopter hovering above sweeping down, the drone attracting attention as it comes lower. Those children who notice what is going on stare excitedly up at the roof. It is a true-life scene out of NYPD Blue – a man on the roof with a gun in his hand. Far from this scaring the children off, more and more come to watch and point, and a few of them run to me: 'Sir, sir, there's this man with a gun on the roof.'

I'm out there with the others by now, the helicopter hovering over the man's head; and at this point – it all happens quickly – the guy leaps down and runs across the yard out into the road, and hares off at full pace in the direction of Grove Lane. The helicopter follows, tracking him down, and a few children chase after him to see what's happened – only to be disappointed. No gun goes off; the gangster disappears from view; and no doubt at some point or other the police pick him up. There were no reports in the press of any violence. No one, fortunately, got hurt.

Sometimes people do get hurt, however. One teacher is attacked at the bus stop just outside the school and runs in shocked and crying. She has fought the attacker off and has grabbed her little daughter, who is a pupil. Another teacher tackles a guy breaking into her car in the playground: he has picked the wrong victim and she bashes him as he runs away.

One teacher is not so lucky. She's a young Asian teacher, who is very talented and very bright, with a top-class university degree. Like others, she sets off home late after an evening of preparing work in school for the next day. At the bus stop she's attacked by two black guys who grab her bag, which gets caught in her arm and she's dragged some distance across the ground, and bangs her head violently on a lamp post. Severely injured, she's left lying semi-conscious in the gutter, while the boys run off. An onlooker, a middle-aged man, stands there doing nothing. But in the end someone comes to her rescue and rings an ambulance. She is in hospital for some weeks, with severe head and back injuries, and then has to stay in bed, in plaster, for many more, unable to move and in considerable pain. We are all deeply distressed. Why should young people come to work in situations that involve such risk? After twelve months she returns to the school, first part-time and then full-time: her commitment is undiminished.

That sadly may be seen as par for the course if you're going to risk working in areas like this. Nurses are attacked on duty in hospitals as well – the local news recently had a report of a young nurse being punched in the face. Social workers, too, are profoundly vulnerable. Why do it? Would I want my daughter to take on this kind of work? I read a piece by Chris Woodhead, the Chief Inspector of Schools, which makes me deeply angry, saying that teachers should stop whining and be more like mountain-climbers, and face up to the toughness of the real world.

There were a number of people, some of whom I knew personally, in management, in Government, who I would have liked to have stood by our teacher's bed, in her house, not so far from the school, where she was strapped up for six months. I had the furious sense that the evil of casual indifference was perhaps not merely the province of young unemployed black muggers in Handsworth, but something more pervasive that was spreading through the machinery of politics and management. This indifference surely comes from a lack of imagination, a failure to understand, or feel for, or care about, the people you employ, such as those who work day by day in places like Handsworth.

52
The Tragedy

In the bonfire season, the local kids burn down the play-slide we have bought partly from money raised ourselves and partly with a Children in Need grant. Others have battered the climbing frames with hammers. We warn the children about fireworks, but this doesn't stop local boys hurling bangers into the playground.

Bashir and Parvinder are amiable nine-year-olds with a touch of roguish villainy. Bashir has a disabled father and by all accounts little moral sense. Caught up in petty theft and unpredictable behaviour from time to time he falls out with his father and disappears for the day. His saving grace in life is his handsomeness. The more naive kinds of girls are attracted to him but a suave, confident swagger conceals an unmistakable impulsiveness and irresponsibility. He's a boy who does things but rarely thinks about what he's doing.

Parvinder's father has left home. He marched out of the house a year ago, leaving his young wife with two small boys to look after. Occasionally he drops by, although he is now living way across the city. Parvinder's mother lives in a little corner house near the school.

Parvinder is elfin-sized, with bright eyes and an appealing open manner. Almost his first act on arriving as a new boy at the school is to show me his stamp collection. I bring some of my own stamps to give him and for a while, through Parvinder's enthusiasm, we run a stamp-club.

That was last year. This year as he is growing older, he's getting wilder. One week he wanders off for the day – a warm summer's day – with his friend, Bashir. They use their Monday's dinner money to fund a bonanza of bus-rides and buzz off to West Bromwich where they ramble round the shops, up to no good. When he finds out, Bashir's father goes ballistic and sends him to bed. I punish Parvinder at the request of his mother. She can manage him, she says, most of the time but he is getting more difficult. He was not a bad boy, but naughtier than his brother.

'He needs a father's hand,' she says, sadly, explaining that she looks after him on her own.

Is she really saying that things are not going well, that she's finding it hard to manage? Are there any indications that she's asking for more help? Should I have taken a closer interest in the family? I visit the home once or twice, but only to check out whether Parvinder is behaving himself. There had been a problem getting him to bed, but that seems to have been resolved. He appears to be back on track: there is no more truancy, and his behaviour at school has never been a problem. He is a happy-go-lucky sort, trouble-free, a child everyone likes. I don't feel it's necessary to visit his home again.

It's a warm night, sultry with no rain, dark by nine o'clock. The local kids play out late and do things they're not supposed to do like climbing fences, knocking on doors and running away, scrambling into backyards, kicking footballs about, until it is hard to see what they're doing. There is plenty of rough ground to explore, an Amazon forest of broken bricks, damp boxes, the rusting entrails of mashed-up old cars, stacks of wooden crates. Every so often the boys light fires. Traders and even households leave stuff lying about, piling up to rot. There's one garden with heaps of dead chicken bits smelling to high heaven, which raise grumbles from the neighbours. Kids sometimes get into parked cars and batter them into the school fences, playing cat and mouse with the police who roam round occasionally in cars, but are for the most part rarely seen. Others get on roofs and throw stones, or pull the slates and crash them into the playground. Some of this behaviour is pure mindless destruction, some of it inventively wicked. One teenage boy called Pinky inscribes his name regularly in giant pink letters across the school windows in indelible spray paint.

It was Bashir's idea to play at the back of the garage where the big tins are. They can be rolled and climbed on and drummed with sticks, which drives people mad so that occasionally they run out of their houses and eff and blind them away.

Bashir, Parvinder and a couple of older boys manage to roll one of the big barrels out of the yard into the street outside the school, where they sit on it and bang on it. Then one of them has the bright idea of setting it on fire. They throw a match into it, and it explodes.

Parvinder is standing too close. He may have been the one to throw the match. When the oily fire explodes volcanically, it showers him and sets his clothes alight, so that immediately he's totally on fire. Screaming, he runs towards his house like a burning firework, while the oil burns through his clothes to the skin. His mother, hearing him screaming, runs out and traps him in the folds of a carpet and rolls him on the floor to try and put the flames out. She could not have done more. Other neighbours run out of their houses, and ambulances, fire-engines, the police are summoned.

Interviews with the police follow. The other shocked boys are checked over and eventually taken home. The man who owns the garage is asked why he'd left such volatile material so accessibly exposed. He argues, no doubt with some justification, that it was on his property at the back and that the boys had effectively broken in. But there were no locks.

Parvinder is rushed by ambulance to hospital and at once into intensive care. He has 90% body burns and visitors are not allowed to see him. He dies a few days later. His teacher is traumatized along with the rest of the school. She points out the irony – absurdly beginning to blame herself – that the class had recently been going through a curriculum programme about safety in the home, and that a week or two back they'd even looked at the dangers of fire and the importance of not carrying matches, and so on. 'Perhaps I put the idea into his head?' she says, knowing, as we all knew, that this was not very likely.

I begin to think that I could have done more: I could have put Parvinder on a yellow home-card to check out his behaviour there, and given his mother more support. There were other children in the school I'd put on curfew: they had to be home and in bed by a certain time. I could have visited him more regularly and taken on more of the role of the absent father. The reality is that little Parvinder is dead. For all the hundreds of other children at school, there seems to be a great hole in their lives.

This is strange. It is as if Parvinder was all along by far the most significant person in the school. Now he is not there you notice every space he used to occupy; you remember every visit he made to you, every contact; his voice seems to be trying to say something; your mind fixes obsessively on the stamps, his work, his tiny neat handwriting. You don't know what to do with his books, his pens and his desk. The whole school is flooded with Parvinder, and even though conversation may be about other things, everyone is thinking of him.

It reminds you how important a single soul is, and how a community is a group of uniquely important individuals. For me it was a reminder of risks and responsibilities. In my hands I have the lives of hundreds of children: how easy it is for one mistake to be made, one thing forgotten that may lead to something terrible happening. The children must above all be safe. But there is no safety in life.

The funeral is the saddest of affairs. Parvinder's mother seems to have aged; for the moment she is like an old woman. Her diminutive second child, the spitting image of Parvinder, stands by her side. I admire and respect her – she had done what she could, and somehow she had kept going – and I try to tell her so.

The women, weeping, pass through the house past the small flowered coffin laid out in the best room. I stand by Bashir, holding his hand. Throughout Bashir shows no reaction, no expression, as though he is imprisoned in some deep, private well of puzzlement. I have told Bashir that it was not his fault, that he should not blame himself. The death of a child is the same for all cultures, and there are people from every ethnic group at the crematorium. It is as if representatives of the whole world have come together in silence.

Afterwards I stand with the little gathering outside in the sunshine and watch the puffs of dark smoke rising slowly from the crematorium chimney – not many of them, frail, hanging together in the air for a moment and then rapidly disappearing in the light autumn breeze.

53
The Children

It is easy to forget the children. A researcher into Ofsted's use of language found to his surprise how rarely the word 'children' featured in their reports. There is a danger of children being seen as an afterthought in a system that is constantly expanding its plans to control schools, to keep everyone's nose to the grindstone. The fashion has been to focus heavily on discipline, on formalities. Children are no longer smacked, at least at school, but they are given rafts of targets and tests in regimes which are ever more intrusive. Children are universally expected to wear school uniform; homework even for the younger ones is demanded by the state; and I visit schools where children are told to remain silent for long periods of time in classrooms, and when moving about in corridors. They are far more likely to be suspended from school, their parents being expected to discipline them in circumstances that ten years earlier would have been handled by the school alone. Since the mid 1980s there has been exponential growth, year on year, in exclusions and suspensions.

There are times when I feel that the world of schooling is closing around these children in a form of tyranny. It's becoming increasingly hard to maintain a multi-dimensional curriculum, to find adequate time for the arts, or for the kinds of calm activities that allow individual learning and space for them to think and play with ideas. A recent Ofsted inspection at a local school is damning about 'circle time', an arrangement where children sit in a circle for a short-time discussing their feelings openly.

'What has this,' said the Ofsted team, 'to do with the National Curriculum? Why aren't they working?'

Children must at all costs achieve their levels in maths, science and language; and if other things get pushed out, so be it. But in the late 1990s schools began to report a reaction from youngsters against this regime with increasing incidence of despondency and disillusionment.

The desire to discipline the children tightly, such a constant concern amongst parents, is accompanied by ever more stringent state intervention for child protection, with the consequence that parents are a great deal less sure than in previous generations how best to manage their children. Some have given up altogether. Others discipline them with little idea of balance or moderating justice or prior discussion, deploying uncontrolled temper tantrums and casual violence – reactions which often seem to be mere cries of desperation. Child management in general is becoming both more liberal and more erratic, and children find themselves increasingly caught between the more permissive world of child management at home, the artificial constraints and structures at school, and the increasingly violent and hazardous world of the streets. There is far more bullying in schools and far more street violence than there was ten years ago. One year a dozen of our children came to me after they had started their new secondary school to arrange a transfer because of the level of personal violence they were experiencing from other pupils at the school. All of them eventually dispersed to other schools.

Traditional deference towards adults has changed. The role of fathers is increasingly uncertain. We in turn are more deferential to our children, more uneasy about punishing them, and more likely to try to negotiate with them, and to walk away from poor behaviour. Children are more likely to be brought up under the authority of their mothers and to have absent or weakly functioning fathers.

Men seem to be increasingly diffident in relating to children, and there are far fewer men coming into teaching. Soon some children's entire first decade of life will be largely free from the influence of an adult male.

Lack of trust in authority and child-protection legislation have had the unforeseen effect of widening the separation between the school and the home. We now have a national procedure for suspension or exclusion which schools everywhere are using more and more often. I am myself still extremely reluctant to suspend children, which seems to me often to be an abdication of authority – the equivalent of washing your hands of the child, saying to parents, sorry, he's your problem not mine. I still think that when they are asked by parents, schools ought to give support in bringing up children, and sometimes take quasi-parental responsibility for them. I'm aware that many homes round here see me as a kind of add-on father, and I'm not sure this is a bad thing.

It is increasingly fashionable to see children as being entitled to the same rights as adults under the law, and we consequently treat them *less like children*. But they sometimes benefit from the containment that comes from knowing that there are appropriate parental sanctions for particular kinds of irresponsible behaviour. Many children no longer know what the boundaries are that adults set, and under what rules these should be obeyed. The school surely does have a role here in supporting parents and offering one more layer of security for children both inside and outside school.

Children's views on these matters are more complex and less predictable than is often assumed. Two girls in my philosophy group wrote an essay on discipline after a moral philosophy discussion. It was subsequently published in a national newspaper (for which they both earned fifty pounds). My group voted for tougher discipline all round, so long as it was imposed within a commonsensical and caring framework. They qualified this tough-guy attitude by arguing that schools and parents should only impose sanctions which have the prior approval of the children – a view that is not so far from my own.

I am conscious of how much childhood has changed since I first came to the school. There is, I think, a loss of innocence. Children are more exposed. I ask in assembly how many people have seen the film *Silence of the Lambs* and half the school put their hands in the air. There is more sexual awareness. In the sex education lessons that are now incorporated into the health programme, children ask uninhibited and remarkably adult questions. There is no possibility that this 1990s generation of children could behave like the group of naughty and innocent ten-year-old girls who twenty years ago once took all their clothes off on a hot day, and lay flat out and naked like impressionist bathers on the grass in the school playground 'for a dare'.

The barriers between childhood and adulthood have become less clear. Unlike twenty years ago, there is now a consumer society that specifically targets children. Children watch adult television, talk fashion, enjoy discos and are sensitive about boy- and girlfriends at a much younger age. They also start to worry earlier about careers, the difficulty of getting jobs, the hazards of the marketplace.

It's understandable that young people should start to carve out their own areas of freedom sooner and look at ways to escape into the alternative worlds of boyfriends, popular music and fashion, the internet and teenage angst.

Meanwhile they become more vulnerable, especially those who suffer inadequate parenting, unable to develop empathy, balance, and to understand the importance of boundaries. The number of children with mental health problems is on the rise, and most headteachers feel that the special needs provision in the city continues to be inadequate.

It strikes me that children these days need a new kind of resilience: their belief in themselves needs to be very strong. It is almost invariably the self-motivated, well-balanced children who in the long run do best. They learn how to *survive*. Such inner toughness, such personal integrity, is enough to hold them firm against the bewildering flow of demands and problems that the changing world throws their way. It is possible that children may increasingly turn away from formal education, disillusioned by what schools have to offer. For this is a generation that will increasingly be in a position to choose; and by early adolescence many are already largely free from their parents' influence.

Some are in fact beginning to opt out completely, especially those who loathe the new educational marketplace of competition and grades. They are more interested in the real-world marketplace, in which they can develop their own values, for better or worse. They can, as it were, choose a lifestyle for themselves.

Many of the Grove children have the advantage of cultural stability, local reference points in religion and child-rearing traditions which, though old-fashioned, continue to give a modicum of security, some protection.

I'm encouraged when one day a class delegates two spokespersons – both of them girls – to complain to me about a supply teacher.

'Can we speak to you privately, sir?'

'Sure – what is it?'

'We're not happy with Mr ... the supply teacher. We think you should do something about him.'

'What's wrong?'

The three of us sit down with the door closed to discuss the matter. I have sometimes talked to the children about 'professionalism', what it means to behave appropriately in a community, or in a job. The two girls remind me of what I have been saying.

'His behaviour is *inappropriate* ...'

One of the girls is in my advanced writing group and understands perfectly what this means. 'He pushed Rashid against the wall ... He shouts too much, and doesn't listen ...'

'He's a bully,' says the other girl, straight to the point.

'Are you being fair to him?' I ask. 'Isn't he just trying to be strict?'

'You should be there. You wouldn't approve. You wouldn't let him push people around. You wouldn't let him hit us ...'

'Hit you? Give me an example.'

And the examples begin to flow, subtle little assaults, verbal abuse and occasional 'accidental' hitting. It is not a difficult class. The girls are measured and calm, presenting their case as though it is in a court of law. I can see them, one day, as lawyers. 'I'll check it out,' I say. Which I do immediately, by questioning the whole class, and collating the overwhelming evidence.

'Why didn't you say anything before?'

'We told him. We wanted to give him a chance.'

'Didn't you tell your parents?'

'We thought you should know first.'

It is a remarkable example of comradeship, of organized collaboration, the whole class working together.

I sent the teacher straight out of the school. 'I've had these complaints,' I said. 'I'm convinced by them. I want you to leave immediately.' He went without a word, although as he was a Local Authority teacher, and had been given a long-term placement, I expected a call from the LEA telling me that I was exceeding my authority. I had not had a full investigation; I had not discussed the incidents with the member of staff; I was subject to a union-driven grievance procedure, and had not gone through the proper disciplinary steps. I had simply sent him away. But I heard nothing of him again, either from the Authority or from anywhere else.

I apologized to the class, and said it should not have happened. The teacher had been dismissed, and I was impressed by the professional way they had handled things. They sat in silence, gravely, and nodded their appreciation and understanding with the quietness of a jury that has considered a case with the greatest care and finally passed judgement.

These days I run a philosophy group with a view to getting children to think clearly, argue cogently, interrogate issues intelligently, and as a side-product revive the ancient tradition of writing good argumentative essays. What I teach for the most part is epistemology: I encourage them to decide why they think what they do. How can they know something for sure? What does it mean in the contemporary world to *know*? This can lead to a discussion of values, a moral debate covering a wide range of issues to do with justice, child-rearing, the law, democratic decision-making and what it means to be an educated person. Even these nine-to-ten-year-olds can deal with such things with surprising subtlety and sophistication if they are helped with the linguistic and thinking processes that are involved.

A small girl talks to an interested visitor who asks whether it is possible to know anything for certain.

'Of course,' says the girl, 'Descartes said "Cogito ergo sum": do you know what that means? *I think therefore I am*. Do you think that's right?' she says. 'Does it mean that my cat doesn't exist unless it can think?'

She pauses to consider and smiles at the visitor.

'Of course it does think, at least I *think* it thinks.'

A balance between encouraging independent thinking and fulfilling the skills-based target-setting expectations of the state is hard to achieve. The state, like the parent, can easily get the balance wrong and forget that not all the best learning is achieved in a behaviourist world of rewards and penalties, test-results and performance-indicators. Education may be more than ever a *business*; but all schools, and maybe primary schools in particular, have a role to play in listening to children, understanding their needs and feelings.

In spite of the current hype about young children and the importance of their education, children remain a very low-budget priority. The state is in many respects an indifferent and parsimonious parent. In 1997 2% of the National Lottery receipts was spent on children under sixteen who make up 25% of the population. A third less was spent by the state on an eleven-year-old child in a primary school than on an eleven-year-old in a secondary school. Yet we know that investment in parenting and the early years makes a disproportionately large impact on health, on emotional stability and on future academic achievement. It is as if our commitment to young children in an age of rapid change and scientific discovery has not moved on since the nineteenth century.

Maybe the school has become something of an oasis. These days, children at Grove seem to grow up much more quickly; but they have become progressively better behaved as the years have gone by, and the school environment is relaxed and happy. The traumas and outbursts of the past are rare. There is an openness and good humour that is exactly, I think, what we have been aiming for all along.

I think the school is at its best when there seems, however fleetingly, to be a resolution of the differences between children and adults – the creation of a culture in which they can come together in a relaxed way, with mutual respect. Above all, children and adults need to find ways in which they can constructively *converse*.

Conversation is losing out in the age of television and computers, especially in large families and in relatively poor homes. When children are young, we have a real opportunity to talk freely and openly with them before they move into the group cultures of adolescence and experience the tribal barriers that modern youth cultures can impose. In primary schools we should take full advantage of a summer of relationships between children and adults when we can talk to each other in depth. There are times when teachers can have a profound influence, by building on trust, discussing issues which children are able to handle at this age. This generation talks much more openly about such matters as sex and drugs, smoking, crime and punishment. A liberal culture, a calm ability to listen to what children have to say, helps serious and sustained thinking on matters of real importance.

I play some Rachmaninov in the hall through the new Bose speakers and ask the children in assembly: 'Who's that composer with the big hands?' 'Rachmaninov,' they all chorus. The music is romantic but tinged as all Rachmaninov is with melancholy. It seems like the music of lovers, or of old age. Yet the children attend closely, and they sit in silence listening. For a moment, there is a compatibility of interest, a harmonious connection between the children and the adults in this place, a common reference point.

We now have a school council and Tracy, our new second deputy, has trained children as mediators to deal with difficult behaviour at breaks and dinner-times. These children handle situations as well as adults. Quarrelsome or misbehaving children at, say, lunchtime are brought into one of the offices to which the child mediators have open access, and two of them listen to their stories, negotiate, conciliate and pass judgement. In some cases they call in a teacher to act in a disciplinary role.

'You may not agree with me,' says one exasperated mediator, 'but I really think that this child needs sorting out.'

On another occasion, I walk into my room and find two

children talking to two dinner ladies who have apparently been shouting at each other in the playground, and the children are dealing with them just as they would with a couple of naughty kids. Tracy and Mandy, two of our expert staff, pilot the 'circle time' I have mentioned, and show us how to get children to discuss their feelings and problems. This turns out to be a powerful device to help them think more sensitively about each other and to counter bullying.

I have a long conversation with Ingrid, one of our Afro-Caribbean teachers, who has now been at the school for ten years. She believes that what affects our children most in the long run is the quality of their day-to-day experience. If their experience has been warm, challenging, memorable for them personally, it will drive them on to greater things. She says that she meets former pupils who were unspectacular at school but have emerged ten years on with all manner of unexpected successes. The problem I have with this – and of course I want to believe it – is how do I *know*, how can anyone know, that it is the way the school *is* that makes the difference? How many individual anecdotes do you need to prove your point? How can it be measured?

This is surely not a generation that is easily soft-soaped. It has been part of our mission to breed a little scepticism. To encourage the children to ask questions, form hypotheses, turn problems into puzzles. Are we training our children to think clearly? For themselves? It seems to me what we need right now is a spirit of questioning in a world where half-truths, sloppy rhetoric, seductive advertising, the misuse of evidence, media-driven opinion command the field. All very remote from that spirit of evidence-based caution in which my jury of children formulated, managed and finally – almost reluctantly – passed judgement on that unhappy supply teacher.

54
Blair's Speech

In May 1996 Tony Blair, the leader of the Labour party, gave an address in Southwark Cathedral during which he named Grove School as a model of good practice, particularly in dealing with more able pupils.

On the following Sunday the BBC Today programme tracked me down to ask for an interview early on Monday morning. In the Pebble Mill Studio, at some unearthly hour, I was closeted on my own in a tiny room, equipped with earphones and a microphone, and answering questions about 'accelerated learning' and 'fast tracking' and ways in which schools could best deal with talented pupils. This was one of those subjects that require you to steer a course between rocks.

> What is a talented child anyway? Aren't you in danger of just hot-housing children like species of tropical plant?

In the interview I noted the dangers of moving children on too fast, and pressuring them too much. Some parents, I said, were over-anxious to do their best for their children, which resulted in such over-pressuring. One of our girls had failed against expectation to make it to the grammar school. (Birmingham still had the old eleven-plus exam.) Her mother wept every time the matter was mentioned, blaming the school, the child herself, the system, even the weather on the Saturday morning of the exam. It had been like a family bereavement, and you could only wonder how the girl herself survived the trauma.

There was plenty of evidence that many children who went to the local comprehensive schools did just as well as their grammar-school peers (given an equal academic starting-point, a level-headed family and good motivation), and went on to sixth forms and university careers. But this didn't cut any ice. Some people refused to believe such things, preferring to worry about all the rough kids in the area, the drop-outs, the truants, the 'riff-raff' – as they called them – who also went to the local schools. Who would want their child mixed up with them?

On the other hand, there seemed to me little doubt that there were also many children with talents that were not only unfulfilled at school, but sometimes not even noticed at all.

I had been down my own road to Damascus on this issue. One day I had come into the large school hall in the Old Building early in the morning – at about eight o'clock when it was normally empty. I was stopped suddenly by the distant sound of the octaves of the opening bars of Rachmaninov's third piano concerto from the school's upright piano. A small Vietnamese boy, eight years old, was playing on it merrily, in the right key (D minor), and more or less accurately. 'Where did you learn to play that?'

'I heard it on the TV.'

'Really?'

(It was the morning after the Leeds Piano Competition that had been televised by the BBC.)

'Can you play anything else?'

'I can play this.'

He strummed with both hands a jangly piece in E flat.

'Where d'you hear that?'

'With my mom in town.'

'How?'

'Shopping. There was this guy playing ...'

'You remember?'

'Yeh. It's easy.'

'You've had piano lessons.'

He looked at me quizzically.

'I've got a keyboard ...'

'Where?'

'At home, under the bed.'

It was a large family, who could hardly have known that the boy had perfect pitch. We arranged for him to have piano lessons, eventually persuading a local trust to cover the cost. But the real issue lay deeper. Why didn't we know that the boy had such a natural gift? He was eight and no one knew. That we knew now was only because by luck I'd happened to wander into the hall at the right time, and caught him being naughty – creeping in on his own when he knew he shouldn't. So how many more children were out there with similar talents, in artistic and other activities? The middle-class child with an attentive parent arranging music or ballet or other activities for them had a huge advantage over our children, and I doubted whether many schools had developed antennae for such talent, and were offering a whole range of experiences and the diagnostic follow-up that identifies signs of the specially gifted. I guessed that many children in areas like Handsworth were falling through the net.

What then was the case for making special arrangements for especially able children? Let's suppose, I would argue, that you have Daniel Barenboim or Vadim Repin, someone with, say, amazing instrumental talent at a very early age. Are you going to stick to teaching them the scale of C? Are you going to say 'You've got to wait until the others catch up', as one of our most able mathematicians was told on arrival in her secondary school? Surely not. You sail, in a measured way, with the following-wind of the child's talent, nurturing it both by creating space for exploration and experiment, and by ensuring that the child moves forward and practises, and that its talent develops.

This takes subtle teaching focused at the level of the child's ability. It often requires special tutoring, and this in turn requires organizational adjustments. The school routine has to adapt to the particular needs of its various individuals rather than children just fitting into established age- and group-orientated systems.

Such complications are of course impossible to put over in a two to three minute interview on the Today programme. The media simplifies. You rarely get the chance to say everything you want to say. The interview scarcely got beyond saying: 'Here's a school fast-tracking ten-year-olds to GCSE. Isn't that different!' If nothing else, it was newsworthy.

But not, I imagined, so newsworthy as to be more than a one-programme wonder. I set off back to school at about eight-thirty, assuming that this was the end of the affair. But I hadn't perceived that the press already saw Blair as the Prime Minister heir presumptive, and it was a day when there was – as is often the case on a Monday – not much in the way of other news.

I arrived back to a mass invasion by the media. Over the next couple of hours, four TV crews from different companies turned up and journalists from virtually all the serious dailies. A phone call came from Millbank, Labour's headquarters, and I was asked to write a piece for the *Daily Mail*, which I did, but which wasn't published. The BBC Midlands Today news programme drove a lorry with a high rig into the Upper School playground, aiming to put out a series of live transmissions during the day.

I found myself positioned in my room with a one-piece earphone, answering a range of questions from interviewers. There was subsequent commentary from parents, teachers' unions (the NASWT was notably hostile), and politicians.

Journalists prowled around the school and TV cameras roved about, filming children at their lessons and in the playgrounds. I gave them carte blanche to go anywhere, to film as they saw fit, and hoped for the best. You had in the end to trust the commonsense of the film and production teams and the children themselves. If negative reports emerged, then they were likely (like positive ones too) to be passing wonders, and to make little difference in the long run. It was easy to get it all out of perspective: today we were besieged with wondrous interest but tomorrow would be another day and the army would march on, turning the spotlight elsewhere.

It was interesting, of course, to be spotlighted, if only for a moment.

Two little girls walking to their maths group chatter in front of the journalist from the *Independent*.

'It's nice to have these cameras all over the place,' says one to the other, 'but doesn't it distract you from your work!'

Two boxes of smarties are quietly given next day. The girls look at me in surprise.

'What's this for, sir?'

'Good PR,' I say.

'What's PR?'

'PR means saying the right thing at exactly the right time. It's very hard to do.'

They still looked puzzled.

'Saying nice things to the visitors yesterday,' I say.

'Oh – yeh.'

But they can't remember what they said.

Tony Blair had mentioned maths in his speech and it was the maths department in part that they wanted to see. Ann, now our deputy, as Gilroy had moved on to a headship of his own, took the fast-track maths group of some thirty-six children and was used to visitors. Besides, she was one of the finest teachers anyone was ever likely to see. For some of the time the class would always run the lesson themselves while she watched – and there was the usual brilliant panache. But then we directed the journalists across the road to film the younger children. Lunchtime came with more live news transmissions and interviews for ITV; and then later in the afternoon an interview for Channel Four News.

It was Channel Four News that won the prize for length and depth, for their measured probing and for their attention to detail and accuracy. They occasionally asked if they'd got it right – and whether I wanted to say more or clarify a point.

'How do children cope in secondary school, when they're so advanced?'

I argued that if their talent had been music and not maths we wouldn't have been asking such questions.

'The advanced maths group is a very large group: does this mean you don't think smaller classes are important?'

This was partly, I said, a matter of resources. But very able children at similar levels of ability can be taught effectively in large groups for at least some of the time. Our advanced maths teacher had a very special ability to communicate and focus on the development of individuals, and to put in a huge amount of time making sure they were keeping up. She also grouped them carefully so that they could work at different levels of ability. On the other hand, without substantial extra resources I doubted whether you could sustain this level of quality across the board for every aspect of the curriculum. *Yes*, the size of this group does have radical implications for the organization of schooling. *Yes*, it is based on thinking about individual children's needs and abilities, and not merely on 'classes' or 'blocks of age-related teaching'.

'Do other children get envious?'

Not, I argued, if they understood the principle of what we were trying to do – which was to bring out individual talent wherever it is to be found. We have advanced clubs for dance; we have made a lot of use of talent in acting, music, badminton. Why should maths be any different?

So the questions flowed on. *Yes*, there are many children with special needs and we're far from solving all our problems. *No*, while my own children went through this school, this is a school servicing a socially and economically disadvantaged community, and the overall results would reflect this.

The camera continued to roll. I had no idea how much of this was going to be on air.

'Should other schools try to copy what you are doing? That seemed to be Mr Blair's message?'

No, the point wasn't that every school should try to copy us. Ours was a large school, which gave us some flexibility in the use of resources, and we had a spare classroom. Ours was simply a particular solution to a particular problem. It wasn't the only solution. There was the potential of information technology, of making increased used of specialist teachers, of closer linking with secondary schools, and of improved out-of-school learning programmes: there were plenty of other approaches that might be more appropriate to local circumstances.

I smiled. The presenter, looking straight at me from behind the camera, smiled back, and it was hard to say how convinced he really was.

The reports the next day were wide-ranging in detail and accuracy, and often comic. One paper, headlined 'Dr Dunkley and his Famous School', got every single factual detail wrong: my name, the name of the school, Handsworth, and so on. One journalist had picked it up that we had a Unit for excluded pupils, and ran a story about 'Excluded pupils who take GCSE'. Only one newspaper, the *Yorkshire Post*, was positively hostile, probably because of its generally Conservative stance. But they hadn't sent anyone to see the school. On the other hand, the Editor rang to offer me a space to put 'my point of view', which I declined to do.

But none of them were *unfair*. The general ethos of Grove came over all right and the spirit of the pieces was positive and balanced. Maybe the folk realized that I was basically supportive of the workaday journalist (which was almost the career I had myself taken up) and felt they had a useful, informative role. More than one journalist tackled me, after spending time in the school, saying rather gloomily: 'Makes me think I've wasted my life – this is what I should have been doing.'

55
Fame

There was a continuing media interest in the school after the panoply of rigs, TV cameras and journalists had gone away.

Over the last few years we'd already had many contacts with the press and the broadcasting media – some of which had looked risky at the time. On one occasion, the *News of the World* rang through to the school at a time when I was out. It was surprising how your whole life could run in front of you. What had we done? What were they up to? I rang back to try to track down the contact from an education department which didn't exist.

'Sorry, boss, have you got a name?'

I hadn't got a name, and tried to explain who I was.

'Sorry, mate, can't help you, it's not my story.'

'It came from your education section,' I said hopefully.

There was a pause, and I heard the young man yell across to someone else, 'Angie, do we have an education section?'

'Nope,' he came back; 'sorry, we don't have an education section. You need a name.'

But the story that finally came out the following Sunday was from an over-enthusiastic parent who lived on the other side of the city, and who had brought her child to our school because, as she explained, 'he was hugely talented, and this school brings out the best in talented pupils.' We read this entertaining piece with some relief.

The BBC approached us to run a feature on the school, to which we agreed. Then at the last minute, a day or so before filming, we were told that a little girl and her mother were to be brought up from a middle-class area in Sussex to 'see how she would get on in a school like yours'. The idea was that she should spend the day in lessons with the Grove children, and follow one or two of the specialist teaching groups with her mother watching. At the end of the day the mother and child would be interviewed separately to get them to talk frankly about the experience. This looked to me at first sight another risky proposition.

The child was at a perfectly reasonable primary school back home, but felt insufficiently challenged. The mother also clearly thought her child was special academically. With my previous experience of such mothers, my heart sank. Handsworth was a very different proposition from leafy Sussex: it probably couldn't be *more* different; and, for an innocent nine-year-old, coming here must seem like flying to a new, exotic country. Things might turn out all right, but they could also go badly wrong. We needn't have worried. There is something moving about the generosity and warmth of our children, their ability to put you at your ease. Their liveliness and immediate confident eye-contact, and pride in themselves, came over in the programme. They seem these days to have an ingrained amiability, and to take life good-humouredly and in their stride.

Sion, the nine-year-old, turned out to be a common-sensical, well-balanced, fun-loving child who was not in the least over-awed by her experience. She was also, just as her mother suspected, unusually smart and inquiring. It wasn't long before she had settled in and was really enjoying herself. She found the school very demanding intellectually: she joined the fast-track maths and language and philosophy groups. She was interviewed both with her mother and on her own at the end of the day, and said how much she loved it here; how she found it really lively and challenging. Her mother was equally enthusiastic. But perhaps the most engaging contribution to the programme was from a Grove girl who, when asked what she thought about new children coming into the school, 'especially children who have special talents', said that there was a 'place for everyone at this school,' and 'wasn't everybody talented in some way?'

The programme led to a shoal of letters from parents across the country asking how they could best encourage accelerated learning in their own children. My response to this was conventional, and no doubt felt by some to be disappointing. There is, I said, no magic way of increasing the abilities of children beyond commonsense, lots of discussion with them and encouragement of the imaginative exploration of all manner of educational experience, and, especially with young children, the arts. Self-confidence, I pointed out, was as crucial as was good humour.

We made a BBC2 programme about 'Special Needs' which featured Baroness Warnock, who spent a day at the school. It was a very enjoyable day with such a sensitive and highly intelligent observer, who talked easily with the staff and children, and obviously really liked the school. We started with the children singing 'This Little Light of Mine' at full volume in the assembly (which Mary loved).

The programme showed various clips of conversation between us, one of them about an extraordinary piece of writing by a beautiful and interesting girl, Usha, who was one of the most brilliant contributors to my philosophy class over the years. A long shot was taken of Mary and myself walking slowly across the playground in the Old Building. It had to be done over and over again, as we either walked too fast or in the wrong direction at the wrong camera-angle. We chatted away, becoming increasingly amused, and at one point collapsed with laughter to the annoyance of the director. It was really an enchanting day and what finally appeared on the programme was a sustained analysis of our efforts to develop children's ability at both ends of the ability spectrum.

We were also featured in a number of Government publications, which highlighted various aspects of the school. At a Government conference to launch the new policy of target-setting, the Secretary of State, Gillian Shepherd, suddenly announced that 'Grove School was the originator of the idea'. It was certainly true that by now we had developed our assessment programme to give more detailed performance-information to the parents (in graphic computer read-outs) and to the teachers. We had long been tracking individual children, as I have mentioned, and could provide indicators on how they were performing which had clear implications for teaching. It allowed us to target groups or individuals for specialist teaching-groups or approaches. But it had been the idea of Tim Brighouse, our Chief Education Officer, to carry the concept one step further, setting 'targets' for whole-year groups for subsequent 'improvement over previous best'.

Everything depended, of course, on what you meant by targets. The subsequent Government policy of setting fixed-percentage targets to 'boost' whole-school performance and then publishing performance outcomes at the age of eleven was, I think, one step beyond what Tim Brighouse had intended, and certainly a long way from what we had in mind. I objected to the notion of there being abstract 'percentages' (e.g. 10% per year) by which a school or a child was expected to improve. This seemed to me plain nonsense, as figures of this kind plucked out of the blue make no allowance for the state of the school or for the individual child. For a special-needs child, a small improvement is often a dramatic breakthrough. For a very able child, massive acceleration was possible. Moreover, it was often beneficial for children to 'plateau' in order to have periods of play and consolidation, and, statistically speaking, make no progress at all for some time. Furthermore, our own data showed just how complicated the notion of 'improvement' and 'accelerated learning' really was – given that year groups vary so considerably in ability.

The purpose of our data seemed to me to be: (i) to give parents an honest view of the progress of their children in basic skills; (ii) to define groups of children for special 'inputs' of support to accelerate their progress; (iii) to give teachers at the beginning of the year a bird's eye view of their children's current performance in maths and language;

and (iv) to give me a full picture of the development of the children as a whole, year on year.

It was apparent from the mass of our data that the gaps between the low-achievers and the high-achievers widen year by year: low-ability special-needs children improve much more slowly than the mean, and so require a very intensive input of a kind that we had not yet – for all our efforts – managed to make available. We had instituted a second specialist unit called 'The Rocket' for intensive support, which was insufficiently equipped but did allow some useful gathering of information about the progressive small steps that the children were (or were not) taking. It also allowed us to experiment with the American IT system, 'Successmaker', which seemed one potentially effective support for children with specific learning difficulties. It was apparent, too, from our data that the younger the child was, the greater the impact you could make.

All this data gathering and 'accelerated learning' was to be turned by the Government into a national programme for schools, with all children being tested en masse, and all schools given 'targets' to reach – a procedure which led to a gross distortion of the curriculum. The schools concentrated heavily on children who might with a push just 'pass their test' and reach the Government's target Level 4, and consequently neglected the very children who needed the most resources and the most intensive support, that is, the very slow movers who in some places amounted to almost a third of the school. There was a good deal of under-the-carpet fixing and cheating. We got the blame for some of this, with the Government using and misusing our original idea to create an internal knowledge-gathering system. Our ambition to develop the database further into other curriculum areas was never fulfilled.

Photographs of children at the school began to appear in various newspapers with one particular photograph being syndicated – a brilliant picture of a little Chinese boy with his hand in the air during one of Ann's maths groups. There continued to be numerous items in the press about the school, and visitors were trekking in from all over the country. An entire town council came from Kilkenny in Ireland, and watched, astonished and amused, a lesson being taught on atomic physics by Ranjit, a university academic, as one of a series which he designed as a module for thirty children who were good at maths. A number of schools came to watch our theatrical productions as well and to sit in on various groups. Both Channel Four and BBC Newsnight filmed our philosophy group, and Ofsted paid us several further visits to look at our 'target-setting' programme and our new approach to computerizing the curriculum. Ofsted also came to puzzle out the success of our advanced-maths teaching. After one visit watching our new second deputy, Pam Matty, teach, an HMI reported ...

> Remarkably high attainment is evident amongst the pupils ... However, an equally interesting feature in my view is that these pupils have made very important progress in 'learning how to learn'. A dozen pupils whom I interviewed were very articulate. They could talk with me and with each other about their mathematics, all sharing in the discussion. Meta-cognition is very much a feature of the free interchange of ideas around the work table in the lesson ... The benefits being achieved at Grove are contained within normal timetable time and within normal staffing resources ... I was impressed by other features of the school though I do not elaborate these in this letter ...

On another visit, two lady HMIs spent time with our lunchtime reading-mentor groups in which twenty older children took on responsibility for helping the reading of younger children in years three and four. They were struck by the maturity of the children, by the way we had trained them to listen and converse and by the diligence with which the children worked. The HMIs had come to talk about our assessment system, but were distracted and amazed by this do-it-yourself reading recovery system, and wrote to tell me so.

We were visited at the same time by the Deputy Mayor of Chicago, and one girl fingered her dangling brooch. 'Nice bit of jewellery,' she commented.

We continued with our own privately commissioned external consultancy exercises (which we found incisive and critically constructive) especially those organized by an Ofsted Registered Inspector, Hugh Protheroe. The Vice-President and Managing Director of Volvo came as one of Hugh's inspection team to carry out an inspection of the management of the school and wrote back ...

> Whilst I have only very limited experience of Primary Schools, I have worked with and in many different types of organisations in my career, but none have made such a dramatic impression on me as your school. I came away with many impressions the most powerful of which came from the children whose confidence, enthusiasm and behaviour was inspiring and rewarding to experience ...

Then one day a journalist from *The Times* arrived. It was an unpromising visit, which began with her expressing some scepticism about the virtues of the state-school system. She spent the day walking uncommunicatively around the school. Some staff felt nervous: they were sure she was going to notice all our weaknesses. It was, therefore, a considerable surprise when in December, down in London, I happened to pick up the paper and found a full-page spread on the school headlined: 'Is this the Best School in Britain?'.[32] It was an odd experience to read this long and extraordinarily glowing account of the school in a newspaper so little noted for its celebration of schools in the state sector, let alone of an insignificant primary school in the heart of a poor part of provincial England.

I felt both moved and strangely detached.

In the centre of the article was a huge photograph of one of our children, Yasmin, with a piece of chalk in her hand demonstrating an algebraic formula on the blackboard to the children in the class. It was a great picture: her scarf was wrapped around her neck, her large glasses were tilted; her face was shining with what seemed like an intense delight. It caught Yasmin as she really was, gentle, lively-minded, enthusiastic and intellectually alert.

I was always surprised by the power of the reactions of so many people who came to the school. But I hadn't expected anything like this. *The Times* piece was an attempt to describe a complex of feelings and impressions, above all the impact the children made. It was, in its way, an old-fashioned eulogy, but it truly reflected the school as outsiders see it: it was in that respect a brilliant article, catching the atmosphere, the energy of the place with accurate detail. It pleased me in one other important respect. It caught a sense of the way the children were.

It made no pretence that the school was easy to run:

> An area of high unemployment, crime and the focus of inner city rioting in the 1980s would seem to have the odds stacked against it. Free school meals – an indicator of social need – are taken by up to 75% of pupils ...

But then the story unfolded:

> An air of industrious calm hangs over the classroom as, having read the story of Rapunzel, the children compose letters to the Wicked Witch. 'You best go away from here, Witch,' inscribes one child in a laborious hand, tongue protruding as he warms to his theme ... A mixed-age group tackles creative writing classes, philosophy and nuclear physics ... Pupils are encouraged to direct the competitive instinct against themselves, each child working with their teachers to set their own targets. A minor improvement by a less capable child is greeted as ecstatically as a huge leap in understanding by a brighter child ... High-quality pastoral care is a priority ... the children and staff both work within a positive culture. 'We respect each other and have high esteem about ourselves ...' The pupils are used to visitors, replying with confidence and enthusiasm to questions rather than seeing it as a welcome distraction ... Pupils of many different social and racial backgrounds mix

> happily with each other, and there is a spirit of genuine kindness ... Asked why they were keen to take on the burden of extra homework, the children came back with 'for the challenge' ... It is extraordinary to hear these children talking about periodic tables, neutrons and positrons with the ease other children talk about *Neighbours* ... Charlotte Barrett, 10, was aghast at the suggestion that they were especially clever ... 'we're all clever at something,' she said ... The emphasis is on the breadth of the curriculum, the strength of pastoral care and a stringent monitoring system ... The school boasts a jazz dance teacher, a specialist music teacher and an artist who incorporates art history into her practical classes ... Good communication with parents is important. A detailed grid of what each child is doing in each subject is sent home ...

It suggested that this was how schools of this kind ought to be, and was like a dazzling picture of a glittering, flat moon. What it didn't do was give a deeper, more rounded view of the continuing problems we faced. It didn't say, as I would have said, that anything achieved had been against a background of scanty resources. That there were far too few computers. That many ambitions seemed impossible to attain. For example, the children couldn't have the instrumental music lessons I would have liked. I couldn't open the school every evening, as I wanted to. Our work with the Rocket was still in its early stages, and there was a long way to go to tackle some of the learning problems. We needed to work intensively with the early-years children. It did not say that the Junior School had two years ago amalgamated with the Infant School, bringing the three-to-six-year-olds under our jurisdiction. It did not say that our curriculum programmes were far from reaching the level of perfection that I thought was required. I felt that the school, which certainly had made progress and had fantastic potential, was in fact working at 80% of its capacity. Worse, I could see no way that we would be able to fulfil the other 20% without substantial extra resources, smaller classes, longer hours and improved programmes both during the day and in the evenings. It did not say that in many respects these children, and children like them, got a raw deal. If we had done anything, we had produced glimpses of light, indicators, ways in which schooling might in the future move forward.

The articles, the impressions in the media, seemed to suggest that this was a school that had reached its goal, one to sit back and admire with satisfaction. This was not my view. Although to some it appeared we had reached Utopia, I knew it was still a long way off.

56

Discouragement

The Times article certainly didn't reflect the tone of articles in the mainstream press about schools in general, which were excessively negative, and often orchestrated, it seemed, by Government propaganda and by a flow of rhetoric from Ofsted that appeared to many to be opinionated and unbalanced, and based on a scattering of undigested and sometimes dubious evidence.

Jefferson once observed that 'bodies of men as well as individuals are susceptible to a spirit of tyranny'. Who now wanted to be a teacher? Fewer of the brightest graduates were opting to teach. Young people had become teachers through idealism and a commitment to public service. They had been prepared to overlook relatively low pay and many had been willing to teach less privileged children in inner cities. If, however, the trust and public respect that sustain teachers' pride and independence are taken away, then graduates will look elsewhere. Why, I asked, should my son want to teach when he can earn a great deal more as a lawyer? The future for education in the 1990s, as for the NHS, seemed to lie not with teachers or medical staff but with administrators and managers. In King's College, London, twenty years ago, more than half the English graduates went in for teaching. By the 1990s there were rarely more than two of them.

Both the popular and the serious press were promoting a rhetorical view of teachers that was based on sweeping generalizations and unquestioned assumptions. The journalist Melanie Phillips demonstrated this well in an article in the *New Statesman*[33] which broadly conveyed the view of successive governments. Schooling, she explained, had long been a disaster because:

> Children were not being taught to read; nor were they being taught history or maths or anything very much.

The teachers were clearly to blame as they:

> had decided teaching children facts or the rules of language or maths might stifle their innate creativity ... This view was said to be progressive.

As part of the decline:

> Moral obligations were in effect junked, opening the way for a libertarian revolution.

This was evidently the consequence of a culture of choice, of individualism which:

> worships autonomy and deems obligation to be oppressive, and is based on hedonistic selfishness.

So teachers had to be dealt with. The popular political view of both Labour and the Conservatives carried the story further. The problem, many argued, had been in allowing too much *independent initiative*, *managerial trust*, *cosy communality*, *cultural diversity*. Schools should be as alike as possible and work to a national programme of expectation and quality. Schools must realize they are in a competitive culture and are expected to be winners against a state-authenticated quality kitemark. What we needed were rational regimes with progress being marked, measured and rewarded, and failures duly punished.

If A happened then B would follow. If teachers were given clear directions then improved teaching would result. Ofsted had by this stage evolved a formulaic view of the 'perfect school' that was constructed on the building bricks of hundreds of 'perfect lessons' and achieved 'exact targets'. Ofsted had a blueprint against which all lessons were to be assessed, and described perfection itself: it told us exactly how teachers must perform. They were allowed one weak lesson out of ten. The school overall was allowed 10% of less-than-satisfactory lessons before going into 'special measures', i.e. failing their inspection. Teams of inspectors, paid at roughly twice the rate of teachers, now watched twenty minutes of lessons and marked them above or below the waterline. Marks and Spencers had managed to standardize and quality-control the practice of their sales hands. Why not schools?

Such utopianism, backed by political mandate, makes unreasonable demands on the very people we rely on to do the job. It ignores the teacher's feelings, her motivation, her intentions, her contribution to the debate, her ability to argue back. It ignores the messy reality that, come what may, the discouraged teachers will have to deal with the children the next day, and the day after that. In real life we are not for the most part dealing with extreme cases of the obviously incompetent. We are dealing with the run-of-the-mill teacher doing her best.

The problem is in part the disabling gap between word and thing, between idea and action. For words such as 'standards', or 'rigorous', or 'targets', or 'improvement', or even 'understanding' and 'knowing', can seem ethereal, distant and even threatening, all too easily turned into verbal weapons against the teacher.

Richard Hoggart, a veteran observer of social and cultural change, noted that:

> Authoritarian governments believe in the – forced – perfectibility of man; their own version of perfectibility. They assume and demand too much of everyone. They believe they can arrange over time for the average sensual human to be made average only in unsensuality, obedient behaviour; that most people can be screwed into a simulacrum of virtue or at least of good routines, as Stakhanovite citizen/workers or onwards and upwards Gauleiters.[34]

Schools are not superstores and children are not commodities. Children are unpredictable and children in the inner city particularly so. Most schools which failed inspections were in areas of high socio-economic deprivation, in the very places where we wanted to encourage some of the best teachers to work. Because of the risk of public failure, such teachers protected themselves by removing – so far as was humanly possible – every vestige of risk. They had been forced onto the defensive. They had been pressed into teaching according to a schedule, to over-valuing control. They focused on routines in order to eliminate problems, to intensify discipline, to accommodate management demands. This was not a world in which creative minds wished to operate. It was becoming ever more difficult for the imaginative, the risk-takers, the divergent thinkers to work in such an atmosphere.

A firm called Brook Street ran an advert which read:

> Waiting for home time? You're on the way out. Evolution favours the professional.

Here was an illustration of contemporary management in action, of its habit of endlessly demanding more, and pressing the troops – the doctors, teachers, social-workers, police – harder and harder, with a cavalier disregard for the quality of their lives.

Successive Secretaries of State suffered from a weakness I sometimes recognized in myself. It was the presumption of claiming to know what other people ought to do without actually having to do it themselves. I still did some teaching of specialist English and philosophy, drama and music, but I was fully aware that this wasn't at all the same as managing a class of thirty children through the week, teaching all subjects day in and day out.

The fact was that the primary-class teacher could be picked off with the greatest of ease like some flailing clown – all Ofsted had to do was to shift its spotlight to the latest weakness in reading or maths or writing or class-management or test results, and sharpen its claws. There was always something you could dig out of the bin to use to create a headline, and there was nothing better for political self-assertion than a flow of critical headlines about someone else – other people out there – which would sustain a righteous national mission to 'sort them out'.

We were, therefore, having serious problems recruiting teachers, especially the brightest people, who demanded, more than anything, intellectual and emotional space for their work. They wanted to work in a lively, questioning atmosphere, not in an intellectual sheep-pen. But by the end of the 1990s we saw a demoralized and depleting profession subjected to a continuing flow of ever-expanding demands.

The counter to the pre-modern European Gnostic vision of the world as engaged in an endless struggle between Good and Evil was *humanitas*, which required a fusion of nature and morality in the natural and the divine cosmos. I liked to think that what we had being trying to achieve at Grove was in some sense to recreate Montaigne's sense of *humanitas*: faith, trust, tolerance.

Learning, the kind I was interested in, surely required that element of freedom, that space, that had in one way or another long preoccupied me. Was it not possible to create an oasis in a school? This was what we had been about all along. Wasn't the best learning effectively achieved in small groups, by the close interacting of one mind with another? Some state secondary pupils had recently been sent for a while to Eton and had produced a penetrating analysis of their experience.[35] They had noted the freedom people had to explore, the space, real and cerebral, the personal tutorials, the facilities. They had experienced high-quality engagement with relaxed, enthusiastic minds, supported by exceptional resources. It was what the rich can buy – and what the rich will pay for because they think it matters. Where were the champions to argue that such an environment matters too to everyone else? Montaigne, an aristocrat expressing a vision of *what ought to be*, would surely have asked such questions.

This was what, ambitiously, I wanted to achieve for our children. It would have been nice to have Eton's resources. But I couldn't afford to provide each child with a musical instrument, to offer suites of rooms for design and technology, to give teachers space and time to hone up their teaching to the highest level of enthusiasm. I surveyed a discouraged profession and diminishing freedoms for both teachers and children.

The philosopher Richard Rorty claimed that education of the feelings 'only works on people who can relax long enough to listen'.[36] From this notably materialist standpoint, Terry Eagleton argued, 'you can be imaginative only if you are well heeled.'[37] It was but a short step to argue that what the children of the poor – and the younger children in particular – needed were basic competencies, apart from which nothing else much mattered. The rest was play, much of it peripheral. If you were, therefore, both a small child and poor, there was a double argument for narrowing the teaching.

This was a philosophy that was now being implicitly promulgated – often without their coming clean – by many of those who formed and administered policy. It denied the ever-growing evidence of neurological science that the young brain develops most effectively in an atmosphere of experiential richness and diversity, using all the senses, sight and sound, physical movement, as well as lively conversational interactions with interested adults, to develop curiosity and intellectual potential.

In this respect I felt that our school had been fighting against a philistinism through which teachers and pupils had been discouraged from evolving the radically different, richly planned and often costly experiences that children not only deserved but urgently needed. Instruction and direction had replaced evolution and self-directed professional growth. We had not only been sold the culture of the second-rate but in some measure *oppressed* by a certain indifference and misunderstanding among people who were themselves an affluent elite.

At this school, for the most part, we held our own. Maybe our success resided more in the things people *didn't* think about and would find hard to enumerate, in the feel of the place, the way people lived together and valued and enjoyed each other's company – the texture, the civility of the place, its creative life.

There was convincing evidence to suggest that schools tend to be more successful when they have strong internal bonding – structurally, organizationally, culturally.[38] Hence the evidence that church schools, for example, have particular strengths; for binding traditions help create common languages and develop common points of view. The teachers in such cultures work better as teams, draw adults and children together in (often) unstated attitudes and behaviours, and seem to care more about each other as members of the school organization. They are more civil.

There was, of course, the danger of cosiness. It was easy to exaggerate, to feel sorry for yourself and mark yourself out as a victim. The kind of bonding culture I had been looking for had a tension, a strong awareness of individuals, a complexity in which there was an edge, a dialectic, an openness.

But schools at their best create a network of social relationships and values. Teachers at best are powerful motivating forces. Schools at their best draw people together, create social capital, act as gathering and reference points for communities. They ensure that children don't miss out. They monitor and persuade, they civilize and act as energizers. All these years I had been living with teachers who, with their various strengths and weaknesses, had by and large worked towards creating such communities, committing themselves sometimes in the most unpropitious circumstances.

At the end of *Middlemarch* George Eliot has an extraordinary description of the invisibility of certain kinds of goodness. I felt I would like to replace the heroine Dorothea with my own sense of what the school – what any school – might be achieving at its best.

> Her fine-touched spirit had still its fine issues, though they were not widely visible. Her full nature ... spent itself in channels that had no great name on earth. But the effect of her being on those around here was incalculably diffusive: for the growing good of the world is partly dependent on unhistoric acts; and that things are not so ill with you and me as they might have been, is half owing to the number who lived faithfully a hidden life.[39]

Though this was far from exact, it was a moving and powerful paraphrase of something I was trying to say. There was an element in the culture of the school that gave out and contributed to a sense of life: a vividness that created its own electricity. That was the beginning of something I was incoherently searching for: in particular to emphasize that a school was not a bag of bones or a radar screen of test marks, or an organization chart, or a set of policy handouts. Not that I was against any of those things – indeed I had been partly responsible for introducing some of them. These were the scaffolding that held the business of schooling together. But the *texture*, the real-life of the school, resided in the lives of the people who lived here, day in and day out, and whose lives were touched and animated by what went on. The true history, the history that mattered, lay in the accumulation of small unheard historic acts by the quiet folk, the teachers.

57
The Dance

Teachers these days, then, have a real sense of oppression. Many of them believe that primary education has changed for the worse. They easily get fired up about politicians. In one school I visited the staff had received a pile of new full-colour, expensively produced Government-sponsored magazines and had shredded them and thrown them in a fury round the room. I suggested setting the American comedian Chris Rock onto the Department for Education and Employment.

> Fuck them man, they don' know a fuckin' chicken wing from a fucking pork chop – they all a bag o' shit.

But you can be carried away by this, get it out of perspective and let it weigh you down. It's important to think positive, mark out and defend your territory, and hold onto the good things.

Just occasionally there are events that astonish you. These rare moments accumulate. They linger, such moments, in the mind. There are times when you feel a sense of closure, as though you have gone through the door into the last room; something which, for once, appears to justify your existence.

When ex-pupils return to school, now grown up, the things that they remember best are the plays, the fun, the great events, those moments of maximum emotional intensity. These seem to make them feel worthwhile; they are reference points for the next step forward in life. Such experiences can be partly planned but very often they come at you without warning. Yet happen they do – and you feel inspired as you stumble into them.

Who would forget the moment when after a heavy snowfall the entire school engaged in a monumental snowball battle, teachers and children together, red-faced and peppered white with snow, their eyes gleaming in the frost? Or the moment when at the end of term one of the school discos with darkened room and twirling lights suddenly metamorphosed into a gigantic, giggling crocodile too big for the hall? To the loud beat of the music, a huge joined-up line of children and teachers danced out of the school into the playground, hundreds of them prancing and singing round the school, snaking out of the front door and across the yard and going in through the back door with a kind of drunken merriment: a wholly unschool-like end-of-term madness; a spontaneous joining of hearts and hands in which not a single child spoiled the line that ended up finally in the hall again – where everyone flopped down laughing. It was a marvellous way to polish off the term.

Who would forget the last day of term before the summer holidays when the children sang the rousing *Building Song*?

> All over the world ... everybody's building in a different way.

Or our slow, sad little leaving song? Or some of the memorable assemblies performed by the children; or the best moments in the school plays? The more I dug down, the more shafts of gold seemed to appear. Was there a moment that stood out, not just for me but for the children as well, above all moments? Perhaps not. But the story of Sarbjit hung longest in the mind.

Sarbjit is a perfectly ordinary boy. He's been three years in the Infants, four in the Junior School, and is seen by everyone who has anything to do with him as quiet, courteous, pleasant and shy. Every year has its characters, the noisy, the smart, the badly behaved and attention-seeking; the teachers' helpers, the organizers, the popular, the charismatic, the sports stars. Sarbjit is none of these. He is by all accounts a boy whom nobody notices very much.

'Who?' says one teacher; 'I'm not sure I can place him ... '

That's Sarbjit. He's neither particularly good at sport nor especially academic. He comes and goes, creating no waves. You can envisage him as a future clerk in a large anonymous office, carrying out his duties without fuss, and conscientiously rising slowly over the years to a minor managerial position. He's one of those children who is more or less invisible; he is unostentatious and under-noticed. There are a lot of people out there like Sarbjit.

At the end of the year, the oldest children organize an Event for the whole school. They write sketches, and they perform comedy, act, sing, recite, dance, fool about. Everyone gathers in the Upper School hall; the curtains are drawn; the spotlights are on; the children sit on three sides of the room; and the performances take place in a central arena. The boys and girls with the most panache and public self-confidence run the show, and host it. They dress in wild clothes, ape TV-show presenters, using microphones and putting on mid-Atlantic accents.

For the most part, the acts are a lot of fun, and get a great response from the audience who clap every act with vigorous approval. They have something of the style, even occasionally the skill, of professionals. The children often seem much older than they really are whilst performing. Act follows act, and the audience continues to clap and cheer.

Then all of a sudden Candice, the star presenter, all confidence and adrenalin, announces the next act in a good clear speaking voice: Sarbjit – to dance. Who? Some of the children look round, and then a slender figure emerges dressed in cut-off trousers and a light-blue silk shirt, his black hair gleaming under the lights. The hall goes quiet. Sarbjit stands still in the very centre of the room. The spotlight fixes on him, pins him to the floor. Someone puts a Michael Jackson record on. Hundreds of children snap their fingers and hum along with the tune, and Sarbjit starts to move.

It's not long before everyone goes quiet. Sarbjit is moving into action, his body beginning to sway elegantly, his feet sliding, his torso upright, and an extraordinary new persona, a brilliant butterfly, emerges before our eyes. His dance, slow at first, now speeds up, showing incredible agility – it is a perfect Michael Jackson imitation, but with an authority all his own. His body bends to the rhythms and he moves like a graceful master, an Astaire, across the centre of the floor, dancing with a glittering brilliance that takes the breath away. All at once he *is* Michael Jackson – with the hypnotic professionalism of a natural performer. The audience's attention is spinning along with him; the children gathered round the edges of the room start to clap and cheer in astonishment. He twirls like a ballerina, on one foot, on one hand, extending his range moment by moment to a dazzling climax, poised and synchronized exactly with the music, and stopping precisely on time. There's a breathless pause and he pulls himself up straight, standing quite still, feet together, smiling gently at the flabbergasted audience. Then he takes his bow, to a chorus of cheers, and lowering his head very slowly, even arrogantly, like a great artist at the end of a performance – a gentle, almost disdainful smile on his lips, which I have occasionally witnessed in great performers, who convey a curious sense of not needing any applause at all, simply existing in some distant and slightly superior world of their own.

We had witnessed something special. The admiration was tangible. Like everyone else who was there, of every age, I felt elated, as if I was dancing on air. It was a life-enhancing performance. Afterwards Sarbjit quietly sat down. No one knew he could dance like this – could dance *at all*. He was not a member of the dance or drama club; he had never danced at school before. Where had he learned to dance?

The following day Sarbjit, along with the other performers, left the school.

58

Dante

> ... deep in myself the burning wish
> to know the world and have experience
> both of men's vices and of human worth.
> So I set out on the deep and open sea
> with just one ship and with that group of men
> those few who never deserted me.

Dante's extended speeches are incomparably seductive and dramatic. The economy of emotion is amazing, especially in the progression through the heavens to the extraordinary descriptions of light and music in Paradiso.

Is Paradiso so unattainable? As I stand outside the school looking back, I survey the little houses around. My eyes scan the horizon of the higgledy piggledy shops. The vegetables burgeon out on the street from the corner shop. The Muslim family working there day and night are expanding into fine new premises round the back. I see some signs of improvement in the area. I've managed some expensive upgrading of the playgrounds, and we now have patches of plants and trees cut out of the tarmac, to brighten things up.

But more prominent are the surveillance cameras and the heavy steel shutters over every window. Cameras survey everything.

The litter is the same, everywhere, the flowers of the streets: swathes of Walkers crisp packets, discarded condoms, empty packs of ciggies. The tiny shop opposite is full during the day of local lads out of school, future – or real – gangsters who hang about all day long. At lunchtimes the place seethes with crowds of children buying crisps and sweets and big 'Grammarbugs', as they are called locally, illegally smoking. The Ravidas temple, burnt down in a mysterious fire, now sports a handsome new building. At night its lights glisten like Piccadilly Circus, firing out the bright message of Guru Ravi Das. The land at the back of the school is still as much of a tip as ever. The new climbing frame has survived all attempts to burn it down, but it is a poor thing in a sea of asphalt.

There has been a wealth of new opportunities across the city for aspiring restaurant owners, entrepreneurs, sweat shops, do-it-yourself businesses, clothing factories; but far too many deprived people have been left behind. The project of the 'bourgeoisification' of the nation – the majority of people are now classed as middle-class – has not yet reached this particular outpost.

This is still the poor inner city suburb it always was. People who get enough cash together leave for better conditions. It strikes me, as I stare at all this, that we have failed. We have failed corporately. The problems – the challenges – are the same as they ever have been. Despite numerous initiatives, the huge commitment of energy, the great departments of the Local Authority and the Departments of State, few of these have made any visible impact.

As for anyone who works in a school like ours, I'm reminded of the colonel in the John Wayne movie who, bitter about his relegation to a third-rate outpost at Fort Apache, immortalizes himself through a wild, heroic gallop into Indian territory, going to his certain death – and destroying most of his cavalry command. What, after all the heroics, have we achieved?

Some achievements are tangible or measurable. You can see the art work; you can touch the children's pottery and read their poems. You can note the progress, or lack of it, of pupils across National Curriculum levels and the like. But such empirical evidence is not enough. On the basis of the data, the schools of Sutton Coldfield, Harborne and Solihull will always win the game. The London Borough of Richmond's results will always be better than Birmingham's.

So maybe it is inwardly that we have achieved the most important things, in the souls of people, in the invisible heart of the community. Life is lived in the real world in the spaces between the numbers. Much of it is hidden and elusive.

What is inward achievement? If a child believes in himself then he can believe in the possibility of making his own achievements. He can, in one way or another, farm his own future. There is an interesting difference between hunters and farmers. The hunters are the kids on the streets, living on their wits, stealing, perhaps robbing, burgling. The farmers plan ahead; they think carefully about the future, and plant today for what can be achieved tomorrow. They have to evolve, to hold onto *cultures*. They have confidence in themselves and their basic skills not merely to do things – such as pass a few exams – but to adapt, to survive hazards, to solve problems. All these are inner capabilities that require mental flexibility, emotional balance, self-control. By comparison, the hunters are driven by hunger, by whim; they are desperadoes of instability, and they are liable to fall apart.

At the same time, much that has happened politically during my period at the school has been about breaking cultures down, about a notion of entrepreneurism that more resembles hunting than farming, of the establishment of pecking orders, of winners and losers, a kind of social lottery. It's no surprise that coincidentally we have a real Lottery, the symptom of a deeper socio-political phenomenon. In this contemporary spirit of entrepreneurism, risk becomes important; trust is downgraded; jobs become more insecure. The stock market is the new hunting ground. We hunt for jobs, tips, investments. The clearest sign of this is to be found in the phenomenon of *instantness*. We require rapid rewards, short-term gains, and we live increasingly for the moment.

But hunters succeed best by far in the middle-class world where hunting can in some measure be an add-on, a game founded on a strong sense of culture, on educational success, on books in the home, cultured conversation and interests, an unshakeable security. For poorer and less stable people, the hunting psychology is a disaster unless the individual has a powerful and sustained self-belief. Which is why strong cultural and family traditions and communal pride are so important. Why the Sikhs do so well, for instance. Such communities survive to the extent that they are farmers, steadily building up their wealth and their domain, whilst holding onto the pride and assertiveness of their own beliefs.

Raymond Williams once noted that the notion of culture is derived from husbandry, the tending of natural growth.[40] It is curious that the word 'organic' which in the 1960s and 1970s HMIs frequently used to apply to the development of the culture of good schools, is now out of fashion in education and has been replaced by a more technical, number-driven language, even though it is very much in fashion for food products.

It may be, then, that what matters most in schools in areas like this is that we should be producing such *farmers* – children with practised skills and pride in their culture, in their background, and most of all in themselves. In the scrubland of the city, where the press constantly bangs on about problems and poverty, crime and disillusionment, these children have to have such an inner pride and self-belief. So it was that Montaigne said on the matter of educating children:

> It is just as in farming: the ploughing which precedes the planting is easy and sure; so is the planting itself: but as soon as what is planted springs to life, the raising of it is marked by a great variety of methods and by difficulty.[41]

It could even be that the language of hunters (league-tables, examinations, losers and winners) *actively damages* the potential of children in communities such as ours. Perhaps it damages the potential of children in all communities.

This is not a romantic thought. It raises the possibility that many schools in areas like this fail the children in every sense, both as farmers and hunters. They give them a poor deal in a world in which the dice are loaded in favour of the the better-off players.

There are differences, too, between boys and girls. Our data shows that our girls are following the national trend and performing better academically than boys. The irony is that girls seem less naturally competitive; and yet they are doing strikingly better in a competitive environment – except in places where the cultural roots of boys are so well laid that they can, as it were, survive the hazards of the jungle. This happens by and large amongst those families with strong, traditional cultural roots. *Tradition* in this respect means *farming* and can compensate considerably for poverty. The problem is that poor families suffer not merely from the indignities of being poor relative to the majority of people around them, but because their family's private or community cultures and traditions are vulnerable to overwhelming and dominant national, racial and global cultures – those of the wealthier majority. The 'fostering' which takes place in a well-trusted school at the heart of a community becomes all the more important. Trust, reliability, the building up of continuity over the years and a 'farming' environment is essential, and one which as a matter of record, we are now finding encouraged through our current Chief Education Officer, and much changed Local Authority.

These days I frequently meet past pupils. They move in many directions, and into many careers. Many of them become graduates. Some get to university late in the day. We have past pupils who are taking PhDs. At least five I know of have gone to Oxford and Cambridge. Medicine and law are popular. A few go in for teaching. Many make a good deal of money. Some stay around in Handsworth; many have families of their own. A few end up in jail. One I know has recently been shot dead in a gang war. When you meet them, they always seem refreshingly welcoming and friendly. 'Hi, sir!' they start, and I ask them how they're getting on.

They seem by and large to be cheery and successful. Many are in good jobs and others are planning for the future, and are on courses, in Further Education, working out where their lives will go next. They speak affectionately, sometimes movingly, about the school and the teachers. A secondary teacher in London posted back a piece of work from an ex-pupil about his teacher, Donal, at Grove:

> He made my days as a pupil with him very memorable. He was a very kind and understanding person and he knew how to make us relax after working hard and how to make us laugh with his hilarious stories. He was strict as well as he did not like to see his students messing around during lesson time, he wanted to enable his students to work and achieve to the best of their abilities and thus he was always re-assuring everyone that they were capable of achieving something in life ... I thought the world of him as he rarely shouted at the class and because he himself was proud of having us as his form class.

This was a deep and significant tribute that penetrated to the heart of what teaching at its best is about.

There are always surprises. Kuldip, one of the most difficult pupils of his day, appears next to me on the top of a bus, and tells me how he is a Karate black-belt. He is strikingly calm and good-humoured. How I remember his screaming outbursts in school. Then there is the Lord Mayor's clerk, an impeccably dressed young man, oh so naughty at school. Also Rajeev, who was a slow-minded, plodding boy at school, no more – in contemporary speak – than a middling level-three boy when he left, who now has a top degree in computer science. There is the seventeen-year-old young lady who asked me to tutor her to get her into Oxford, having been told by her secondary school that she hadn't a hope. She went to Oxford, gained a first in law, and became a London barrister. And Randolph, too, who meets me in the City Centre on my own on a dark, wet night, a huge young man. He pauses to bow slightly. 'Hallo, sir', he says, and tells me of his years in jail for grievous bodily harm. Another young man visits me recently – Roger, handsome, quick-witted, has a smart car and four women, each of them with a child and each living in a different quarter of the city.

How much did we – the school – influence them? The children who do best are those who are quietly determined. There's a point as they grow older when self-motivation becomes the main driving force of progress; and underlying that is self-confidence, and a belief that, come what may, all hurdles will eventually be overcome. Add to this a modicum of good humour and emotional balance. Academic success without a sustaining emotional maturity and balance seems to me a largely worthless commodity. Exam-passing, game-playing, gets you to the job interview but doesn't take you much further on in your career or your life. On the other hand, slower movers, children who rest for a while on an academic plateau, or need extra time to master a particular competency, are perfectly capable of personal and career success if they keep going. Which reminds me, reassuringly, of the times – hundreds of them – in assemblies, in classes, when I've told the children that the most important thing is their own self-belief. 'You can do it if you really want to.' Value your own self-confidence; 'look people, teachers, visitors, everyone in the eye;' 'don't ever believe anyone is better than you.' 'Take risks. If you don't get there first time – try again and keep on trying.' And hold onto your own integrity. Don't undervalue yourself. Don't let yourself down. And if you have let yourself down, accept it and learn from it. Try and learn from everything: new things all the time. Be alert. Ask questions. Don't be put down by anything. 'And,' I always used to add, 'smile. People like people who smile.'

59

Twenty-first Century Schooling

The Old School is empty. As I walk through the hall, it feels like an abandoned cathedral. I sit at the piano and play a tune or two and the sound disappears into the roof. The classrooms lie there clustered round the edge of the hall with their rows of abandoned desks. This old building – now Grade III listed – is almost a hundred years old, as I have said, and it feels its age, the heritage site that it has become.

Of all our traditional institutions schools have perhaps changed least, stubbornly clinging to ancient traditions, old ways of working. Children still crowd into classrooms at the ringing of an antique school bell, and attend to the teacher who wields the chalk.

State schooling was set in place in the nineteenth century to give basic competencies to the masses. My story shows how disillusionment with schooling in the 1970s slowly shifted us back to focus on the time-worn basics and equated our economic failures as a nation with our failings in schooling, especially in literacy and numeracy. The consequence has been a radical shift in authority from the Local Authorities to the centre, accompanied by a raft of legal reforms aimed at imposing an authentic national voice on what was seen as a dislocated service.

We are in the age of the supermarkets, when every high street in the land seems to look much the same, with its W.H. Smith, its Boots, Marks and Spencer and its Next. Standardization and standards are all the rage, and commentators on education constantly make comparisons between the unevenness of schools and the wondrous reliability of the chain-store. Every child in the land is now expected to be taught to an acceptable level of competence – to be taught the same things, and if possible in much the same way.

Teachers are exhorted to return to 'whole-class teaching', school uniform, formal discipline. Parents, too, are given guidelines and advice on how to manage their children. The national political mood mostly favours control and command. Deviation from the norm is to be highlighted and punished, with constraints being imposed on irresponsible parents ever more rigorously through the threat of legal sanctions. The standardized society has become the *audit* society, in which traditional notions of trust and local cultural norms of behaviour are replaced by national guidelines and directions. And all this passes under the banner of improved choice and 'responding to market forces'.

The good contemporary school is the formulaic school. The key is commanding leadership, good test results, quality lessons based on clear blueprints. It is possible now to grade every product, every lesson, every child, every teacher, and every school according to a formula based on numerical scales, like *Radio Times*' assessments of films. One day I take some amusement from watching a retired BBC Producer employed as an Ofsted Inspector spending the best part of a day counting our attendance registers to see if we're a percentage above or below the national average. (We're below, as I told him for free.) He also walks round the Upper School playground with a notebook and counts the holes in the fences and the uprooted hedges. 'Look,' he says, like a latter-day King Lear, 'look there,' as though I haven't already noticed it a hundred times.

How successful has this vigorous politicization of education been? By the end of the 1990s, it looks as if there has been some demonstrable raising of standards, as reflected in test results. But more wary commentators have pointed out that there are a number of statistical and other extraneous factors that might account for this, and it's certainly the case that if you practise tests with sufficient energy, children naturally tend to improve their pass rate.[42] Such improvements, defined by limited test data, don't necessarily reflect cleverer or better educated children, and in the USA (the model for our standard attainment tasks testing regime) there are clear signs of a downside to testing, both in narrowing the curriculum and demotivating students. Moreover, for all our efforts to equalize opportunity and standardize school cultures, differences between the most and the least able performers are evidently as wide as ever.

The proportion of failing children has remained stubbornly constant at 20–25% for decades, and this is a phenomenon in education systems in most large urban conurbations in the Western world. Only countries with high levels of cultural and economic homogeneity, like Japan and Finland, seem to have cracked the problem of the underachievement of the urban poor. Despite all our efforts and good intentions, our difficulties remain. Winson Green prison, no more than a mile from here, is full of neglected, academically slow youngsters, many of them with mental-health problems, and mostly from poor backgrounds. If creating equity of provision for the mass of the population through standardization of procedures is the main purpose of public education, then we have transparently failed.

It is a failure which can be accounted for in different ways. One is our inability to link social and educational policy. There is a view that schools can carry the main load, and can on their own make all the difference; but this, on the evidence, is misconceived. In fact, school league-table performance can be determined by the Micawber-like formula:

> Add mean household income to mean per capita school income and multiply by a measure of pupil selection (on a scale, say, of 1–5). The resulting figure will be reliably indicative of school league-table status.

Hence a school with relatively well-off parents, well endowed and with a selective intake, will invariably figure at the top end of the tables. Conversely, a school in a poor community, with little in the way of financial assets and with a non-selective intake, will figure at the bottom.

Other minor variations can be accounted for by local cultural factors. There are subtle differences between ethnic and cultural make-up in school catchment areas that help predict local variations in league-table performance. Our school, for example, gets a relatively high proportion of children to grammar schools (10–15%), a fact that results from the disproportionate number of out-of-the area middle-class parents who send their children here, although this is not sufficient to distort the overall league-table performance. Levin and Kelly, after a rigorous examination of the evidence, summed the matter up succinctly:

> Education has the potential for powerful impacts ... if the proper supportive conditions are present. It has the potential for a very nominal impact when the complementary requirements are not in place.[43]

Standardization of schooling in a pluralistic society, in which the variations and gaps between haves and have nots are widening, seems unlikely to touch the problems at their core. Schools are, in the event, not supermarkets. We can pile children into classrooms, but they are never as predictable as tins of baked beans piled on supermarket shelves. If one child in a class of thirty decides to throw a pencil during an Ofsted inspected lesson, this will lower the lesson grade. Baked-bean tins, when weighed and counted, will not move, or have moods, or cry.

Set against the larger picture of international comparisons

of the effects of spending on improving teacher-child ratios, then, policies in the UK over the last three decades have looked more to the low-cost options of exhortation and control than to serious attempts to address funding needs in rational ways.

I have argued all along that resources have not been aimed at those who most need them: surely the most rational and effective way of achieving equality of educational provision is to put extra resources into primary education. Yet pupil numbers in the classes at our school are as high at the end of the century as they were twenty-five years ago when I first walked into this hall, although a new Labour Government is showing a determination to bring down class sizes in infant schools to a maximum of thirty, and an increasing awareness of the importance of pre-school provision.

This is, ironically, a moment in time when great commercial chains like Marks and Spencer and Sainsbury's are suddenly facing a downturn, and smaller niche competitors are starting to make inroads into their traditional markets. Similar problems may face the standardization model for schools, with the appearance of new, radical possibilities on the horizon. Information and communication technology is to the twenty-first century what electricity was to the nineteenth. Old-style classrooms will start to look out of date in a world in which every child has a laptop, and can access the internet and access distance-learning opportunities and video links with teachers across the globe. It is possible that the whole school building as currently constructed may go the way of the abandoned church next door and become redundant in the age of new technologies.

Even for young children, schools will look more like universities, with pupils attending courses for a range of different subjects that are run at different ability levels. We will be required to focus much more specifically on the needs of individuals, and we will have to become increasingly sophisticated in the business of *diagnosis* as a means of analysing pupils' needs and potential.

More refined diagnosis and awareness will lead institutions to rethink their traditional ways of working in order to respond to the diversity of pupils for whom they are responsible. More complex organizational arrangements involving small-group teaching, tutorial teaching, large-scale lectures are likely to become the norm. We will certainly be expected to offer a much wider range of learning experiences to children in response to the growing heterogeneity of society and pupils' interest in a growing range of subjects. The consumer-led society will require schools to be ever more responsive to parent expectations. The school will be pressed to extend its activities beyond the school day, and to offer extra-curricular activities in more structured ways, with children having more of a say in what they choose to do, and with more systematic ways of identifying and developing skills and talents being adopted.

We will need to employ a greater diversity of people in the teaching-tutoring business, and to make more use of specialists to work (especially) with children with particular talents or needs. The 'class teacher' will increasingly become a 'learning manager' with responsibility for the overview of, and support for, the broader needs of each individual pupil. Schools will need to ensure competencies in basic skills, but this is likely to demand a much more vigorous attempt to tackle the learning difficulties of pupils, with a strong focus on the 0–5 age group, involving parents during the early years before formal schooling.

Children are likely to become increasingly assertive and better educated about their rights and responsibilities. The new idea of *pupil entitlement* is likely to spread – under which the state has to guarantee that each pupil has access, in or out of school, to a range of appropriate experiences, including, say, learning a musical instrument, participation in a range of sports from an early age, and access to involvement in theatre. Schools will also have the responsibility to offer emotional and counselling support for children who need it, to integrate health and educational issues more closely, to give much more comprehensive support to children with real or potential mental-health difficulties. The services offered to children will be more comprehensive, and involve a wider range of personnel, and ever more sophisticated technical back-up.

There will be counter forces. How shall we now ensure that all this doesn't lead towards a new form of post-televisual anomie – towards the individual who is engaged in personal and personalized pursuits, spending too much time penned up in a solitary environment in front of a computer screen, which results in a diminished social life and a narcissistic life-style? There will be issues for local democracy, for the teaching of the importance of community and civility and the support of local cultures. It will be important to develop children's abilities to analyse, to think clearly, to be inventive as well as appropriately sceptical. There will be the question of how to ensure that the teaching process at its core remains somehow intact; that Montaigne's vision that at the heart of learning lies dialectic, conversation, debate and human encounters, is not lost: that schools remain institutions with a deeply caring, stimulating environment – which is particularly important for primary-aged children.

One virtue of the best independent schools is their ability to protect their teachers from hassle that is unrelated to their work in the classroom, and to retain an emphatic emphasis on the quality of discourse between teachers and pupils. Smaller classes help with this and so does a protective 'professionalism' that allows the teacher the time and space to develop and plan his/her teaching through vastly improved resource back-up and administrative support. Smaller groups allow for much freer and deeper exchanges between teachers and pupils.

The challenge for teachers in the future will be defending

and retaining the old virtues of knowing (and loving) their subject and being able to communicate in a free, personal and relaxed way with the pupils. At the same time, they may need to accept that many aspects of the job, especially the teaching of many basic skills, the technical tasks involved in pupil diagnosis, and the management of information technology, can be carried out by classroom assistants or administrative staff, with an increased role being given to external specialist tutors.

Centralism discourages trust and participation. It is an important and difficult question whether political action can succeed in the absence of self-confident professionals who will work closely over long periods with strong local communities. A failure to get the right balance between centre and periphery will lead to the very people you need most jumping ship. Some of the best teachers and heads are at present profoundly disillusioned. Primary teaching is rapidly becoming an almost exclusively female profession, and many outstanding women teachers are no longer interested in shouldering the strains of management responsibility. When I left Grove there were only three serious applicants for my job, in a school now of over 700 pupils. Fortunately one of them was outstanding.

Maybe national standardization will continue for some years to come and traditional classrooms and traditional lessons will also continue as we have always known them. Maybe children will continue to be taught in groups of thirty and mass-tested at intervals to achieve various targets. Maybe the parameters of choice for teachers will be even more constrained by a theoretical blueprint of 'what a good lesson is'. Maybe teachers will be ever more tightly scrutinized and their daily lives prescribed by various laws and impositions. There may be a 'freeing up' of schools in relation to the 'market', allowing them to cherry-pick their pupils, and (at least theoretically) an extension of parental choice through expanding popular schools: an attempt to bring the opportunism and culture of the private sector into state schools.

The battle is on between the standardizers and the diversifiers. Between a national culture struggling to impose national norms and identities and an ever diversifying pluralism of cultures. Between a middle class that commands the field, and the socio-economically deprived, who have more challenging and perhaps different educational requirements. Between professionals, instinctively conservative in practice who want to protect old values, and a high-tech world that offers radically different ways of thinking about teaching and learning. Between those who think they know all there is to know about good teaching and those who suspect that we have a great deal still to learn. A dialectical war lies ahead between different models, requirements, possibilities, pressures and expectations; between teachers, governments, Local Authorities and philosophers. And in the meantime, information technology rolls in like a tidal wave.

I stand in this old hall a long time thinking about these things. This school is like every other school, on the cusp between the past – a long tradition of formal schooling – and a future of dislocation and change, which will throw up those new sets of demands, issues, problems and puzzles.

'No form of the market economy,' writes the American political analyst Peter Unger, 'will do any good – for growth or for democracy – if it denies space to the individual or the collective entrepreneur who says, "to hell with you, I'll do it my way."'

Coleridge put in a counter-claim for the need to ground civilization 'in the harmonious development of those qualities and faculties that characterize our humanity'.

These are two very different propositions, over a century apart, and they both seem to carry weight. We need both individuality and corporateness; entrepreneurism along with a sense of what it means to be fully human; independent-mindedness together with an understanding of the critical importance of culture and cultivation. The best contemporary teaching is caught between these propositions, expressed in the tension of the drama of the classroom, the quality of the teacher-pupil engagement. Indeed, it is determined *by* them. Like good jazz, good teaching is both structured and improvised. It makes use of the finest instruments and themes available but deploys them in personal, original ways. Similarly for the headteacher, over and above the daily task of keeping the ship on course, there's the excitement of learning to adapt to the unpredictable, of shaping a personal vision of how things can be best directed in an insecure world, of keeping a weather-eye on the horizon.

I came into this job partly for the opportunities it gave me to explore, to discover. I have learnt that the deep things happen slowly, and that as the journey unfolds you need great patience. *Possibility* needs balancing against *practicality*; but for all the slowness of the evolving stages as we travel into deeper seas, there is the undeniable prospect of transformations, new and wonderful.

60

Leaving

From where I stand I can see the shops, the roving eyes of security cameras, local mums floating in the direction of the Soho Road, and I can smell the scent of curries, garlic, lemons. The air seems hazy, half asleep. People walk more slowly than they normally walk. There are no doubt all the familiar noises, but I hear none of them. My mind is elsewhere. What have we achieved in all these years? The children, the teachers inside the school today, what are they achieving? Samuel Johnson once said that the problem with writing poetry is to know when you have done it well. How much more truly can that be said of teaching.

At the end of a teaching career, you feel swathed in silence; a strange conclusion to an activity which is so full of *noise*. But what is there to point to as evidence of success in an age when you have to produce measurable data to prove and justify everything? Children grow up, pursue careers, carry on their lives. Like Virgil's stone, they pass through many hands. Of course ex-pupils will occasionally say that such-and-such a teacher had an exceptional influence on me, was extraordinarily memorable or life-enhancing, or motivated me, gave me a sense of self-respect, opened doors. But precisely *how* this was achieved – exactly what it was you did that made the difference, if indeed it really was you that made the difference – is hard to put your finger on. It is curious, though, that pupils invariably seem not so impressed by the fact that you got them through a test or exam as by the fact that you *influenced* them and made them feel good about themselves in what seems, at a distance, unclear and mysterious ways.

I stand and hear nothing. In the pervasive silence, people flow past: flickering shapes in shadows. I don't hear the old bell ring for the end of school, but parents are clustering in small hoops in the front playground and the children are beginning to surge out.

This companionable silence seems to stretch across the years as I think about all the thousands of children, generation after generation of them, who have heard the bell and passed through the gates. Some may see in this a hint of nostalgia, the fanciful Old Romantic. Right now, however, standing outside in the sunshine I am far from dewy-eyed and nostalgic. What I actually feel is a sense of dissatisfaction at not having achieved what I think might have been achieved in more propitious circumstances, and regret that so much of my work has been such an exhausting struggle. I feel I have travelled at least once round the world with many amazing things happening on the way. I've met and worked with a great many remarkable and talented people. But the promised land? That still seems far off, an abstraction in the mist.

I can now see hundreds of children pouring out of school, spilling out down the road. 'Hi, sir,' one of them yells and doffs his red baseball cap. I wave back. His friend kicks a white ball into the air and three little girls dance and twirl, chasing each other and shouting and laughing as they run into the distance.

Notes and References

1. Igor Stravinsky, *Poetics of Music*, trans. A. Knedel and I. Dahl, Cambridge, Mass., 1947, p.75.
2. Keith Joseph's 1974 Conference speech, reported in the *Times Educational Supplement*, 1st November 1974.
3. Alec Clegg, 'Much to Wrong Us', in the *Times Educational Supplement*, 11th October 1974.
4. Black Papers. The first of these right-wing polemical essays was published in March 1969 by C. Cox and A. H. Dyson, and a series followed. They were seen as a useful way of generating public debate, taking the view that standards were falling because of fashionable 'permissive' teaching methods.
5. N. Bennett, 'Plowden's Progress', in the *Times Educational Supplement*, 18th October 1974.
6. M. Rutter et al., *15,000 Hours*, Open Books, 1979.
7. K. Brooksbank (ed.), *Educational Administration*, Councils and Education Press, 1980, p.166.
8. D. H. Hargreaves, *Interpersonal Relations and Education*, Routledge and Kegan Paul, 1972, pp.166–7.
9. R. Auld, *William Tyndale Junior and Infant Schools Public Inquiry*, HMSO, 1976.
10. D. R. Winkley, 'From Condescension to Complexity: post-Plowden schooling in the inner-city', in *Oxford Review*, Vol.13, No.1, 1987, p.54.
11. R. Skynner and J. Cleese, *Families and How to Survive Them*, Methuen, 1983.
12. Cf. the discussion of the developing inspectorates and advisory services in D. R. Winkley, *Diplomats and Detectives*, Robert Royce, 1986, pp.29–31.
13. Keith Joseph's speech, reported by Stuart Maclure in D. Lawton (ed.), *The Educational Reform Act: Choice and Control*, Hodder, 1989, p.35.
14. The Yellow Book, DES, 1976. This provided a programme for reform for the 1980s, proposing a National Curriculum, a regime of testing, inspection for value for money and work on school effectiveness.

15. The *Times Educational Supplement*, 7th April 1978.
16. Rhodes Boyson, speech to the National Council for Educational Standards, reported in the *Times Educational Supplement*, 17th March 1978.
17. Letter to the *Times Educational Supplement*, 10th March 1978.
18. M. Stone, *The Education of the Black Child in Britain*, Fontana, 1981.
19. Cf. D. Murphy, *Tales from Two Cities*, Penguin, 1987, p.181.
20. The Swann Report, *Education for All*, HMSO, 1985.
21. George Eliot, *Felix Holt*, Penguin, 1972 edn, p.129.
22. S. Szreter, 'Staff and Resources in the State Education System', in *Primary Practice*, No.13, January 1998.
23. J. G. Chubb and T. M. Moe, 'Politics, Markets and the Organization of Schools', in A. H. Halsey et al., *Education, Culture, Economy and Society*, Oxford University Press, 1997, p.378.
24. E. Midwinter, *Schools in Society*, Batsford, 1980, p.131.
25. For further discussion of the curriculum, cf. D. R. Winkley in *Managing the National Curriculum*, T. Brighouse and B. Moon (eds), Longman, 1990.
26. Stuart MacClure, at the Primary Educational Study Group Conference, Ambleside, 1989.
27. DES growth figures: by 1996 the cost was £8.2 billion, or just over 20% of education spending. This was a real-term rise of more than 300% since 1979.
28. D. R. Winkley, *Diplomats and Detectives*, Robert Royce, 1986.
29. Ofsted costs. The annual budget of Ofsted in 1999 was £160 million. The total cost since 1991 has been £1.3 billion. These are central costs and do not allow for the substantial costs that are additional to those being inspected.
30. Marc W. Kruman, *Between Authority and Liberty*, University of North Carolina Press, 1997.
31. Health data for the area remains appalling. The Rowntree study, *Reducing Health Inequalities in Britain*, September 2000, specifically highlighted the area, pointing out that amongst children aged 0–14 there are about thirteen more deaths per year than the national average.

32. *The Times*, 2nd December 1997.
33. M. Philips, 'Why I am Really a Progressive', in the *New Statesman*, 14th February 2000, pp.25–7.
34. R. Hoggart, *First and Last Things*, Aurum Press, 1999, p.84.
35. Cf. report by Elizabeth Udall on the exchange between Eton College and Harlesden City Challenge, summer 2000.
36. R. Rorty, 'Human Rights, Rationality and Sentimentality', in *The Politics of Human Rights*, London, 1999, p.80.
37. T. Eagleton, *The Idea of Culture*, Blackwells, 2000, p.47.
38. Cf., for example, J. Murphy, 'School Effectiveness and School Restructuring', in *School Effectiveness and School Improvement*, 3rd February 1992, p.96:

    One of the most powerful and enduring lessons from all the research on effective schools is that better schools are more tightly linked – structurally, symbolically and culturally – than the less effective ones. They operate more as an organic whole and less as a loose collection of disparate sub-systems.

39. George Eliot, *Middlemarch*, Riverside Press, Cambridge, Mass., 1956 edn, pp.212–13.
40. R. Williams, *Culture and Society*, London, 1958, p.334.
41. Michel de Montaigne, 'On Educating Children', in the *Complete Essays*, trans. M. A. Screech, Allen Lane, 1997, p.167.
42. Note, for example, M. Cresswell and J. Gubb, *The Second International Maths Study in England and Wales*, National Foundation for Education Research, 1987. This identified 17% of test improvement as linked to opportunity to learn test items. Also cf. F. A. Hanson, 'Testing Testing; Social Consequences of the Examined Life', in *Harvard Educational Review*, Vol.64, spring 1994.
43. H. M. Levin and C. Kelly, 'Can Education Do It Alone?', in A. H. Halsey et al., *Education, Culture, Economy and Society*, Oxford University Press, 1997, p.250.

Glossary of Abbreviations

BBC	British Broadcasting Corporation
CEO	Chief Education Officer
DfEE	Department for Education and Employment
DES	Department of Education and Science
FE	Further Education
GCSE	General Certificate of Secondary Education
HMI	Her Majesty's Inspector of Schools
HMSO	Her Majesty's Stationery Office
JTC	Joint Teachers' Council
LEA	Local Education Authority
MP	Member of Parliament
NASWT	National Association of Schoolmasters and Women Teachers
NCC	National Curriculum Council
NF	National Front
NUT	National Union of Teachers
Ofsted	Office for Standards in Education
PE	Physical education
PTA	Parent-teacher association
QC	Queen's Counsel
RE	Religious education
TES	*Times Educational Supplement*